To Liana

Contents

Foreword

This book was originally written in 1957, in Kelantan, one of the north-eastern states of Malaya. I was at the time working as head of the English Department in the Federal Training College at Kota Bharu, and I recognised that my students, who were of many races and cultures, needed an easy book to provide them with the historical background which would make some of their set books more intelligible. The result was this short history of English literature which, in the thirteen years or so since it first appeared, has been used fairly widely in Europe as well as in what used to be the Colonial Empire. It is perhaps discourteous to European students to make the book still appear to be a kind of tropical production, but it was written against a background of snakes and jungle drums, and there seems to me a harmless piquancy in letting these go on hissing and beating somewhere behind a discussion of *Paradise Lost*. But other changes have been necessary, particularly the bringing up to date of the account of contemporary British literature. I am aware of the unchanged naïveté of the prose, and of some of the literary judgements made, but all this can be put right only by the writing of a new book, a task for which I am not yet ready. The facts remain solid enough, and I hope they will continue to feed whatever hunger for facts students of English literature possess. I mean, of course, students at the elementary level. If they learn a bigger hunger, I trust they will be led to the great Cambridge History of English Literature, or to the shorter work of Legouis and Cazamien.

A. B.
Bracciano, Italy.
August 1, 1971.

Acknowledgements

We are indebted to the late Mr. Ezra Pound for an extract from 'The Seafarer'.

We are grateful to the following for permission to reproduce copyright material: Camera Press for page 202 top right; William Gordon Davis for pages 67, 74, 96 bottom; Mary Evans Picture Library for page 138; Fitzwilliam Museum, Cambridge for page 202 top left; Mansell Collection for pages 47, 192; National Portrait Gallery for page 202 bottom left and right; Radio Times Hulton Picture Library for pages 88, 116, 184, 195; Reunion des Musees Nationaux for page 4; Sir Stanley Spencer Memorial Trust for page 10; Trustees of the British Museum for pages 16, 30 top and bottom, 40, 96 top, 152, 179; Victoria & Albert Museum (Crown Copyright) for page 54; Laurence Whistler for page 156.
The photograph on page 123 is reproduced by gracious permission of Her Majesty The Queen.

The illustrations on page 216 are by Robin Wiggins.

1. *What is Literature?*

The subjects we study at school can be divided roughly into two groups—the sciences and the arts. The sciences include mathematics, geography, chemistry, physics, and so on. Among the arts are drawing, painting, modelling, needlework, drama, music, literature. The purpose of education is to fit us for life in a civilised community, and it seems to follow from the subjects we study that the two most important things in civilised life are Art and Science.

Is this really true? If we take an average day in the life of the average man we seem to see very little evidence of concern with the sciences and the arts. The average man gets up, goes to work, eats his meals, reads the newspapers, watches television, goes to the cinema, goes to bed, sleeps, wakes up, starts all over again. Unless we happen to be professional scientists, laboratory experiments and formulae have ceased to have any meaning for most of us; unless we happen to be poets or painters or musicians—or teachers of literature, painting, and music—the arts seem to us to be only the concern of schoolchildren. And yet people have said, and people still say, that the great glories of our civilisation are the scientists and artists. Ancient Greece is remembered because of mathematicians like Euclid and Pythagoras, because of poets like Homer and dramatists like Sophocles. In two thousand years all our generals and politicians may be forgotten, but Einstein and Madame Curie and Bernard Shaw and Stravinsky will keep the memory of our age alive.

Why then are the arts and sciences important? I suppose with the sciences we could say that the answer is obvious: we have radium, penicillin, television and recorded sound, motor-cars and aircraft, air-conditioning and central heating. But these achievements have never been the primary intention of science; they are a sort of by-product, the things that emerge only when the scientist has performed his main task. That task is simply stated: to be curious, to keep on asking the question 'Why?' and not to be satisfied till an answer has been found. The scientist is curious about the universe: he wants to know why water boils at one temperature and freezes at another; why cheese is different from chalk; why one person behaves differently from another. Not only 'Why?' but 'What?' What is salt made of? What are the stars? What is the constitution of all matter? The answers to these questions do not necessarily make our lives any easier. The answer to one question—'Can the atom be split?'—has made our lives somewhat harder. But the questions have to be asked. It is man's job to be curious; it is man's job to try to find out the truth about the world about us, to answer the big question 'What is the world really like?'

Truth and Beauty   'The truth about the world about us.' 'Truth' is a word used in many different ways—'You're not telling the truth.' 'The truth about conditions in Russia.' 'Beauty is truth, truth beauty.' I want to use it here in the sense of *what lies behind an outward show*. Let me hasten to explain by giving an example. The sun rises in the east and sets in the west. That is what we see; that is the 'outward show'. In the past the outward show was regarded as the truth. But then a scientist came along to question it and then to announce that the truth was quite different from the appearance: the truth was that the earth revolved and the sun remained still—the outward show was telling a lie. The curious thing about scientific truths like this is that they often seem so useless. It makes no difference to the average man whether the sun moves or the earth moves. He still has to rise at dawn and stop work at dusk. But because a thing is useless it does not mean that it is *valueless*. Scientists still think it worthwhile to pursue truth. They do not expect that laws of gravitation and relativity are going to make much difference to everyday life, but they think it is a *valuable* activity to ask their eternal questions about the universe. And so we say that truth—the thing they are looking for—is a *value*.

A value is something that raises our lives above the purely animal level —the level of getting our food and drink, producing children, sleeping, and dying. This world of getting a living and getting children is sometimes called the world of *subsistence*. A value is something added to the world of subsistence. Some people say that our lives are unsatisfactory because they are mostly concerned with things that are impermanent— things that decay and change. Sitting here now, a degree or so above the equator, I look round my hot room and see nothing that will last. It won't be long before my house collapses, eaten by white ants, eroded by rain and wind. The flowers in front of me will be dead tomorrow. My typewriter is already rusty. And so I hunger for something that is permanent, something that will last forever. Truth, I am told, is a thing that will last forever.

Truth is one value. Another is beauty. And here, having talked about the scientist, I turn to the artist. The scientist's concern is truth, the artist's concern is beauty. Now some philosophers tell us that beauty and truth are the same thing. They say there is only one value, one eternal thing which we can call x, and that truth is the name given to it by the scientist and beauty the name given to it by the artist. Let us try to make this clear. There is a substance called salt. If I am a blind man I have to rely on my sense of taste to describe it: salt to me is a substance with a taste which we can only call 'salty'. If I have my eyesight but no sense of taste I have to describe salt as a white crystalline substance. Now both descriptions are correct, but neither is complete in itself. Each description concentrates on *one way of examining salt*. It is possible to say that the scientist examines x in one way, the artist examines it in another. Beauty is one aspect of x, truth is another. But what is x? Some people call it ultimate reality—the thing that is left when the universe of appearances, of outward show, is removed. Other people call it God, and they say that beauty and truth are two of the qualities of God.

Anyway, both the artist and the scientist are seeking something which they think is real. Their methods are different. The scientist sets his brain to work and, by a slow process of trial and error, after long experiment and enquiry, he finds his answer. This is usually an exciting moment. We remember the story of Archimedes finding his famous principle in the bath and rushing out naked, shouting 'Eureka!' ('I've found it!') The artist wants to make something which will produce just that sort of excitement in the minds of other people—the excitement of discovering something new about x, about reality. He may make a picture, a play, a poem, or a palace, but he wants to make the people who see or hear or read his creation feel excited and say about it, 'That is beautiful.' Beauty, then, you could define as the quality you find in any object which produces in your mind a special kind of excitement, an excitement somehow tied up with a sense of discovery. It need not be something made by man; a sunset or a bunch of flowers or a tree may make you feel this excitement and utter the word 'Beautiful!' But the primary task of natural things like flowers and trees and the sun is perhaps not to be beautiful but just to exist. The primary task of the artist's creations is to be beautiful.

Let us try to understand a little more about this 'artistic excitement'. First of all, it is what is known as a *static* excitement. It does not make you want to *do* anything. If you call me a fool and various other bad names, I shall get very excited and possibly want to fight you. But the excitement of experiencing beauty leaves one content, as though one has just achieved something. The achievement, as I have already suggested, is the achievement of a discovery. But a discovery of what? I would say the discovery of a *pattern* or the realisation of *order*. Again I must hasten to explain. Life to most of us is just a jumble of sensations, like a very bad film with no plot, no real beginning and end. We are also confused by a great number of contradictions: life is ugly, because people are always trying to kill one another; life is beautiful, because we see plenty of evidence of people trying to be kind to one another. Hitler and Gandhi were

Artistic excitement

Still-life with onions by Cézanne.

both human beings. We see the ugliness of a diseased body and the come-liness of a healthy one; sometimes we say, 'Life is good'; sometimes we say, 'Life is bad'. Which is the true statement? Because we can find no single answer we become confused. A work of art seems to give us the single answer by seeming to show that there is order or pattern in life. Let me show how this works.

Artistic unity   The artist takes raw material and forces or coaxes it into a pattern. If he is a painter he may choose from the world about us various single ob-jects—an apple, a wine-bottle, a table-napkin, a newspaper—and arrange them into a single composition on canvas—what is called a 'still-life'. All these different objects are seen to be part of one pattern, a pattern bounded by the four sides of the picture-frame, and we get satisfaction out of seeing this unity, a unity created out of objects which previously seemed to have nothing in common with each other at all. A sculptor will take hard, shapeless stone and force it into the resemblance of a human figure; there unity has been established between completely different things; soft flesh and hard stone, and also between the shapely human figure and the shapeless inhuman rock. The musician takes the sounds produced by scraping a string and blowing down a tube, and he creates order out of them by forcing on them the *shape* of a tune or the order of harmony. The novelist takes incidents from human life and gives them a plot, a beginning and an end—another pattern.

Unity, order, and pattern may be created in other ways too. The poet may bring two completely different things together and make them into a unity by creating a metaphor or simile. T. S. Eliot, a modern poet, takes two completely different pictures—one of the autumn evening, one of a patient in a hospital awaiting an operation—and joins them together like this:

> Let us go then, you and I,
> When the evening is laid out against the sky,
> Like a patient etherised upon a table.

Beethoven, in his Ninth Symphony, makes the chorus sing about the starry heavens, and accompanies their song with a comic march on bassoons and piccolo. Again, two completely opposed ideas—the sublime and the grotesque—have been brought together and fused into a unity. You see, then, that this excitement we derive from a work of art is mostly the excitement of seeing connections that did not exist before, of seeing quite different aspects of life unified through a pattern.

That is the highest kind of artistic experience. The lowest kind is pure sensation: 'What a beautiful sunset!' means we are overwhelmed by the colour; 'What a beautiful apple-pie!' means that our sense of taste—either now in the act of eating or else in anticipation—is being pleased. Between this kind of experience and the experience of 'patterns' comes another kind: the pleasure of finding an artist able to *express* our feelings for us. The artist finds a means of setting down our emotions—joy, *Artistic expression* passion, sorrow, regret—and, as it were, helps us to *separate* those emotions from ourselves. Let me make this clear. Any strong emotion has to be relieved. When we are happy we shout or dance, when we feel sorrow we want to weep. But the emotion has to be expressed (i.e. pressed out, like juice from a lime). Poets and musicians are especially expert at expressing emotions for us. A death in the family, the loss of money and other calamities are soothed by music and poetry, which seem to find in words or sounds a means of getting the sorrow out of our systems. But, on a higher level, our personal troubles are relieved when we can be made to see them as part of a pattern, so that here again we have the discovery of unity, of one personal experience being part of a greater whole. We feel that we do not have to bear this sorrow on our own: our sorrow is part of a huge organisation—the universe—and a necessary part of it. And when we discover that a thing is necessary we no longer complain about it.

Artistic methods   Our concern is with literature, but the student of literature must always maintain a live interest also in music and painting, sculpture, architecture, film, and theatre. All the arts try to perform the same sort of task, differing only in their methods. Methods are dictated by the sort of material used. There are *spatial* materials—paint, stone, clay—and there are *temporal* materials—words, sounds, dance-steps, stage movements. In other words, some arts work in terms of space, others in terms of time. You can take in a painting or building or piece of sculpture almost immediately, but to listen to a symphony or read a poem takes time—often a lot of time. Thus music and literature have a great deal in common: they both use the temporal material of sounds. Music uses meaningless sounds as raw material; literature uses those meaningful sounds we call words.

Use of words   Now there are two ways of using words, one artistic, one non-artistic. This means that words themselves can be viewed in two different ways. There is, in fact, the meaning that a word has in the dictionary (what is called the *lexical* meaning or the *denotation*) and the associations that the word has gained through constant use (the *connotations* of the word). Take the word 'mother', for instance. The dictionary definition is designed only to make you *understand* what the word means. It means the female parent of an animal. That is denotation. But the word, because we first use it in connection with our own mothers, carries many associations— warmth, security, comfort, love. We feel strongly about our mothers. Because of these associations 'mother' is used in connection with other things about which we are expected to feel strongly—our country, our school (thus 'motherland' and 'alma mater', which means 'dear mother'). We say then that 'mother' is rich in connotations. Connotations appeal to the feelings, denotations to the brain. Thus various activities which involve the use of words and are concerned with giving orders or information—the framing of club rules, for instance—will try to restrict words to denotation only. The writer of a science book, the creators of a new constitution for a country—these do not want to appeal to the emotions of the reader, only to his brain, his understanding. They are not writing literature. The writer of literature is much more concerned with the connotations, the ways in which he can make his words move or excite you, the ways in which he can suggest colour or movement or character. The poet, whose work is said to represent the highest form of literature, is most of all concerned with the connotations of words.

Connotations can be likened to the clusters of sounds you hear when you strike a single note on the piano. Strike middle C forcefully and you will hear far more than that one note. You will hear fainter notes rising out of it, notes called harmonics. The note itself is the denotation, the harmonics the connotations.

The writer of literature, especially the poet, differs from the scientist or lawyer in *not restricting* his words. The scientist has to make his word mean one thing and one thing only, so does the lawyer. But once the word—like our note on the piano—is allowed to vibrate freely, it not only calls up associations but also, at times, suggests other completely different meanings and perhaps even other words. Here is an extreme example:

> Action calls like a bugle and my heart
> Buckles . . .[1]

Now what does 'buckle' mean there? We use it to denote the fastening of a belt and also the collapsing of any solid body—sheet metal, a bicycle wheel. Now in a piece of scientific or legal writing the word must have one meaning or the other. But in this fragment of verse we are not so restricted. The word can carry two meanings, can suggest two different things at the same time. So that this passage means: 'I am called to action and I get ready for it: I buckle on my military equipment. But at the same time I am afraid; my heart seems to collapse inside me, like a wheel collapsing when it meets an obstacle.'

This may serve to illustrate how the creator of literature makes his words work overtime. It is not only dictionary meaning that counts—it is sound, suggestion of other meanings, other words, as well as those clusters of harmonics we call connotations. Literature may be defined as words working hard; literature is the *exploitation of words*.

But literature has different branches, and some branches do more ex-
ploiting of words than others. Poetry relies most on the power of words, on their manifold suggestiveness, and in a sense you may say that poetry is the *most literary* of all branches of literature; the most literary because it makes the greatest use of the raw material of literature, which is words. Once upon a time, the only kind of literature that existed was poetry; prose was used merely for jotting down laws and records and scientific theories. With the ancient Greeks, poetry had three departments—lyric, dramatic, and epic. In lyrical poetry the author was concerned with expressing certain emotions—love, hate, pity, fear—relying all the time on the power of his words. In dramatic poetry (or plays) he did not have to rely quite so much on words (although Greek drama was packed with lyrical poems) because there was action, a plot, human character. In epic poetry he could tell a tale—again making use of character and action—
and there perhaps his skill as a narrator and his constructive power would be more important than the suggestive qualities of words.

Literary forms

[1] Compare a similar use of the word 'buckle' in 'The Windhover' by Gerard Manley Hopkins, and also William Empson's discussion of the poem in his *Seven Types of Ambiguity*.

We still have these three ancient divisions, but two of them are no longer—except very occasionally—presented in the form of poetry. The epic has become the novel, written in prose. (Sometimes people still write novels in verse, but they are not very popular.) The dramatic poem has become the film or the play (only rarely in verse nowadays). Lyrical poetry is the only kind of poetry left. In other words, there is very little room for the epic poet or the dramatic poet nowadays: the poet, as opposed to the playwright or the novelist, writes short lyrical poems, publishes them in magazines, and does not expect to make much money out of them. There is no living poet who can make a living out of his poetry. This is a bad sign and perhaps means that there is no future for poetry. But this is something we can discuss later.

There are other branches of literature and 'near-literature' which we shall consider in this book, particularly the essay, which is what a man writes when he has no gift for poetry or the novel. But I should like you to keep those three main forms in mind—the novel, the drama, the poem —for they are the forms which have attracted our greatest names during the last few centuries. In our own age it seems likely that only the novel will survive as a literary form. There are few readers of poetry, and most people prefer to enjoy drama in the form of the film (a visual form, not a literary form). But before we come to the problems of the present we have a good deal to learn about the past, and the past of English Literature is the subject of the pages that follow.

2. *What is English Literature?*

English literature is literature written in English. It is not merely the literature of England or of the British Isles, but a vast and growing body of writings made up of the work of authors who use the English language as a natural medium of communication. In other words, the 'English' of 'English literature' refers not to a nation but to a language. This seems to me to be an important point. There is a tendency among some people to regard, for instance, American literature as a separate entity, a body of writings distinct from that of the British Isles, and the same attitude is beginning to prevail with regard to the growing literatures of Africa and Australia. Joseph Conrad was a Pole, Demetrios Kapetanakis was a Greek, Ernest Hemingway was an American, Lin Yutang was a Chinese, but English is the medium they have in common, and they all belong—with Chaucer and Shakespeare and Dickens—to English literature. On the other hand, a good deal of the work of Sir Thomas More and Sir Francis Bacon—both Englishmen—is written not in English but in Latin, and William Beckford and T. S. Eliot have written in French. Such writings are outside the scope of our survey. Literature is an art which exploits language, English literature is an art which exploits the English language. But it is not just an English art. It is international, and Chinese, Malays, Africans, Indians reading this book may well one day themselves contribute to English literature.

But in this brief history we must confine ourselves to the literature produced in the British Isles, chiefly because the 'international' concept of English literature belongs to the present and the future, and our main concern is with the past. In the pages that follow we shall hardly move out of England, and the term 'English' will refer as much to the race as to the language. Let us therefore begin by considering very briefly both the race and the country, for, though the subject matter of the writer is humanity, and humanity is above race and nation, yet he is bound to take humanity as he finds it in his own country and, to a lesser extent, in his own age. But, to the writer, geography seems to be more important

England and the English

9

Cookham Moor by Sir Stanley Spencer.

than history, and it is the geography of England that is perpetually reflected in its literature, far more than the pattern of events which we call the history of a nation. England is an island, and the sea washes its literature as much as its shores. It is a cold, stormy sea, quite unlike the placid Mediterranean or the warm waters of the tropics. Its voice is never far away from the music of English poetry, and it can be heard clearly enough even in the novels of a 'town' writer like Dickens. The landscape of England is varied—mountains and lakes and rivers—but the uniform effect is one of green gentleness—downs and farms and woods. The English landscape made Wordsworth; tropical jungles could never have produced a poet like him, and, often, when we read him in the tropics, we find it hard to accept his belief in a kindly, gentle power brooding over nature—it does not fit in with snakes and elephants and tigers and torrential rain. We have to know something about the English landscape before we can begin to appreciate the English nature poets.

Ruling sea and land is the English climate. In the tropics there are no seasons except the rainy and the dry, but in England one is aware of the earth approaching and retreating from the sun—spring, summer, autumn, winter, and the festivals associated with these seasons. The longing for spring is a common theme with English poets, and Christmas, the winter festival, is the very essence of Charles Dickens. The Christian year in England is very much the natural year—the resurrection of the earth at Easter, the hope of new life expressed in joy at the birth of Christ at the dead time of the year. Four distinct seasons, but all comparatively gentle —the summer never too hot and the winter never arctic. But it is the cold of England that is hardest for the dweller in the tropics to understand:

> When icicles hang by the wall,
>   And Dick the shepherd blows his nail.

Snow and frozen ponds and bare trees are common images in English literature, but it is only by a great effort of the imagination that the inhabitant of a perpetually warm land can bring himself to appreciate their significance for the English poet and his English reader. It has been said that the English climate is responsible for the English character: the English are cold rather than hot-blooded, temperate rather than fiery, active because of the need to keep warm, philosophical under difficulties because—so an unkind person said—if you can stand the English climate you can stand anything.

The English are also said to be conservative, disliking change (this is generally true of island-dwellers), but also, because the sea makes them a nation of sailors, adventurous and great travellers. The English have, for nearly a thousand years, been free of domination by foreign powers (an island is not easy to invade), and this has made them independent, jealous of their freedom, but also a little suspicious of foreigners. The English

are, in fact, a curious mixture, and their literature reflects the contradictions in their character. The English rebels and eccentrics—people
like Shelley and Byron and Blake—are as typical as the rather dull die-
hards who sit at home and never change their opinions in fifty years: the
very fact of a conservative society—social stability, no foreign domination—explains the rebels and eccentrics, for only in a country where
tradition is respected will you find men who say that tradition should not
be respected. In other words, to have rebels you must have something to
rebel against.

The English are sometimes said to be mad: this is certainly a tradition
in some European countries. It is hard to say what this means, but possibly it refers to impatience with restrictions, dislike of anything which
interferes with personal liberty. 'Englishmen never will be slaves,' said
George Bernard Shaw. 'They are free to do whatever the Government
and public opinion allow them to do.' But both these can restrict so far
and no farther: the Englishman has always been able to change his
Government and what an Englishman calls 'public opinion' is usually
what he himself thinks. The English love justice but hate laws, and it is
this hatred of laws which makes so much English literature seem 'mad'.
A French writer obeys the Academy rules which govern the employment
of the French language, but a typically English writer like Shakespeare
is always ready to make language do 'mad' things, to invent new words
or use metaphors which take the breath away with their daring. And it
follows that much English literature is 'formless'. Shakespeare breaks all
the dramatic rules, Dickens's novels proceed, seemingly without rhyme
or reason, not like a controlled and organised work of art, but like a river
in full spate. The French and Italians have always liked traditional verse-
forms—the sonnet, the rondel, the line with a fixed number of syllables—
but the English have usually preferred to invent their own forms and,
eventually, to have as many syllables as they wished in a line of verse.
English literature, in short, has a freedom, a willingness to experiment,
a hatred of rules which has no parallel in any other literature.

English language   So much, briefly, for the country and the people. We must now consider the English language itself and ask: What do we mean by 'English'?
This is not an easy question to answer. We use terms like 'Chinese',
'Malay', 'French', and 'Russian' very loosely when talking about language, always assuming that each of these names refers to a single fixed
thing, like a house or a tree. But language is not a thing of dead bricks
and wood like a house, nor a simple organism like a tree. A house can
decay and a tree can die, but when a language seems to die (as Latin may
be said to have died) it has really only undergone great change. Change
implies time, and time suggests history, and so the term 'language'
should really mean: a system of sounds made by the vocal organs of a
particular group of people, possessing meaning for that group of people,

and existing continuously for a given period of history. But, if language changes, is it not likely that it will change, as we say, 'beyond all recognition'? There may well be so great a difference between the Chinese of 1000 A.D. and the Chinese of 1980 A.D., that the two kinds of Chinese are really two completely different languages. That is certainly the case with English. English has been spoken continuously in England for over fifteen hundred years, but the English spoken in 1000 A.D. is a language that the Englishman of today cannot understand. And yet it is the same language, it is still English. This seems absurd. If a modern Englishman cannot understand a particular language he calls it a foreign language. But how can it be a foreign language when it is the language of his own country and his own ancestors? We solve the difficulty by talking about the 'historical phases' of a language and using the terms 'Old English' and 'Modern English'.

Old English

Old English has to be treated like any 'real' foreign language. It has to be learnt—with grammar books and dictionaries. If we want first-hand knowledge of the first English literature we have to get down to the learning of Old English first. But this is not a thing I expect you to do, at least not yet. For the moment you will have to be content with knowing roughly what Old English literature is about, roughly what kind of poetry was written by the ancestors of the English and what kind of prose. We have to know something about these things, we cannot just ignore them, because they have had, and still have, a certain influence on the literature of Modern English.

That is the concern of this book—the literature of Modern English. But again we are faced with a question: when does Modern English start? As far as we are concerned, it starts as soon as we find an old poem or prose-work which we can understand without getting out a grammar-book or a dictionary. Between Old English and Modern English there is a 'phase of transition' when what is virtually a foreign language is becoming like the language we use today. This phase is known as Middle English. Some Middle English books we can read without much diffi-culty; others are just as 'foreign' as Old English. There is a reason for this. Time, as we have seen, is one of the 'dimensions' of language; another dimension is space. 'English' means all the different kinds of English spoken from the very moment the first speakers of the language settled in England up to the present day. But it also means all the varying kinds of English spoken in different places, at any given moment in time. Today, for instance, in England itself a local dialect of English can be heard in Lancashire, another in Kent, another in Northumberland, another in Essex, and so on. But they all have a sound claim to be re-garded as 'true English', though we find it convenient to call them *English dialects*. It usually happens in any civilised country that one dia-lect establishes itself as the most important. Thus Kuo-yü is the dialect

Middle English

Dialects

taught in Chinese schools, and Johore Malay the dialect taught in Malay schools. The dialect chosen is usually the one which is spoken in the capital city, in the royal court, or in the universities. The English dialect which has established itself as the most important is that now known as Standard English or King's (or Queen's) English, historically speaking a mixture of the old East Midland dialect (north of the Thames) and the old Kentish dialect (south of the Thames). This is the dialect that I am writing now; this is the dialect that all foreigners who want to know English start to learn. Having been for a long time the dialect most favoured by royalty, by learned men and statesmen, it tends to have more *texts* than any other, and indeed some of the other dialects have no Modern English texts at all. It is chiefly the literature of Standard English that we are concerned with.

In the Middle English phase—the 'phase of transition'—all the dialects of England seemed to be as good as each other, and all of them had literatures. There was, as yet, no thought of a supreme dialect with a monopoly of English literature. This explains some of our difficulties. Chaucer wrote in the English of London and we find him comparatively easy to understand, for this English became the language we ourselves write and speak. But there were other poets writing in Worcestershire English and Lancashire English and Kentish English, hard for us to understand, and so we become frustrated. But by about 1400 the confusion is cleared up, and the history of English literature becomes the history of the literature of one dialect.

Or very nearly so. Even in the Modern period, a number of writers have preferred to write in their own county dialects. Robert Burns was one, clinging to the dialect of Ayrshire in Scotland, although he knew Standard English perfectly well. William Barnes, a brilliant language scholar of the nineteenth century, liked to write in the Dorset dialect. And today English literature contains works in the many English dialects of America, and even in the dialect of the West Indian negro. We should rejoice in this richness and variety.

English literature, then, is vast, extending long in time and wide in space. Our task now is to examine its beginnings in the temperate, misty, rainy island where the English nation came into being.

3. The First English Literature

The first Englishmen were foreigners. In other words, they came to England from abroad when England was already inhabited by a long-settled race and blessed by a fairly advanced civilisation. That long-settled race was the British race, and the beginnings of its settlement cannot be traced: they belong to pre-history. That race still exists, to be found mainly in Wales, to the west of England, speaking a language quite unlike English, different in temperament and culture from the English invader, still cultivating a literature which has never influenced—nor been much influenced by—the literature we are studying. It is ironical that this people should now be called the Welsh (from the Old English word for 'foreigner') when they are much less foreigners than the English. The ancient Romans called them 'Britanni' and their country 'Britannia'. We can call them Britons.

Roman Britain

These Britons were ruled for a few centuries by the Romans, and Britannia—or Britain—was the most westerly and northerly province of the Roman Empire. The Romans brought their language (of which traces still survive in the names of the towns of England) and their architects and engineers as well as their garrisons and governors. Britain was given towns, villas with central heating, public baths, theatres, and a system of roads which is still more or less in existence. But, as we know, the Roman Empire eventually fell, the Roman legions withdrew, and a people softened by civilisation and colonial rule was left to itself and to any tough invader who cared to cross from Europe. The time of the fall of the Roman Empire is also the time of the migrations of peoples from the East of Europe—such peoples as the Goths and Vandals, who themselves broke the power of Rome. Disturbed by these movements westward by barbarous and ruthless hordes, certain peoples from the north-west of Europe crossed the seas and settled—over a number of years—in Britain, driving the British west and claiming the country for themselves. These peoples included the Angles and Saxons, who still give their names to what is sometimes called the Anglo-Saxon race. Their language,

Anglo-Saxon England

15

Anglo-Saxon illumination from the Lindesfarne Gospels.

or group of dialects, is sometimes called Anglo-Saxon, but, in the interests of unity, we shall keep to the name Old English.

We have few historical details of these invasions and settlements, which you can think of as being completed by the end of the seventh century. The legends of King Arthur and his Knights of the Round Table tell of the defenders of the old Roman civilisation fighting a brave rearguard action against the new barbarians. The Angles and Saxons and, along with them, the Jutes were barbarians perhaps only in the sense that they were not Christians. The Roman Empire had ended as a Christian Empire and Christianity had been well-established as the religion of Britain. But the Angles and Saxons worshipped the old Germanic gods who still give their names to the days of the week—Thor and Woden and the rest. Yet they had some civilisation. They were farmers and sea-men, they knew something of law and the art of government, and it seems that they brought a literature with them from Europe to England, as the country must now be called.

By the end of the sixth century, the new masters of England had become a Christian people, chiefly because of the energy of the Christian evangelists from Ireland, who came over to convert them. And all the records of the early literature of the Anglo-Saxons belong to a Christian England, written by clerks in monasteries, kept stored in monasteries, and only coming to light at the time of the Reformation, when Henry VIII dissolved the monasteries. We must think of this literature as being *oral*, passed down by word of mouth from generation to generation, its creators for the most part unknown, and only being given a written form long after its composition. This literature is almost exclusively a verse literature. There is prose, but this is not strictly literature—history, theology, letters, biography—and the names of the writers of much of this prose are known. There is a lot of anonymous poetry in the world, but very little anonymous prose. Sound is the essence of verse, and hence verse is chiefly a matter of mouth and ear. But prose is a matter for the pen and it has to be composed on paper. When a man composes on paper he usually signs his name. A poem is recited, remembered, passed on, and its origin is forgotten—at least as far as early literatures are concerned.

The oldest poem in the English language is *Beowulf*. It was not composed in England, but on the continent of Europe: the new settlers brought it over along with their wives, goods, and chattels. It was not written down till the end of the ninth century. It is a stirring, warlike, violent poem of over three thousand lines, and it is perhaps difficult to think of it as being set down by a monk, a man of peace, in the quiet of a monastery. These Anglo-Saxon monks, however, had the blood of warriors in them, they were the sons and grandsons of Vikings. *Beowulf* is essentially a warrior's story. It tells of the hero who gives his name to the poem and his struggle with a foul monster—half-devil, half-man—called

Beowulf

Grendel, who has for a long time been raiding the banqueting-hall of King Hrothgar of Jutland (land of the Jutes) and carrying off and devouring Hrothgar's warriors. Beowulf sails from Sweden and comes to the help of Hrothgar. His fights with Grendel—and Grendel's equally horrific mother—are the subject of the poem, a poem whose grim music is the snapping of fangs, the crunching of bones, and whose colour is the grey of the northern winter, shot by the red of blood. It is strong meat, no work for the squeamish, but it is in no way a crude and primitive composition. It shows great skill in its construction, its imagery and language are sophisticated. It is not a Christian poem—despite the Christian flavour given to it by the monastery scribe (e.g. Grendel is of the accursed race of the first murderer, Cain)—but the product of an advanced pagan civilisation.

Old English
Language

Much of the strength and violence of *Beowulf* derive from the nature of Old English itself. That was a language rich in consonants, fond of clustering its consonants together, so that the mouth seems to perform a swift act of violence. The following Modern English words are to be found in Old English, and are typical of that language: *strength* ('in which seven muscular consonants strangle a single vowel'),[1] *breath*, *quell*, *drench*, *crash*. Compared with the softer languages of the East and South, Old English seems to be a series of loud noises. And the violence of the language is emphasised in the technique that the Old English poet employs. Here is a line from *Beowulf*:

> Steap stanlitho—stige nearwe
> (Steep stone-slopes, paths narrow)

The line is divided into two halves, and each half has two heavy stresses. Three (sometimes four, occasionally two) of the stresses of the whole line are made even more emphatic by the use of *head-rhyme*. Head-rhyme means making words begin with the same sound (this is sometimes called alliteration, but alliteration really refers to words beginning with the same letter, which is not always the same thing as beginning with the same sound). Although, since the Norman Conquest, most English verse has traditionally used *end-rhyme* (or ordinary rhyme, as we may call it) this old head-rhyme has always had some influence on English writers. In the twentieth century some poets have abandoned ordinary rhyme and reverted to the Old English practice. Certainly, the use of head-rhyme seems natural to English verse and it even plays a large part in everyday English speech: *hale and hearty; fat and forty; time and tide; fit as a fiddle; a pig in a poke*, etc., etc. This modern revival was perhaps started by Ezra Pound, an American, who translated the Old English poem *The Seafarer*

Head-rhyme

---

[1] *A History of English Literature*, Book I, by Emile Legouis, translated by Helen Douglas Irvine. J. M. Dent, 1937.

into Modern English but retained the technique of the original:

> Bitter breast-cares have I abided,
> Known on my keel many a care's hold,
> And dire sea-surge, and there I oft spent
> Narrow nightwatch nigh the ship's head
> While she tossed close to cliffs. Coldly afflicted,
> My feet were by frost benumbed.
> Chill its chains are; chafing sighs
> Hew my heart round and hunger begot
> Mere-weary mood. . . .

This use of head-rhyme in Old English verse, while it produces an effect of violence, is also responsible for a certain inability to 'call a spade a spade'. The need to find words beginning with the same sound means often that a poet has to call some quite common thing by an uncommon name, usually a name that he himself invents for his immediate purpose. Thus the sea becomes the swan's way or the whale's road or the sail-path. Fog becomes the air-helmet, darkness the night-helmet. The Old English language was well fitted for playing this sort of game, because its normal way of making new words was to take two old words and join them together. Thus, as there was no word for *crucify*, the form *rod-fasten* had to be made, meaning 'to fix to a tree'. The word *vertebra* had not yet come into English, so *ban-hring* (bone-ring) had to be used instead. A lot of Old English words thus have the quality of riddles—'guess what this is'—and it is not surprising that riddling was a favourite Old English pursuit. Indeed, some of the loveliest of the shorter poems are called riddles. There is one on a bull's horn. The horn itself speaks, telling how it once was the weapon of an armed warrior (the bull) but soon afterwards was transformed into a cup, its bosom being filled by a maiden 'adorned with rings'. Finally it is borne on horseback, and it swells with the air from someone else's bosom. It has become a trumpet. The actual guessing—essence of a riddle—is less important than the fanciful description of the object whose name, of course, is never disclosed.

It is time we examined a piece of Old English verse, and we cannot do better than take a poem composed by Caedmon. This poem is perhaps the first piece of Christian literature to appear in Anglo-Saxon England, and it is especially notable because, according to the Venerable Bede, it was divinely inspired. Caedmon, a humble and unlearned man, tended the cattle of an abbey on the Yorkshire coast. One night, at a feast, when songs were called for, he stole out quietly, ashamed that he could contribute nothing to the amateur entertainment. He lay down in the cow-shed and slept. In his sleep he heard a voice asking him to sing. 'I cannot sing,' he said, 'and that's why I left the feast and came here.' 'Nevertheless,' said the mysterious voice, 'you shall sing to me.' 'What shall I sing?'

asked Caedmon. 'Sing me the Song of Creation,' was the answer. Then Caedmon sang the following verses, verses he had never heard before:

> Nu we sculan herian   heofonrices weard,
> Metodes mihte   and his modgethonc;
> Weorc wuldorfaeder,   swa he wundras gehwaes,
> Ece dryhten,   ord onstealde.

Those are the first four lines, and they can be translated as follows: 'Now we must praise the Guardian of the kingdom of heaven, the might of the Creator and the thought of His mind; the work of the Father of men, as He, the Eternal Lord, formed the beginning of every wonder.' If you look carefully at these lines you will see that Old English is not a completely foreign language. Certain words we still possess—*and, his, he, we*—while other words have merely changed their form a little. Thus, *nu* has become *now* (still *nu* in Scotland), *mihte* has become *might*, *weorc* has become *work*, *swa* has become *so*, *faeder* has become *father*. *Heofonric* (heavenly kingdom) suggests *bishopric*, which we still use to describe the 'kingdom' of a bishop. Other words, of course, have died completely. Note the form of the poem: the division of the line into two halves, the four stresses, the use of head-rhyme. You can think of this poem as having been composed about 670, a key year for English literature.

There is a good deal of Old English verse, some dealing with war, like *The Battle of Maldon*, whose heroic note still rings over the centuries:

> Thought shall be braver, the heart bolder,
> Mightier the mood, as our might lessens.

There is a larger body of verse on Christian themes, sometimes beautiful, but generally duller than the pagan, warrior poems. There are two great poems—*The Seafarer* and *The Wanderer*—whose resigned melancholy (the laments of men without fixed abode) and powerful description of nature still speak strongly through the strange words and the heavy-footed rhythms. Resigned melancholy is a characteristic of much Old English verse: even when a poem is at its most vigorous—dealing with war, storm, sea, the drinking-hall, the creation of the world—we always seem to be aware of a certain undercurrent of sadness. Perhaps this is a reflection of the English climate—the grey skies and the mist—or perhaps it is something to do with the mere sound of English in its first phase—heavy-footed, harsh, lacking in the tripping, gay quality of a language like French or Italian. Or perhaps it is a quality added, in odd lines or even words, by the scribes in their monasteries—monks aware that this world is vanity, that life is short, that things pass away and only God is real. But the sense of melancholy is there all the time, part of the strange haunting music of Old English poetry.

It remains to say something of Old English prose. Before we can do this we must remind ourselves of the fact of dialect, the fact that Old English was not a single language but is—as with Modern English—merely the name we give to a group of dialects. Think of England, about the end of the ninth century, as divided into three main kingdoms—Northumbria, the long thick neck of the country; Mercia, the fat body; Wessex, the foot, stretching from the Thames to Land's End. Of these three, Northumbria was the centre of learning, with its rich monasteries crammed with manuscript books bound in gold and ornamented with precious stones. Up to the middle of the ninth century, all the poetry of England was recorded in the Northumbrian dialect. But in those days, as any monk would tell us, nothing was permanent, and the ninth century sees the end of Northumbria as the home of learning and the library of England. The Danes invaded England (*The Battle of Maldon* tells of a bitter fight against the Danes) and sacked Northumbria as the Goths had sacked Rome. The monasteries were looted, the precious books were ripped to pieces for their rich ornaments, the monks fled or were slaughtered. Now Wessex, the kingdom of Alfred the Great, became England's cultural centre.

Old English prose

Alfred

When Alfred came to the throne of Wessex he was not happy about the state of learning he found there. (There is a very interesting letter he wrote about this to one of his bishops.) But then was no time for improving it: the Danes were savaging the country and Alfred's task was to organise armies and beat back the invader. In 878, when it looked as though the Danes would become masters of England, Alfred defeated them in a series of decisive battles and then made a treaty which confined their rule to the north. Now, in a peaceful kingdom, he began to improve the state of education, founding colleges, importing teachers from Europe, translating Latin books into West Saxon (or Wessex) English, preserving the wealth of verse which had left its old home in Northumbria. So now the dialect of English culture became a southern one.

Alfred is an important figure in the history of English literature. He was not an artist (that is, he wrote no poems, drama, or stories), but he knew how to write good clear prose. Also, with helpers, he translated much Latin into English (including the *Ecclesiastical History* of the Venerable Bede), and so showed writers of English how to handle foreign ideas. English had been mostly concerned with sheer *description*: now it had to learn how to express *abstractions*. And also, because of his concern for education and books, Alfred may be said to have established the continuous cultural tradition of England—despite the foreign invasions which were still to come.

For much of the later history of Anglo-Saxon times we are indebted to what is known as the *Anglo-Saxon Chronicle*—a record of the main happenings of the country, kept by monks in seven successive monasteries, and covering the period from the middle of the ninth century to 1154, when Henry II came to the throne. This is the first history of a Germanic people, in some ways the first newspaper, certainly the most solid and interesting piece of Old English prose we possess. And in it we see Old English moving steadily towards Middle English, that transitional language which is slowly to develop into the tongue of our own age.

Our brief story ends at the close of the first thousand years of the Christian era. It ends with the impassioned prose of an Archbishop of York, Wulfstan, crying out that the end of the world is coming, the Anti-Christ is here: 'Repent, for the day of the Lord is at hand.' And indeed it was the end, not of the world but of Anglo-Saxon England. The Danes over-ran the whole country and, after only a brief moment of independence, the Anglo-Saxons were to know an even greater servitude. In 1066, the Normans came over to make England theirs, to change the old way of life and also the language. Heavy-footed Old English was to become—through its mingling with a lighter, brighter tongue from sunnier lands—the richest and most various literary medium in the whole of history.

4. The Coming of the Normans

'Norman' means 'North-man'. The Normans were, in fact, of the same blood as the Danes, but they had thoroughly absorbed the culture of the late Roman Empire, had been long Christianised, and spoke that offshoot of Latin we call Norman French. Thus their kingdom in France had a very different set of traditions from those of the country they conquered. You may sum it up by saying that the Norman way of life looked south— towards the Mediterranean, towards the sun, towards wine and laughter, while the Anglo-Saxon way of life looked towards the grey northern seas—grim, heavy, melancholy, humourless.

Not that the conquering Normans were irresponsible or inefficient (qualities which, wrongly, people often associate with the southern races). William the Conqueror made a thorough job of taking over the country, and had everything neatly inventoried—down to the number of deer in the forests, so it was said—and this inventory carried the frightening name of Domesday Book. So the first piece of Norman writing in England is a catalogue of the king's property, for William saw himself as the owner of the country. He owned the land and everything in it, but granted land to the nobles who had helped him achieve his conquest, and so set up that feudal system which was to transform English life. Feudalism may be thought of as a sort of pyramid, with the king at the apex and society ranged below him in lower and lower degrees of rank, till at the base you have the humblest order of men, tied to working on the land, men with few rights. Few rights, but yet rights, for one of the characteristics of feudalism was responsibility working two ways— up and down. The barons were responsible to the king, but the king had his responsibilities towards them, and so on down to the base of the pyramid.

Domesday Book

With the coming of the Normans, their laws, their castles, their knowledge of the art of war, the Anglo-Saxons sank to a position of abjectness which killed their culture and made their language a despised thing. Old English literature dies (though in the monasteries the *Anglo-Saxon*

Chronicle ticks away and with the common people the old poems are still half-remembered) and, to take the place of Old English literature, the Normans produce little of value. But, of course, the Normans remembered the literature they shared with much of the rest of France, and it is the qualities of old French literature which are to appear in England later, when, in fact, the country has recovered from the shock of change and the culture of the north has begun to mix with the culture of the south. We can only give here a very general impression of the old French

*Old English
Literature*

literature. Its themes, like the themes of Old English literature, were often warlike, as in the great *Song of Roland*, but, if one may take a metaphor from the cinema, Old English verse is in black and white, French literature in colour. Old English verse is drenched in mist, grey and grim, while French literature is drenched in sunlight. In the *Song of Roland* we see the silver of the armour, the bright red of the spilt blood, the blue of the sky. A characteristic word in the poetry of France is, as Legouis points out, *'clere'*—clear—as though the author is always aware of the light shining on to and through things. Along with this colour and clarity goes the lighter melody of end-rhyme. French, moreover, is a light-footed language, lacking the heavy hammerstrokes of Old and, for that matter, Modern English. To the Anglo-Saxons French must have appeared a feminine language, softer and gayer than their own masculine tongue. But out of the mingling of feminine and masculine was to come something like an ideal language, a language made 'complete' by marriage.

The Normans in England wrote a literature which was neither one thing nor the other—neither a true English literature nor a true French literature. Living in England, they were cut off from French culture, and the kind of French they used lost its purity, its flexibility—something that always happens to a language when it is exported to a foreign land and has no opportunity for refreshing itself through frequent contacts with the mother-country. The Anglo-Saxons who tried to use the language of the conqueror were not very skilful. And so Latin—rather than Norman French or Old English—tended to be employed as a kind of compromise. In the twelfth and thirteenth centuries we find songs and histories in Latin, some of the latter throwing a good deal of light on the changing *mythology* of England.

Mythology

By a mythology we mean a body of beliefs—not necessarily based on true happenings or true historical characters—which touch the imagination of a race or of an age, inspire its literature and sometimes its behaviour, and provide a kind of romantic glamour to colour the dullness of everyday life. In our own age we find many of our myths in film-stars or popular singers or even strip-cartoon characters. These myths are bigger than life, they are midway between gods and men, they are, in the old Greek sense, heroic. A religion does not provide mythical figures while it is still alive: as long as we believe in the religion, its great names are divine—like Christ or Krishna—or linked with divinity, like Mohamed. But when a religion dies, is no longer seriously believed in, then its figures can become part of a mythology. Thus the old Greek gods belong to European mythology still, and so do the old Greek warriors who gained so much of their strength and skill from the gods—Agamemnon, Ulysses, Aeneas, and so on. These heroic figures began to appear in the Latin writings of England after the Norman Conquest, and so did Brutus (the legendary grandson of Aeneas), who was presented in Geoffrey of Monmouth's *History of the Britons* (written about 1140) as the father of the British race. (This work was translated into French by Wace, and his translation was translated—about 1200—into English by Layamon. Layamon's work is in verse and it is called, after the mythical founder of the British, quite simply *Brut*.) But—and this is interesting— a far greater hero than any of Greece or Rome emerges in the figure of King Arthur. This is interesting and curious because Arthur belongs to the mythology of a race—the Welsh or true Britons—that the Anglo-Saxons drove out of England and that the Normans, invading their borders, struck with a heavy fist. Why this renewed interest in the shadowy British king and his Knights of the Round Table? Well, Geoffrey of Monmouth himself had been brought up in Wales and lived close to the myth; but even Norman writers seemed fascinated by it. It is possible that the Anglo-Saxons—a defeated race—were drawn closer to the race they had themselves defeated, and helped to spread the Arthurian myth through England. It is more likely that the Normans, through their invasions of Wales, became interested in the Welsh and their culture. Anyway, the myth of King Arthur is as powerful today as ever it was— we can see this not only from films and children's books but also from the curious rumour that circulated in England in 1940—that Arthur had come again to drive out the expected invader, that Arthur would never really die. Soon another powerful—but not quite so powerful—myth was to arise among the English—that of Robin Hood and his followers, the outlaws who would not accept Norman rule but lived, free as the green leaves, in the forest.

King Arthur

Time passes. The Normans learn the language of the English and some of the English learn the language of the Normans. But English, not Norman French, is to prevail. We see slowly developing a kind of English that enriches itself with borrowings from Norman French; we see the words creeping into books, often introduced with translation into Old English: 'Despair, that is to say, wanhope.' But sometimes, even today, the mingling does not seem really complete. (Words like 'walk' seem more natural to Englishmen than words like 'promenade'.) The coming of Norman French to England also opened the door to the borrowing of long Latin words (Latin being the parent tongue of French), so that what is, in fact, quite good English can sound strange and even absurd to the English ear. Dr. Johnson, in the eighteenth century, spoke of a certain play, saying: 'It has insufficient vitality to preserve it from putrefaction.' He could have said, and actually did say earlier: 'It has not wit enough to keep it sweet.' The second is nearly pure Old English; the first is a mixture of French and Latin. The date which you can keep in mind as marking the beginning of the Normans' interest in the language of the conquered is 1204, when Normandy was lost and the connection of the Normans with the Continent was severed.

There is plenty to say about the literature written in Middle English—the language of transition—but, as you are not at present likely to be interested in reading anything written between, say, 1200 and 1340 (the year of Chaucer's birth), I shall merely state very briefly what one needs to know about the writers who pave the way for the first great English poet.

Middle English Religious writing

There was a good deal of religious writing—works like the *Ormulum*, a translation of some of the Gospels read at Mass, made by the monk Orm about 1200. There is the *Ancrene Riwle*—advice given by a priest to three religious ladies living not in a convent but in a little house near a church. This is rather charming, and it seems that, for a time in the literature of England, there is an awareness of woman as woman—a creature to be treated courteously and delicately, in gentle language. There is a connection here with the devotion to the Blessed Virgin, Mother of Christ, a cult which the Normans brought over, practised by them in prayers and homage even when it was forbidden by Rome. Chivalry, which demanded a devotion to womankind almost amounting to worship, is another myth of old Europe, killed finally by Cervantes in his satire *Don Quixote*, written in Shakespeare's time. There is a curious book written about 1300—a translation from the French spoken in England—by Robert Mannyng, called *Handlyng Synne*, setting out in verse stories the various paths of sin—satirical, amusing, as well as edifying. There is the *Pricke of Conscience*, probably written by Richard Rolle about 1340, which deals with the pains of hell in horrifying detail—the damned souls, tortured by thirst, finding that fire will not quench it, suck instead the heads of poisonous snakes. Demons yell, strike with red-hot hammers, while their victims shed tears of fire, nauseated by unspeakable filth and smells of an indescribable foulness.

Middle English non-religious writing

Of the non-religious works in Middle English, one can point first to certain lyrics, written with great delicacy and skill, but signed by no name, which still have power to enchant us and still, in fact, are sung. This is known everywhere, together with its delightful tune:

> Sumer is icumen in,
> Lhude sing cuccu!
> Groweth sed and bloweth med,
> And springth the wude nu—
> Sing cuccu!

There is love poetry, like the fine song *Alison* (a common name for girls in the Middle Ages), which has the refrain:

> An hendy hap ichabbe y-hent,
> Ichot from hevene it is me sent,
> From alle wymmen my love is lent
> Ant lyht on Alisoun.

We may translate this as follows:

> By a gracious chance I have caught it—I know it has been sent from heaven.
> From all other women I have taken away my love: it has alighted on Alison.

There are patriotic songs, carols for Christmas and Easter, even political songs.

Longer poems are *The Owl and the Nightingale*—the story of a dispute between the two birds as to which has the finer song; *Pearl*—a long lament in very ornamental language on the death of a child and a vision of the heaven to which she has gone. Contained in the same manuscript as *Pearl* (and belonging with it to the middle of the fourteenth century) is a remarkable work written in the Lancashire dialect called *Sir Gawayn and the Green Knight*. This takes its tale from the myths of the Round Table and tells of the knight Gawain and his curious encounter with the Green Knight of the title, a giant who, having had his head cut off by Gawain, calmly picks it up, tucks it under his arm, and walks off. But he had made a compact that after a year he should deliver a return blow, at the Green Chapel where Gawain undertakes to meet him. On the way there Gawain stays at a castle and is subjected to various temptations by the lord's wife. He resists them, but when the lord of the castle proves to be the Green Knight, Gawain conceals from him the girdle of invulnerability the lady had given him. The Green Knight had himself planned the temptations, and because of the one deception Sir Gawain is given a blow which, however, only slightly wounds him, his merit in resisting the main temptations being sufficient to save him from receiving a fatal blow. The poem is written (appropriately enough) in head-rhyme, in language which shows little Norman influence but is nevertheless notable for a lightness of touch, a certain humour, and great power of description.

Of the other works of the fourteenth century we must mention a very strange book of travel written by a certain 'Sir John Mandeville'— probably the name is fictitious. The writer seems to have been fond of

Longer Middle English poems

his own book, for apparently he wrote it in Latin first, then in French, finally in English. It is an interesting book in many ways, and seems to have been a popular one, for it was copied out again and again (printing had not yet been invented) and in the British Museum there are, at this day, twenty or so manuscript copies of it. Mandeville introduces a great number of French words into his English—words which have now become common coinage, such as *cause* and *quantity*. As a record of travel in the East it is a ludicrous work; there are fantastic tales of cannibals and men with only one foot—a large one which they use to shield themselves from the sun—dog-headed men and the most incredible monsters. Nevertheless, it fed the hunger for knowledge of strange lands, and— living in a world whose every corner is known—one rather envies the thrill Mandeville's readers must have derived from marvelling at the strangeness of the foreign parts so few could visit. The English is quite intelligible to us. Muslim readers may be interested in the following transliteration of the Prophet's name:

> Machamete was born in Arabye, that was a pore knave that kept cameles that wenten with marchantes for marchandise.

Piers Plowman

Finally I must mention William Langland (1332–1400), the last writer of any merit to use the Old English technique of head-rhyme for a long poem. *The Vision of Piers Plowman* attacks the abuses of the Christian Church in England, but also calls upon the ordinary people—the laity— to cease their concern with the things of this world and to follow the only thing worth following—'holy Truth'. The ploughman who gives his name to the poem appears before the 'field full of folk' which represents the world, and shows them the way to salvation. The poem is allegorical; that is to say, as in John Bunyan's *Pilgrim's Progress*, we meet figures with names like Covetousness, Gluttony, Theology, and, like that later work also, the story is that of a pilgrimage—a following of the hard road to salvation. *Piers Plowman*, however, too often wanders from the way, the story becomes shapeless, but the author's dramatic power is considerable and his verse has beauty—as well as vigour—perhaps only matched by that greater poet, Geoffrey Chaucer, who uses a vastly different technique from Langland. Chaucer looks forward to the future, while Langland, in many ways, sums up the past. The future lies with regular rhyme-patterns, French stanza-forms, classical learning, wit, and colour. The past, with its head-rhyme, its formlessness, its concern with sin and its love of a sermon, nevertheless has a perfect swan-song in Langland's poem. This music has haunted me almost from my childhood:

> In a somer seson, when soft was the sunne,
> I shope me in shroudes, as I a shepherd were,
> In habite as an hermite, unholy of werkes,
> Went wide in this worlde, wonders to here.

5. *Chaucer and After*

Geoffrey Chaucer lived in an eventful age. He was born, so we believe, in 1340 or thereabouts, when the Hundred Years' War with France had already begun. Three times in his life the plague known as the Black Death smote the country. When he was in his twenties the English language was established, for the first time, as the language of the law-courts. When he was in his late thirties the young and unfortunate Richard II ascended the throne, to be deposed and murdered a year before Chaucer's death by Bolingbroke, the rebel who became Henry IV. In 1381 there came the Peasants' Revolt, and with it a recognition that the labourers and diggers had human rights quite as much as the middle class and the nobility. Chaucer died in 1400, about forty years before a really important event in our literary history—the invention of printing.

Chaucer belonged to that growing class from which, in the centuries to follow, so many great writers sprang. He was not a peasant, not a priest, not an aristocrat, but the son of a man engaged in trade: his father was a wine merchant. But young Geoffrey was to learn a lot about the aristocracy through becoming a page to the Countess of Ulster. Promotion and foreign service as a young soldier (he was taken prisoner in France but ransomed by the King of England himself), marriage into the family of the great John of Gaunt, the opportunity to observe polite manners, to study the sciences and the arts, the literatures of France and Italy—all these had their part to play in making Chaucer one of the best-equipped of the English poets. Granted also intelligence, a strong sense of humour, a fine musical ear, and the ability to tell a story—how could the young poet fail?

Chaucer's achievements are many. First, despite his knowledge of the 'politer' languages of the Continent, he patriotically confined himself to using the East Midland dialect of English that was spoken in London. He found this dialect not at all rich in words, and completely lacking in an important literature from which he could learn. In a sense, he had to *create* the English language we know today and to establish its literary traditions. To do this he had to turn, chiefly, to the literature of France and bring something of its elegance to East Midland English; he had to

1381 Peasant's Revolt from Froissant's Chronicles.

Part of the Luttrell Psalter produced at the time of Chaucer's birth.

ransack the tales and histories of Europe to find subject matter. But, finally, in his masterpiece *The Canterbury Tales* he stood on his own feet and gave literature something it had never seen before—observation of life as it is really lived, pictures of people who are *real* (not just abstractions from books) and a view of life which, in its tolerance, humour, scepticism, passion, and love of humanity, we can only call 'modern'. Chaucer is a living poet: he speaks to us today with as clear a voice as was heard in his own age. It is this living quality that makes him great.

Chaucer is also modern in that the language he uses is, for the first time in the history of English literature, recognisably the language of our time. At least it *looks* like it; to listen to it is still to hear what sounds like a foreign tongue. To look at it and listen to it at the same time is perhaps the only way really to appreciate it. But certainly the following can only be called 'Modern English'. (It comes from the Pardoner's Tale; the teller of the story is attacking the sin of gluttony.)

Chaucer's language

> Adam our fader, and his wyf also,
> Fro Paradys to labour and to wo
> Were driven for that vyce, it is no drede;
> For whyl that Adam fasted, as I rede,
> He was in Paradys; and whan that he
> Eet of the fruyt defended on the tree,
> Anon he was out-cast to wo and peyne . . .

And also the modernity of Chaucer's English is attested by the number of phrases from his works that have become part of everyday speech: 'Murder will out'; 'The smiler with the knife beneath his cloak'; 'Gladly would he learn and gladly teach', and so on.

For the reading aloud of Chaucer I would recommend that you follow a few simple rules of pronunciation. Give the vowels a 'Continental' quality—that is, sound them as if they belonged to Italian or Spanish or, for that matter, Romanised Malay, Chinese, or Urdu. It is very important to pronounce the 'e' at the end of words like 'shorte', 'erthe', 'throte', 'bathed', 'croppes', otherwise Chaucer's rhythm is lost. An 'e' right at the very end of a word, however, is not sounded if 'h' or another vowel comes immediately after. The consonants are pronounced almost as in present-day English, except that 'gh' in 'cough' and 'laugh' and 'droghte' has a throaty choking sound and 'ng' is pronounced as though it were spelt 'ngg'. In other words, 'singer' and 'finger' rhyme. Try reading the following aloud (it is the opening to *The Canterbury Tales*):

Pronunciation of Chaucer

> Whan that Aprille with his shoures sote
> The droghte of Marche hath perced to the rote,
> And bathed every veyne in swich licour
> Of which vertu engendred is the flour;

> Whan Zephirus eek with his swete breeth
> Inspired hath in every holt and heeth
> The tendre croppes, and the yonge sonne
> Hath in the Ram his halfe cours y-ronne,
> And smale fowles maken melodie,
> That slepen al the night with open ye,
> (So priketh hem nature in hir corages):
> Than longen folk to goon on pilgrimages.

The differences between Chaucer's English and our own can be seen clearly enough from this extract, and they will strike you as not very important. For instance, plural verbs have an ending (-en) which present-day English no longer possesses. You see this in 'maken', 'slepen', 'longen'. Instead of 'them' Chaucer uses 'hem', from which we get the ''em' in 'Kick 'em'. 'Hath' and 'priketh' we know from Shakespeare's English and from the Bible. 'Y-ronne', with its prefix 'y-', is far closer to Middle High German or to Dutch than to present-day English: Middle High German, for instance, gives us *gerunnen* and *gewunnen* for 'run' and 'won' when these words are used as past participles. Chaucer's 'hir' has become 'their'. But, for the rest, his language is substantially the same as our own, and we are justified in calling him the first poet to use Modern English.

Chaucer's realism   In any case, when we are really immersed in a tale by Chaucer, his brilliant descriptive gifts and his humour carry us along and make us forget that we are reading a poet who lived six hundred years ago. Take this, for instance, from the Nun's Priest's Tale. The cock, Chauntecleer, has been carried off by a fox, and a general hullabaloo follows:

> . . . Out at dores sterten they anoon
> And syen the fox toward the grove goon,
> And bar upon his bak the cok away;
> And cryden, 'Out! Harrow! and Weylaway!
> Ha! Ha! The fox!' and after him they ran,
> And eek with staves many another man;
> Ran Colle, our dogge, and Talbot, and Gerland,
> And Malkin, with a distaf in hir hand;
> Ran cow and calf, and eek the very hogges,
> So were they fered for berking of the dogges
> And shouting of the men and women eke,
> They ranne so, hem thoughte hir herte breke.
> They yelleden as feendes doon in helle;
> The duckes cryden as men wolde hem quelle;
> The geese for fere flowen over the trees;
> Out of the hyve came the swarm of bees;
> So hideous was the noise . . .

That vigour and swiftness is something new in English poetry.

The Canterbury Tales—a long work, but still unfinished at Chaucer's death—is partly a new idea, partly an old one. Collections of short stories had been popular for a long time on the Continent (and also in Islam, as the *Arabian Nights* reminds us). Chaucer's masterpiece is no more than a collection of stories, and very few of them are original. That is one way of looking at *The Canterbury Tales*. But what had never been done before was to take a collection of human beings—of all temperaments and social positions—and mingle them together, make them tell stories, and make these stories illustrate their own characters. Chaucer's work sparkles with drama and life: temperaments clash, each person has his own way of speaking and his own philosophy, and the result is not only a picture of the late Middle Ages—in all its colour and variety—but of the world itself.

Pilgrimages were as much a part of Christian life in Chaucer's time as they are today of Muslim and Hindu life. When spring came, when the snow and frost and, later, the floods had left the roads of England and made them safe for traffic again, then people from all classes of society would make trips to holy places. One of the holy towns of England was Canterbury, where Thomas à Becket, the 'blissful holy martyr' murdered in the reign of Henry II, had his resting-place. It was convenient for these pilgrims to travel in companies, having usually met each other at some such starting-point as the Tabard Inn at Southwark, London. On the occasion of the immortal pilgrimage of *The Canterbury Tales*, Harry Bailey, the landlord of the Tabard, making the pilgrimage himself, offers a free supper to whichever of the pilgrims shall tell the best story on the long road to Canterbury. We never find out who it is that wins the land-lord's prize; we can only be sure of one thing—that it is not Chaucer himself. He, a shy pilgrim, tells a verse story so terribly dull that Harry Bailey stops him in the middle of it. Then Chaucer—the great poet—tells a *prose* story hardly less dull. (This, I think, is the first example in litera-ture of that peculiar English humour which takes a keen delight in self-derision. It is a kind of humour which you find at its best in the British army, with its songs about 'We cannot fight, we cannot shoot' and its cry of 'Thank heaven we've got a navy'. The Englishman does not really take himself very seriously.) The other tales are delightful and varied— the rich humour of the Carpenter's Tale and the Miller's Tale, the pathetic tale of the Prioress, the romantic tale of the Knight, and all the rest of them. The Prologue to the Tales is a marvellous portrait-gallery of typical people of the age—the corrupt Monk, the dainty Prioress, the gay young Squire—people whose offices for the most part no longer exist, for the society that produced them no longer exists. We do not have Summoners and Maunciples and Pardoners nowadays, though we do have Physicians and Parsons and Cooks. But, beneath the costumes and the strange occupations, we have timeless human beings. There are no ghosts in Chaucer; his work palpitates with blood, it is as warm as living flesh.

Troilus and Criseyde

The next greatest work of Chaucer is *Troilus and Criseyde*, a love-story taken from the annals of the Trojan War, a war which has provided European writers with innumerable myths. Shakespeare also told the bitter tale of these two wartime lovers. Chaucer's version, with its moral of the faithlessness of women, is not only tragic but also full of humour, and its psychology is so startlingly modern that it reads in some ways like a modern novel. Indeed, it can be called the first full-length piece of English fiction. Of Chaucer's other long works I will say nothing. With some of them, after making a good start, he seems suddenly to have become bored and left them unfinished. But we must not ignore his short love-poems, written in French forms, extolling the beauty of some mythical fair one, full of the convention of courtly love which exaggerated devotion to woman almost into a religion:

Love-poems

> Your eyen two wol slee me sodenly,
> I may the beauté of hem not sustene,
> So woundeth hit throughout my herte kene.

But, even in the serious world of love, Chaucer's humour peeps out:

> Sin I fro love escaped am so fat,
> I never think to ben in his prison lene;
> Sin I am free, I counte him not a bene.

Chaucer opened the way to a new age of literature, but it was a long time before any poet as great as he was to come along to build on his foundations. The year 1400 should, we think, usher in a great century, but it does not. Chaucer seems to have been in advance of his time, never fully appreciated even by the men who called themselves his disciples. And, unfortunately for Chaucer's work, big changes began to take place in English pronunciation, changes which quite swiftly brought something like the pronunciation of our own times. The final 'e' of words like 'sonne' and 'sote' was no longer sounded. Henceforward people could find no rhythm in Chaucer's carefully-wrought lines; they regarded him as a crude poet—promising but primitive—and he was classed with dull men like Gower and Occleve and Lydgate, men who we remember now only because they catch something of the great light which blazes on their master. In Shakespeare's time, certainly, Chaucer was not much esteemed, and a hundred years after Shakespeare poets thought it necessary to translate Chaucer, polish up his 'crudities' and make him fit reading for a 'civilised' age.

Scottish literature

Only in Scotland did something of the Chaucerian fire still burn, in poets like King James I (1394–1437) whom we read now not because he was a king of Scotland but because he was a true poet. Here is part of a love-song of his, a joyful welcome to the spring:

> Worschippe ye that loveris bene this May,
>   For of your blisse the Kalendis are begonne.
> And sing with us, Away, Winter, away!
>   Cum, Somer, cum, the suete sesoun and sonne!
> Awake for schame! that have your hevynnis wonne,
>   And amorously lift up your hedis all,
>   Thank Lufe that list you to his merci call!

And later came Robert Henryson (1425–1500) to sing in the dialect of the Scottish lowlands, and William Dunbar (1465–1520) to bring a richness of texture that is like a return to pre-Chaucerian days, as in his poem in praise of the City of London:

> Gemme of all joy, jaspre of jocunditie,
>   Most myghty carbuncle of vertue and valour;
> Strong Troy in vigour and in strenuytie;
>   Of royall cities rose and geraflour;
>   Empress of townes, exalt in honour;
> In beawtie beryng the crone imperiall;
> Sweet paradys precelling in pleasure;
> London, thou art the flour of Cities all.

Gavin Douglas (1475?–1522?) is another interesting Scot, whose important achievement was a translation of Virgil's *Aeneid* into couplets. But Douglas seems to push the language back into the past again—we have to struggle with learned words, obscure dialect words, words seemingly invented by Douglas himself, and we feel we are a world away from the clarity of Chaucer. But translation was to play an important part in the development of Modern English literature, and Douglas— despite the limitations of his language—did honourable pioneer work in this field.

The only considerable poet that England—as opposed to Scotland— seems to have produced in the fifteenth century is *John Skelton* (1460?– 1529) who, after a long period of neglect, came into his own again in the twentieth century. It was Robert Graves, the modern poet, who pointed out his virtues and allowed these virtues to influence his own work. A modern British composer, Ralph Vaughan Williams, set five of his poems to music, and introduced to mere music-lovers the humour, pathos, and fantastic spirit of this strange writer. 'Strange' because it is hard to classify him: he seems to owe nothing to Chaucer nor to anybody else. He is fond of a short line, a loose rhyme-pattern, and the simplest of words:

Skelton

Merry Margaret,
As midsummer flower,
Gentle as falcon
Or hawk of the tower:
With solace and gladness,
Much mirth and no madness,
All good and no badness;
   So joyously,
   So maidenly,
   So womanly
   Her demeaning
   In every thing,
   Far, far passing
   That I can indite,
   Or suffice to write
Of Merry Margaret,
As midsummer flower,
Gentle as falcon
Or hawk of the tower . . .

His themes range wide: he gives us a picture of the drunken customers of a Suffolk public-house; he writes at length, and tenderly, on the death of a sparrow; he produces a powerful monologue of Christ on the cross; he satirises the great Cardinal Wolsey in *Speak, Parrot*. He is one of the oddities of English literature—an eccentric, but no fool.

Ballads

We must mention briefly, too, a species of poetry which seems to lie outside the main current of English literature—the *Ballad*. We give this name to that kind of popular verse which flourished mainly on the border between England and Scotland, was passed down orally, and hence—like Old English poetry—cannot be assigned to any author or authors. A good deal of this poetry has power and beauty—qualities which seem to come from the conciseness of the technique. There is never a word wasted. A ballad usually tells a simple story, sometimes about war, sometimes about love, sometimes about the world of the supernatural. There is never any lack of art in the telling of the story, and one would willingly trade all the poetry of Gower or Lydgate for a single ballad like that of *Sir Patrick Spens*:

The king sits in Dunfermline town
  Drinking the blude-red wine;
'O whare will I get a skeely skipper
  To sail this new ship o' mine?'

O up and spak an eldern knight,
  Sat at the king's right knee;

'Sir Patrick Spens is the best sailor
    That ever sail'd the sea.'

Some of the best of these ballads may be read in the *Oxford Book of English Verse*. Most of them seem to belong to a later age than the fifteenth century, but that century can certainly claim the finest of all, *The Nut-brown Maid*, which is a long dialogue between a man and woman, highly dramatic and moving. The man announces that he has killed an enemy and must now disappear, an outlaw, to the forest:

Wherefore adieu, mine own heart true!
    None other rede I can:
For I must to the green-wood go,
    Alone, a banished man.

Alone, he says. She must not follow him, however great her love. He tells her of the perils and hardships of the forest, but she is unmoved: she loves him so much that she can bear any hardship in his company. He tells her he has another love in the forest, but still she cannot be bent from her purpose, for she will gladly serve this other woman to be near her love. And now the man reveals that he has only been testing her fidelity; he is no banished man, he is a lord of Westmoreland, and is proud to call such a woman as she has proved herself his lady:

I will you take, and lady make,
    As shortly as I can:
Thus you have won an Earles son,
    And not a banished man.

And so to the prose of the age. Prose had still, in the fifteenth century, to come into its own as an artistic medium worthy to be classed with verse. Chaucer's prose is not important, and the *Paston Letters*—which tell us so much of interest about a typical middle-class family of the age—cannot properly be classed as literature. William Caxton (1421–91) realised where the trouble lay. When he set up his printing-press in 1476 he was bewildered to know exactly what kind of English to print. Thanks to Chaucer, the East Midland dialect of London had become firmly fixed as the medium of poetry, but no great writer had provided a standard for prose. English prose was chaotic, the language was changing rapidly, so that, within the lifetime of one man, nothing seemed fixed, everything seemed flowing. Caxton, when he wrote prose, wrote as he spoke, often giving alternatives for certain words that he thought might not be generally understood. Caxton was a business-man who aimed to make money out of printing: his livelihood depended on producing books that as many people as possible would find intelligible. Though Caxton printed Chaucer's poetry and also the works of Gower and Lydgate, he

C15 prose

was most interested in producing books of prose. And so he had to pro-vide most of this himself, usually translating from French romances, stimulating and satisfying an appetite for stories, in a small way antici-pating the taste of such an age as our own age, an age which will read a million words of prose to one word of poetry.

Malory

But one important prose-writer did emerge. In 1484 Caxton printed the *Morte D'Arthur* of *Sir Thomas Malory*. Malory's is the fullest record we have of the work of the mythical Knights of the Round Table, their loves, treacheries, their search for the Holy Grail. Malory has become our main source for the Arthurian legends, and it is satisfying to know that these stories are set out in a prose-style that, though simple, is digni-fied and clear.[1] But it is curious that, as we move towards the modern period, with its new spirit of enquiry, its sense of a bigger world than the Middle Ages could provide, our first important printed work in prose should evoke that misty ancient world of myth, should look to pre-history rather than to the future.

[1] A fifteenth-century manuscript of Malory's work was discovered in Winchester College library in 1933 and it has been published by the Oxford University Press. A comparison of this and Caxton's edition shows how many liberties Caxton was prepared to take with the manuscripts of his authors.

Interlude *The English Bible*

Let us consider very briefly a book whose influence on English writing, speech, and thought has been, and still is, immense. The Bible is not primarily literature—it is the sacred book of Christianity—but recently there has been a growing tendency to appreciate the Bible for its artistic qualities, to view it not only as the 'Word of God' but as the work of great writers. Whatever our religious beliefs, if we wish to have a full appreciation of the development of English literature we cannot afford to neglect the Bible: its purely literary impact on English writers is almost too great to be measured.

The Bible is a composite book, consisting of two main sections—the Old Testament and the New. The Old Testament, originally written mainly in Hebrew, is a collection of poems, plays, proverbs, prophecy, philosophy, history, theology—a massive anthology of the writings of the ancient Jewish people. The New Testament, originally written in Greek, contains the Gospels and the story of the spreading of Christianity by its first propagandists. In addition there are certain odd books whose origins, particularly from the religious viewpoint, are obscure. These are generally known as the Apocrypha.[1] Present-day Jews and Muslims share the Old Testament with Christians—the Old Testament provides three different religions with something in common.

Since the sixteenth century, Christianity in Western Europe has been divided into two main bodies: the international Catholic Church and the national Protestant Churches. The Catholic Church has always insisted that the Word of God is enshrined within the Church itself, as Christ's own foundation; the Protestants seek the Word of God in the Bible.

[1] The term is more generally applied to the additions to the Old Testament, the 'suspect' books of the New Testament being known as the 'New Testament Apocrypha.' The Old Testament Apocrypha consists of historical and philosophical writings. The New Testament Apocrypha gives, or purports to give, further details of the lives of the Apostles, the birth and resurrection of Christ, etc. These were added for the most part between 150 and 500 A.D.

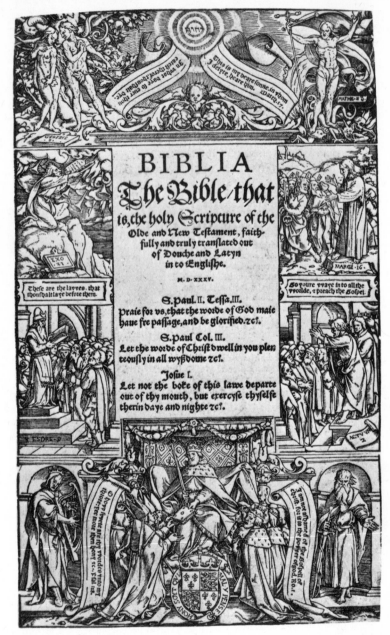

Title page of first printed English Bible.

And so the history of early Protestantism is also the history of making the Bible accessible to everyone, translating it into the vernacular tongues so that even the humblest and least learned can read it.

Mediaeval Europe knew the Bible in Latin. Parts of this Latin Bible had been translated into Old English—either as 'cribs' written over the Latin words themselves or in the form of very free verse translations. It was not until the fourteenth century that a prose translation of part of the New Testament was made into Middle English. The Church was not happy about such translations: they were tolerated in the hands of monks or nuns whose Latin was poor or non-existent, but considered dangerous when made available to the common people. Why dangerous? Chiefly because there was always the possibility that a reader might interpret texts of the Bible in his own way as opposed to the way of the Church, or might regard the sacred text as a greater authority than the words of the priests and bishops. And so, before the Reformation, translations were for the most part made against the wishes of the Church authorities.

John Wyclif (1324–84) was a clergyman who found many abuses in the Church of his time and wanted to reform them. He also wanted the man in the street to have access to the Bible, and to him we owe the first complete translation. We do not know whether he himself did any of the translating, but we do know that his example and fervour inspired his followers to produce a translation of both Testaments in about 1380. John Purvey came along about fifteen years later and revised this 'Wyclif' Bible, making its English more natural and flowing, more like the spoken English of the time. This Bible was widely read. *Wyclif*

But in 1408 it was laid down by the authorities that any man attempting to translate the Bible—without permission from a bishop—was to be punished with excommunication, that is to say, with being deprived of full membership of the Church. Thus William Tyndale (1484–1536) had to defy an ecclesiastical ban in order to start his translation. Admittedly, he asked permission of the Bishop of London, but this permission was not granted, leaving Tyndale with no alternative but to go overseas and do his work in a country where no ban on translation of the Bible existed. Tyndale translated the New Testament from the Greek, and started to print it in Cologne in Germany in 1525. But the authorities did not approve, and so he fled to Worms (also in Germany), where he was able to bring out the first Modern English version of the New Testament in safety. This translation is important, being in many ways the basis for all later translations. *Tyndale*

Tyndale was a slow worker, and in 1535 his translation of the Old Testament (straight from the Hebrew) was not yet completed. So Miles Coverdale rushed in with his own full version (owing much to Tyndale and also to the German Bible). It is hard to appreciate today the storms which these translations aroused. When Coverdale was revising and reprinting his Bible in Paris, in 1538, the sheets were confiscated and many of them burnt, while Coverdale had to escape to England. (The Reformation was now under way in England and a copy of the Bible had been ordered to be placed in every church.) Tyndale, still on the Continent, fell into the hands of the Papal authorities and, at Antwerp, was condemned to death for heresy, strangled, and burnt. Bible translation in those days was high and dangerous adventure.

*Authorised
Version*

In 1604, King James I of England appointed forty-seven learned men to produce an English version of the Bible which should be more or less official and final. Fuller, one of our early historians, says that this body 'vigorously, though slowly, proceeded in this hard, heavy and holy task, nothing offended with the censures of impatient people condemning their delays for laziness'. In 1611 the work was done and that translation known as the Authorised Version was printed. This is the version everybody means when using the term 'English Bible' or just 'the Bible'. For over three hundred years the words of this Bible have been familiar to every Protestant Christian in England. There have been other versions since, but none of them has ever been able to usurp the place which the King James translation holds in most English hearts. Today, the English of the Authorised Version seems quaint and sometimes it is obscure, but there is no doubt of its beauty and power. There is no writer who has not been influenced by it—even writers like Bernard Shaw and H. G. Wells, though not Christian, have fallen heavily under its spell. Even people with little learning tend, when writing letters, to use the rhythms and language of the Bible. This translation, a little conservative in its idiom and vocabulary, which may be regarded as a monument of Tudor, not Stuart, prose.

Through the Old Testament, English literature makes its first contact with the East. The 1611 version keeps closely to the structure and idiom of the Hebrew language and, when translating such poetry as the Book of Job or the Song of Solomon, to the peculiar rhythm of Hebrew poetry, with its balance of images and its repetitions. Old Hebrew had an almost childish way of joining its sentences together, and this is faithfully reproduced in the English:

> And there was war between Rehoboam and Jeroboam all their days. And Rehoboam slept with his fathers, and was buried with his fathers in the city of David. And his mother's name was Naamah an Ammonitess. And Abijam his son reigned in his stead.

Old Hebrew poetry had a richness and a sensuous quality appropriate to a warm and passionate land. This, through the Old Testament, has found its way into the literature of a cold northern country. So, despite what Kipling said about East and West, the twain *can* meet, and have met joyously in the 1611 Version of the Bible, to the enrichment, certainly, of the West.

1970 saw the completion of the most scholarly and exact translation of the scriptures that the modern age can expect—the New English Bible. Unfortunately it cannot compare for majesty, beauty or even earthy homeliness with the King James Version. It may be read as a most scrupulous literal rendering of the original, but it is difficult to enjoy it as literature. It will be a long time before the Speaker complaining of Emptiness (a ghastly whiff of a dull debate in the House of Commons) supplants the Preacher with his cry of Vanity and again Vanity.

New English Bible

6. The Beginnings of Drama

A survey of literature is like a railway journey. We travel through time, stopping at the great city stations, rushing through the tiny village stations, noticing little more than the names of the latter. Chaucer was our first important station; soon we must be ready to stop at that huge junction called Shakespeare. Shakespeare is England's—and the world's—greatest dramatist, and before we can talk about his achievements, and the achievements of his fellow-dramatists, we must find out first what drama is and how drama began.

Imitation

Drama is the most natural of the arts, being based on one of the most fundamental of the human and animal faculties—the faculty of imitation. It is through imitation that animals learn to fight, climb, hunt; it is through imitation that human children learn to talk and to perform a great number of complicated human functions. This imitative faculty or, as we may call it, *mimetic* faculty, makes us all actors almost from the cradle. Children play at being doctors, cowboys, Wild West pioneers, spacemen, kings and queens. Kittens play at being tigers; puppies play at being dogs. This is acting, but it is not yet drama. It is believed that the first drama was not play, but a serious activity performed by grown men, expressing man's highest instinct—the religious instinct.

Magic

To learn about the first drama we have to leave literature behind and go to anthropology—the study of primitive human societies. To build a society at all, let alone to progress to the stage of a civilised human society, man has to learn to control the outside world. The civilised way is through science; the primitive way is through magic. Science really succeeds in controlling the outside world; magic only seems to succeed. If I am a hunter, science will make for me a perfect gun by experiment, observation, and logic. Magic will try to give me the perfect spear or blowpipe, but it will not work logically on problems of sharpness or ballistic experiments; it will try to add power to my weapon by something quite irrelevant—an inscription or a charm or a prayer or an invocation of spirits. A few miles from where I am sitting, in the jungle

44

which almost surrounds my house, there are tiny people whose lives are based on magical beliefs. They see connections between things which to the civilised mind have nothing to do with each other at all: for instance, it is dangerous to laugh at butterflies or to wear a hair-comb during a thunderstorm.

The most interesting and important kind of magic is known as *sympathetic magic*. As you know, many races believe that one way of killing your enemy is to make a wax image of him and melt that image over a slow fire. I have met something like this even in England. One of my pupils there stuck pins into the clay effigy of an unpopular teacher; he said it was a common practice in the village where he lived. This is sympathetic magic, so called because the image of the person is supposed to be in sympathy with the person himself: whatever happens to the image must also happen to the person. Similarly, some of my jungle neighbours connect their own lives with the lives of particular trees. If anything happens to a tree (cut down, or struck by lightning) something terrible must happen to the person whose life is in sympathy with it. It is rather like two piano-strings, both tuned to the same note. Even if these two strings are some distance from each other, if I strike one the other will vibrate also. The strings are in sympathy. But science can explain sympathetic strings; it cannot explain away sympathetic magic.

Many people believe that the first drama was based on four things: the mimetic faculty, sympathetic magic, a belief in gods, and a fear of starvation. Supposing a primitive society has taken to agriculture. It grows rice or corn and relies on the products of the earth for the bulk of its food-supply. Having no science, the members of such a society tend to think that the granting of this food is in the hands of certain natural forces beyond their control. As they cannot think, like the scientists, in terms of abstractions, they think instead in terms of *personified* forces— in other words, gods. In a climate with clearly defined seasons they will be aware of a living time of the year—when things grow—and a dead time of the year, when nothing grows. There is no science to teach them about the turning of the earth, the regular appearance of spring after winter. When winter comes it must seem to them that the god of life has died, killed perhaps by the god of death. How can the god of fertility— the life-god, the corn-god, the rice-god—be brought back to life again? Obviously by sympathetic magic.

And so come magical ceremonies. If a wax or wooden image represents a man, a man should represent a god. And so perhaps a member of the community pretends to be the life-god and another pretends to be the death-god. They fight and the life-god is killed. But then the life-god miraculously rises again, kills the winter-god, dances over his corpse in triumph. Now, according to the law of sympathetic magic, what has happened in mere representation must happen in fact. The real god of

Fertility myths

fertility must come back to life. And, in fact, he does. The earth turns, the earth is fruitful again. Magic has triumphed.

Resurrection — Here you have acting, here you have a plot; action (fighting) leads to a climax (death of the god) and the climax leads to a happy denouement—resurrection. This is drama, but it is also religion. As a primitive agricultural society advances, perhaps there develops a more subtle idea—that, because the resurrection of god is such a glorious thing, his death also must be glorious: you cannot have resurrection without dying first. The god is sacrificed so that he can rise again for the good of the people. Here you see how even a subtle religion like Christianity is connected remotely with what we can call 'fertility myths'. The Mass of the Catholic Church celebrates the sacrifice of Christ: it is religious ritual, but it is also drama.

There still exist in England certain plays—conceived many centuries ago—which are recognisably based on fertility myths. Often the myth is overlaid with historical characters, and the plot itself seems to have travelled some way from its agricultural origins, but the theme of death and resurrection is clearly there. There is a play performed in England at Christmas—usually in villages—which has the following simple story. Saint George—patron saint of England—kills in turn the Dragon, the Turkish Knight, and the Giant Turpin. Three deaths, but also three resurrections, for Father Christmas, who acts as compère, calls for a doctor who can raise the dead. This doctor has a 'little bottle of alicumpane' which he administers to each of the victims of Saint George in turn.

> Here Jack, take a little of my flip flop,
> Pour it down thy tip top;
> Rise up and fight again.

And they do rise and fight again. This resurrection theme one still finds sometimes in popular drama. Recently I saw a musical parody of *Othello* performed by Chinese, Malay, and Indian girls. Othello killed Desdemona at the end, then killed himself, but the doctor came in with his miraculous cure and everybody stood up to sing:

> Now they're up who once were down,
> Toast of all the nation. . . .

I should like to think that the word 'toast' referred back to bread and then to wheat, thus pointing the influence of a fertility myth; but perhaps that is taking things too far.

Greek drama — We shall see religion and drama closely mixed throughout the early history of the art in Europe. With the Greeks, two thousand five hundred years ago, drama had reached a more sophisticated stage of development than the mere representation of the death and resurrection of a god, but it had its beginnings in very crude village ceremonies: *tragedy* comes from

Classical theatre of Dionysus in Athens.

tragos, the Greek word for a goat, and perhaps the first tragedies were merely dances round a sacrificial goat, or songs from a chorus dressed as goats. (The goat has an interesting history in the older religions: it was regarded by the Greeks as the most lustful of the animals and hence, perhaps, the most fertile: animal fertility was closely connected with the fertility of the earth. The Hebrews used, symbolically, to load a goat with their sins and drive it out into the desert; Christ is sometimes compared to this *scapegoat*.) *Comedy* comes from *komos*, meaning a revel, the sort of rough country party which honoured the god Dionysus—'a god of vegetation, a suffering god, who dies and comes to life again, particularly as a god of wine, who loosens care'.[1]

The great Greek tragic dramatists—Aeschylus, Sophocles, and Euripides—wrote religious dramas which were concerned with the moral relation between gods and men and usually had an instructive moral purpose. Performances of these plays were less an entertainment than a religious ceremony: the vast amphitheatres were crowded, the actors, wearing masks, went through stately movements, mouthed noble lines, while a chorus cut in occasionally to comment on the story and point the moral. The story was rarely original; it was usually taken from a myth already well known to the audience. A tragedy deals with the fall of a man from power, a fall brought about by some unsuspected flaw in his character or by some specific sin. King Oedipus,[2] for instance, finds his kingdom ravaged by disease and famine. The gods are obviously angry with someone, but with whom? Nobody in the kingdom will confess to any grave sin. Eventually, Oedipus discovers that he himself is the sinner, and his two sins are the most detestable known to society—parricide and incest. He killed an old man on the road; he married a widow. But, having been cut off from his parents from birth, how was he to know that the old man was his father and the widow his mother? He has committed these sins without intention and without knowledge. Yet the gods are just: the suicide of his mother–wife and his own self-inflicted blindness are means of expiating crimes which, though unconscious, are still crimes. We view Oedipus' tragedy with a mixture of emotions. We feel pity for Oedipus and horror at the situation he finds himself in, but we do not protest at what seems an unfair trick played by the gods—driving him to his downfall for something that we regard as not really his fault; instead, we accept the pattern of fate and, at the end of his story, feel resigned to the will of the gods rather than angry and resentful—we feel 'purged' of emotion, in a state that Milton describes as 'calm of mind, all passion spent'.

Catharsis
This word 'purge' is a significant one. Aristotle, the Greek philosopher, said that the function of tragedy was purgation of the feelings

[1] *The Oxford Companion to Classical Literature*, ed. Sir Paul Harvey.
[2] *Oedipus Tyrannus*, a tragedy by Sophocles.

through the arousing of pity and terror. The technical term is *catharsis*, the Greek word for 'purgation'. It is good for civilised people to have primitive emotions aroused occasionally, so long as these primitive emotions do not get out of hand. In fact, we go to football matches and to films in order to become excited. But there is a big difference between the excitement aroused by a game and the excitement aroused by a play or film. At the end of a football match the excitement still goes on, sometimes leading to fights. At the end of a dramatic performance the excitement which has been artificially aroused is also artificially quietened. We go to see *Hamlet*. We develop slowly a certain feeling of pity for the hero and horror at the circumstances he finds himself in. But at the end of the play we think, 'This is how it had to work out. The hero had to die like this. Nobody could do anything to prevent it. Because of a flaw in Hamlet's character, a flaw he could not control, all this tragic disturbance had to happen.' The pity and terror are purged out of our systems, to be replaced by a mood of resignation.

But there is one big difference between the Greek conception of tragedy and the Shakespearian. The Shakespearian hero has the power of choice; he has free will. It is his own faults of character that bring about his downfall. Macbeth is ambitious but weak; Othello is jealous; Hamlet cannot make up his mind—but all these three *might* have made themselves into better human beings, they *might* have learned how to control the flaws in their characters. Nothing outside themselves prevents them from choosing the right way as opposed to the wrong, or tragic, way. But with the heroes of Greek tragedy there is no free will. The gods control a man's destiny, and one cannot fight the gods.

It is because of the big difference between the Greek view of life and the Christian view of life—the difference between fate and free will—that the Greek tragedies have had so little influence on English drama. When Englishmen began writing tragedies they needed a model of some kind, but the Greek model was not attractive. What was attractive was the work of a Roman playwright, Seneca (4 B.C.–65 A.D.). He modelled his tragedies on the great Greeks, but his plays are no mere copies, either in language, form, or spirit. The gods are still in complete control, but man, though he must accept the divine rule, does not necessarily have to think that it is right to do so. The gods have the monopoly of power, but that does not mean that they have also the monopoly of virtue. The gods can defeat a man, crush him, but the man can still feel, somewhere deep inside, 'I am better than they are. They can kill me, but they cannot kill the fact that I am their moral superior. Whatever they say or do, I've done no wrong—I, not they, am in the right.' This is the attitude of the man going into the Nazi gas-chamber or facing the firing-squad: his enemies are strong, but wrong; he, though powerless and defeated, is right. This peculiar attitude is sometimes known as a *stoical* one, and it seems to have

Stoicism

had a great attraction for Shakespeare and his fellows. Certainly, the essence of stoicism is free will. Free will suggests 'activity'; submitting to fate implies 'passivity'. The language of Seneca is fuller of 'activity' than that of the great Greeks—it has a violence, sometimes a blood-thirstiness, that appealed to the Elizabethan dramatists far more than the calm dignity of Euripides or Sophocles could have done.

One admirable thing about the Greek tragic dramatists is their sense of form. Their main concern is to tell a story and to emphasise the moral significance of that story; everything is subordinated to that end. The Greek tragedian does not want any distractions—no comedy, no second-ary plot—and he wants his action to be a continuous whole, which means no spreading of the story over several weeks, months, or years, for weeks, months, and years cannot be realistically portrayed on the stage. Hence we have the traditional 'unities' of Greek drama—one plot, one day. In other words, Sophocles does not tell us several different stories at the same time (as Shakespeare does in, say, *Cymbeline*); he restricts the action of his plot to a single day (no 'Three Days Later' or 'Five Years Elapse Between the Actions of Act I and Act II'). In the Renaissance period, admirers of the Greek dramatists sometimes took all this a stage further, adding a third unity, that of place. Ben Jonson, for instance, is rarely willing to rush from city to city (as Shakespeare so often does): he prefers to set his action solidly in London or in Venice and stay there for the whole play. In *The Alchemist* he never even moves from the house where all the alchemical roguery takes place. But Shakespeare had no patience with these formal restrictions: the unities meant nothing to him.

Dramatic unities

Of the comedies of the Greeks and the Romans I will say little. The main purpose of 'classical' comedy is to make us laugh at the follies of mankind and, perhaps, correct those follies in ourselves. But most comic writers like to lash the follies they see immediately in front of them, and this means that most comedies take as their subject matter the more ridi-culous manners of the day. Human manners change rapidly, and hence comedies have a habit of becoming quickly out of date. The greatest comedians, of course, deal with the eternal qualities of mankind: a Greek or Roman, or a man of the twenty-second century would certainly find humour in Charlie Chaplin—the eternal 'little man'. But Aristophanes in ancient Greece, Plautus and Terence in ancient Rome, have dated far more than their tragic counterparts. Plautus and Terence have given something to English comedy—certain stock comic types, like the 'boastful soldier', complicated plots in which mistaken identity plays a big part, the division of a play into five acts. But English comedy owes less to these writers than English tragedy owes to Seneca.

Greek and Roman comedies

We are anticipating, however. We must go back to the Middle Ages, when English drama is yet crude and amateur and, like all primitive drama, still in the service of religion.

7. The Beginnings of English Drama

In 1935 a play by T. S. Eliot, dealing with the martyrdom of Thomas à Becket, was produced in Canterbury Cathedral. It was followed by a rash of religious plays, written for performance in churches and cathedrals up and down England. The wheel had come full circle. The English Drama had returned to its place of origin, the Christian Church.

And yet the Christian Church has never been over-friendly towards the Drama. If we go back to the last days of the Roman Empire we can understand why. The plays presented to a jaded, perverted public in the reigns of the last Emperors were marked by a love of sheer outrage and horror that seem hardly credible. Condemned men were executed as part of the action; copulation took place openly on stage. The Church condemned such a prostitution of art, and, when the Roman theatres were closed, the Drama lay, as it were, stunned by its own excesses for many centuries. When Drama came back to Europe, it came back shyly and modestly, in the service of the Church itself.

I have already commented on the dramatic qualities of the Mass of the Catholic Church. The Mass has movement, dialogue, colour, development, and climax. It would seem that the Church is concerned with conveying to its members the majesty of the theme of Christ's sacrifice, through dramatic means. Ritual is one aspect of a religion, another aspect is doctrine. And so, by a natural transition, we can expect that dramatic means might also be used for conveying to the common people —people unable to read or to take pleasure in sermons—the more important of the teachings of the Church.

As early as the ninth century, we find genuinely dramatic dialogue inserted into the Mass for Easter Sunday. The Resurrection of Christ is celebrated on that day, and this Resurrection is made actual and immediate through a dialogue between the Angels at Christ's tomb and the three Maries who have come to look at His body:

Angels: 'Whom do you seek in this tomb, O followers of Christ?'
Women: 'We seek Jesus Christ Who was crucified, O Angels.'
Angels: 'He is not here: He has risen again as He said He would. Go, proclaim that He has risen from the sepulchre.'

There were similar dramatic presentations on Good Friday and at Christmas. At Christmas especially, for the story of Christ's birth and the circumstances of that birth are rich in dramatic possibilities—the star appearing to the Wise Men, the song of the Angels announcing the birth to the sheperds, the coming of the Three Wise Men to the stable, Herod's Slaughter of the Innocents. There is a thirteenth-century manuscript in France which contains very simple dramatic scenes on these last two subjects, and also on the miracles of St. Nicholas (Santa Claus, or Father Christmas), on the conversion of St. Paul, on Lazarus rising from the dead, on Christ's appearance to the two disciples on the road to Emmaus. The language of all these early dramatic pieces is, of course, Latin. The vernacular had, as yet, no part to play in religious drama, for religious drama was still a part of Church ceremonial.

Miracle plays

It is certain that no religious dramas of this type existed in England before the Norman Conquest, and that it was the Normans themselves who introduced sacred drama to England. This drama became popular. Plays about the Gospel characters and the miracles of the saints became more elaborate, demanded more 'stage managing', eventually turned into complete presentations divorced from the ritual of the Church. In fact, they moved out of the church building, into the churchyard, and then into the town itself, where the process of *secularisation* began. By secularisation we mean control and participation by the non-religious, by the man in the street as opposed to the priest in the church. The clergy still performed for a time, but then citizens of the town took a hand, and sometimes also wandering actors, singers, and jugglers. As soon as these plays became divorced from the services of the Church, the Church itself began to frown on them and to forbid clerical participation in them. Robert Mannyng, in his *Handlyng Synne* (see Chapter 4), says that a priest

> May yn the Cherche, thurgh thys resun,
> Pley the resurrecyun . . .
> To make men be yn beleve Gode,
> That he ros with flesshe and blode;
> . . . Gyf thou do hyt in weyys or grenys,
> A syght of synne truly hyt semys.

In other words, a priest could act Christ's resurrection in the church, for that was part of church instruction, but on highways and greens it was a different matter—there it tended to be regarded as entertainment rather than as religious teaching. Incidentally, the word used by Mannyng to describe these plays is *Miracles*. The term Miracle Play is often used to cover all the religious plays of the Middle Ages; I think it best to apply it to these plays that came out of the churches into the towns and, for the most part, dealt with the miracles of Christ and his followers. We come now to a much more important kind of religious play in which the Church plays no part—either literally or figuratively.

In 1264 Pope Urban instituted the feast of Corpus Christi (Body of Christ). This feast was never observed until 1311, when a Church Council decreed that it should be celebrated with all due ceremony. This day—the longest of the northern summer—was chosen by the trade-guilds of the towns of England for the presentation of a cycle of plays based on incidents from the Bible, plays which we can call Mystery Plays (the term 'mystery' meaning a craft, skill or trade; compare the French *métier* and the Italian *mestiere*). These trade-guilds, or craft-guilds, were organisations of skilled men, men banded together for the protection of their crafts, for the promotion of their general welfare, and for social purposes. This presentation of plays on the feast of Corpus Christi became one of the most important of their social activities.

Mystery plays

Each guild would choose an episode from the Bible, and the episode would usually be appropriate to the craft or trade practised. How appropriate—sometimes amusingly so—can be seen from the following list of plays presented by the Chester guilds:

> The Fall of Lucifer, by the Tanners.
> The Creation, by the Drapers.
> The Deluge, by the Dyers.
> The Three Kings, by the Wine Merchants.
> The Last Supper, by the Bakers.
> The Passion and Crucifixion of Christ, by the Arrow-makers,
>   Coopers and Ironmongers.
> The Descent into Hell, by the Cooks.

That is just a selection from the total catalogue; the total number of plays amounts to twenty-four. Wakefield guilds presented thirty-three; Coventry forty-two; York fifty-four. The actors and audience needed the long daylight of Corpus Christi to get through such a formidable schedule.

Each guild had its own decorated cart, called a 'pageant', a sort of portable stage to be dragged through the town, set up at different spots, and, at the end of the long day's acting, dragged back to its shed for another year. The upper part of the pageant was a kind of stage 'in the round'—the audience in the street would be able to surround it and see the action from any angle. The plays were presented in strict chronological order—starting with the Fall of Lucifer or the Creation of the World, ending with the Day of Judgement—a comprehensive dramatisa-

Each guild had its own decorated cart called a 'pageant'.

tion of the Jewish and Christian stories. Archdeacon Rogers, who died in 1595, saw one of the last of the Chester performances; he tells us all about it:

> Every company had his pagiant, or parte, which pagiants weare a high scafolde with two rowmes, a higher and a lower, upon four wheeles. In the lower they apparelled themselves, and in the higher rowme they played, being all upon the tope, that all beholders mighte heare and see them. The places where they played them was in every streete. They begane first at the abay gates, and when the first pagiante was played it was wheeled to the highe crosse before the mayor, and so to every streete; and soe every streete had a pagiant playinge before them at one time, till all the pagiantes for the day appointed weare played.

These plays were taken very seriously by the guilds, who have left us detailed inventories of dress, make-up (the man who played God wore a white coat and had his face gilded) and money spent. The following were a few of the sums expended by the Coventry Smiths' Guild in 1490:

> Item for a Rybbe of befe, iijd.
> Item for a quarte of wyne, ijd.
> Item payd at the Second Reherse in Whyttson weke, in brede,
>> Ayle and Kechyn, ijs. iijd.
> Md. payd to the players for corpus xisti daye.
>> Imprimis to God, ijs.
>> Item to Heroude, iijs. iiijd.
>> Item to the devyll and to Judas, xviijd.

All these plays are anonymous, but they have a certain art in language and construction, a certain power of characterisation, which no minor poet need have been ashamed to put his name to. And they also have humour. The Chester play of the Deluge (performed by the Water-leaders and Drawers of the River Dee) exploits, for the first time in English dramatic history, the comic potentialities of the self-willed wife and the exasperated husband. Noah's wife refuses to board the Ark, despite Noah's appeal and warning that the Flood is about to commence; she wants to bring her women-friends on board too, and, if Noah will not let her, she proposes, flood or no flood, to stay with them:

> Yea, sir, set up your sail
> And row forth with evil heale,
> For, without any fail,
> I will not out of this town.
> But I have my gossips every one,
> One foot further I will not go;
> They shall not drown, by St. John!
> If I may save their life.

> They loved me full well, by Christ!
> But thou wilt let them in thy chest,
> Else row forth, Noah, whither thou list,
> And get thee a new wife.

Noah and his sons together manage to get her on board. Noah sarcastically says, 'Welcome, wife, into this boat', to which his wife replies, 'And have them that for thy note!' accompanying the words with a slap on his face.

We see in such episodes as that the gradual drawing-away of the drama from a purely religious content. In the Wakefield Second Shepherds' Play, which deals, of course, with the homage paid by the 'certain poor shepherds' to the new-born Christ, the Bible story itself occupies very little of the poet's or the actors' time. The play is really a purely secular story about Mak the sheep-thief, his theft of a new-born lamb, and his punishment for the theft. Mak steals the lamb from the three shepherds and, when they come to search his house for it, he and his wife put it in a cradle, pretending it is a child. The episode that leads to the uncovering of the lamb and of Mak's villainy is really very amusing. (You can read the play and others in *Everyman, with Other Interludes*, in Everyman's Library.) The singing of the Angels announcing Christ's birth, the arrival at Bethlehem of these very English shepherds, their adoration of the Child—this is a mere epilogue to what is a very satisfying comic one-act play.

The writers of these Mystery plays are capable of taut dramatic action and strong characterisation as well as humour. Two powerful characters that emerge are Herod and Pontius Pilate. The Wakefield play of the Crucifixion opens with a powerful speech from Pilate which must have caused some tremors of pleasurable fear in the audience:

> What? peace, in the devil's name!
> Harlots and dastards all bedene
> On gallows ye be made full tame.
> Thieves and michers ken
> Will ye not peace when I bid you?
> By Mahoun's blood! If ye me teyn,
> I shall ordain soon for you
> Pains that never e'er was seen,
>   And that anon:
> Be ye so bold beggars, I warn you,
> Full boldly shall I beat you,
> To hell the de'il shall draw you,
>   Body, back and bone.

After which, presumably, he gets silence from the audience and the play can proceed. The realism of the play is remarkable. The four 'Torturers' are responsible for nailing Christ to the cross and for erecting that cross afterwards. Their words are the words of Yorkshire workmen and their insults to Christ have a terrifying ring of authenticity:

> *4th Torturer:* So, sir, gape against the sun! (*To Christ.*)
> *1st Torturer:* Ah, fellow, wear thy crown!
> *2nd Torturer:* Trowest thou this timber will come down?
> *3rd Torturer:* Yet help, to make it fast.
> *4th Torturer:* Bind him well, and let us lift.
> *1st Torturer:* Full short shall be his shrift
> *2nd Torturer:* Ah, it stands up like a mast.

In the Coventry Nativity Play of the Company of Shearmen and Tailors, Herod makes an impressive appearance:

> *Qui status in Jude et Rex Israel,*[1]
> And the mightiest conqueror that ever walked on ground;
> For I am even he that made both heaven and hell,
> And of my mighty power holdeth up this world round.
> Magog and Madroke, both them did I confound,
> And with this bright brand their bones I brake asunder . . .
> I am the cause of this great light and thunder;
> It is through my fury that they such noise do make.
> My fearful countenance the clouds so doth encumber,
> That often for dread thereof the very earth doth quake. . . .

In this play Herod makes claims that the real historical Herod would never have dreamt of making. Herod, in fact, is a special myth to the dramatists of this age: he is descended from Jupiter, related to Mohamed, he is himself a kind of false god. He is also, in my view, the prototype of the big raging character we are to find later in at least two of Marlowe's plays. Shakespeare may or may not have learnt from the mediaeval stage Herod how to rant and bluster, but it is certain that he saw a representation of Herod in a guild play. Hamlet tells the players who have just come to the palace:

> O, it offends me to the soul to hear a robustious periwig-pated fellow tear a passion to tatters, to very rags, to split the ears of the groundlings; which for the most part are capable of nothing but inexplicable dumb-shows and noise; I would have such a fellow whipped for o'erdoing Termagant; it out-Herods Herod—I pray you, avoid it.

In fact, Shakespeare knew what Herod stood for, and how this old stage-type had influenced the dramatists and actors of his own age. But, at the time of writing *Hamlet*, he preferred a subtler art.

---

[1] He that reigns as king in Judea and Israel.

Starting in the fourteenth century, these guild dramas had in all nearly three centuries of life, for we still find mention of them in the reign of James I. But it is not to them that we have to look for the origins of the great Elizabethan drama. Before this drama can come into being, we need a new tradition—a tradition of secular subjects for plays and of professional actors to act them.

Morality plays

The secular subjects are slow in coming, but they make their way into drama through a new kind of religious or semi-religious play—the *Morality*. The Morality was not a guild play and it did not take as its subject a story from the Bible. Instead, it tried to teach a *moral* lesson through allegory, that is, as in *Piers Plowman*, by presenting abstract ideas as though they were real people. A fine example of the Morality tradition is *Everyman*. This is a translation from the Dutch *Elckerlijk*, and it tells, in simple, dignified language, of the appearance of Death to Everyman (who stands for each one of us) and his informing Everyman that he must commence the long journey to the next world. Everyman calls on certain friends to accompany him—Beauty, Five-wits, Strength, Discretion— but they will not go. Only Knowledge and Good-Deeds are ready to travel in his company to the grave. Everyman learns that the pleasures, friends, and faculties of this world avail a man nothing when death comes; only spiritual strength can sustain him at his last hour. This is a simple moral, but it is made extremely forceful by being given dramatic form: the play, in fact, seems to be telling us something that we did not know before. This is always a sign of good art. And *Everyman* is good art. It is one of the later morality plays, printed in the sixteenth century but probably composed before the end of the fifteenth (presumably by the priest who speaks the final words of the play). It comes towards the end of the religious morality tradition, but it should be read before its predecessors.

Professionalism Secularisation

For its predecessors, certainly in England, are not very enlightening. *Mind, Will, and Understanding; Mankind; The Castle of Perseverance*, and others parade their cardboard characters: Wisdom, Mischief, Pleasure, Folly, Backbiting, Indignation, Sturdiness, Malice, Revenge, Discord, and so on. The playwrights wish to instruct us, but we long for the earthy humour of Noah and his wife or Mak the sheep-stealer, for more humanity and less morality. But that, of course, is like asking for beer in a milk-bar. Yet we do learn something of value from these plays. We learn, for instance, that *The Castle of Perseverance* was performed by a group of players who travelled from town to town or village to village, setting up their scenes as a modern circus sets up its tents and cages, and performing for money. In other words, we can begin to associate morality plays with professional companies. And also, to our satisfaction, we find that the moralities are capable of cutting themselves off from stock religious piety (not at all sincere) and dealing with purely moral themes.

This is an advance, for it means complete secularisation; it means that, fairly soon, drama will be capable of presenting a moral theme in terms of *personal conflict* (as in Shakespeare's tragedies, where the interest lies in the moral struggle within a living human being) and not as a mere illustration of a religious doctrine. We can put this in another way: even in a morality play as good as *Everyman* everything is cut and dried; we are listening to a superb dramatic sermon, but it is still a sermon. In a play like *Othello* we do not feel: 'This is an illustration of what happens to a man who is jealous.' True, we see the terrible consequences of Othello's jealousy, but Shakespeare is not just clarifying a religious doctrine. He is saying, in effect, 'Religion warns us about the consequences of our sins, but sometimes we can't help sinning, because our nature is made that way. Let us try to be compassionate towards a human being who, like the rest of us, is burdened with a ghastly load of human imperfection. In other words, let us not just condemn sin; let us try to understand it.'

The later morality plays—like *The World and the Child*, *Hickscorner*, and *Youth*—are about the reforming of vice, not through the exhortations of priests but by the acquisition of wisdom. Religion does come into these plays, but a greater stress seems to be laid on the value of experience, the great teacher, and it is notable that the theme of youth growing up is popular with the later morality playwrights.

In the last days of the fifteenth century we find it rather hard to distinguish between the Morality and the *Interlude*. The main difference seems to lie, not in theme, but in place and occasion of performance. An interlude was, as the name suggests, a short play performed in the middle of something else, perhaps a feast—a sort of incidental entertainment. We now see two dramatic traditions, an aristocratic one and a plebeian or lower-class one. We can think of the great lords in their castles, or rich men in their fine houses, watching a kind of refined morality play; we can think also of the common people watching—in the streets or inn-yards, or on the village green—a rather cruder kind of morality play. The aristocratic morality play—the interlude—can often be assigned to an author, and names like Rastell, Bale (the first Englishman to divide a play into acts), and Medwall appear. These men have learning and are interested in controversy. Medwall, for instance, writes *Fulgens and Lucrece*, which is a sort of dramatised discussion of the nature of true nobility. It is the first English play to have a title suggesting an Elizabethan play (like *Antony and Cleopatra*), and its Roman setting, its adaptation of an old story for the setting-forth of its argument, and its humour relate it to the great period of English drama which is to follow. Rastell wrote *Gentleness and Nobility* and *Calisto and Melibea*—again, plays of 'disputation' on moral themes. Bale's *Interlude of God's Promises* breathes the new spirit of the Reformation: he argues about free will and grace,

Late C15 drama

saying that man cannot achieve salvation through good works, but only the power of Christ's sacrifice, only by the grace that God bestows freely. But the real interest of all these plays lies in the fact of an aristocratic audience and the need for taste, learning, and skill in composition. Perhaps the most enjoyable of all the interlude dramatists is *John Heywood* (1497–1580), whose plays have no instructive purpose. In *The Four P's*, a Palmer, a Pardoner, a 'Pothecary and a Pedlar do nothing more than talk, but their purpose is only to see who can tell the biggest lie. In the *Play of the Weather* a number of people have asked Jupiter (not God!) for the kind of weather that they prefer to be granted all the time; but the various requests are contradictory—the laundress wants perpetual sun to dry and bleach her linen, the schoolboy wants perpetual winter so he can play with snowballs, the man who runs a water-mill wants nothing but rain, and so on. No two people can agree, and so things are left as they are. These plays are sheer entertainment, and their humour is gentle and in excellent taste.

That is more than can be said for the morality plays with which the ordinary people were entertained. There was a growing tendency here for Sin or Vice or the Devil to indulge in humour of the dirtiest kind—ostensibly so that the virtuous characters could condemn it. But this was pure hypocrisy, as we may guess—rather like saying, 'He's really a horrible man and his funny stories are disgusting; to show you what I mean I'll tell you a few of them.'

Now the raw materials for Elizabethan drama are being gathered together. The noble houses have their groups of interlude-players, wearing the livery of their master—these are to become the Elizabethan companies, with names like the Lord Admiral's Men, the King's Men, and so on. The wandering players of moralities, playing in inn-yards, are soon to take over these inn-yards as permanent theatres. Learned men are writing dramas—like the 'University Wits' who are going to lay the foundations for Shakespeare. We even have the Clown, or 'Vice', waiting to become Touchstone in *As You Like It* or the Fool in *King Lear*. Even Seneca is waiting to show Englishmen how to write tragedies, and Plautus and Terence to give advice on comedy. Soon—surprisingly soon—we shall be able to ring up the curtain on the greatest drama of all time.

8. Early Elizabethan Drama

The story of Elizabethan drama begins not in the theatres but in the Inns of Court of London; it begins with tragedies written by gentlemen who practise the law and, in their spare time, try to copy Seneca.

I say again that the influence of Seneca on the Elizabethan dramatists was very considerable. There was something in this Roman philosopher, tutor to Nero and amateur playwright, that appealed to the Tudor mind. Certainly, the first true English tragedy owes everything—except the plot—to him. This first tragedy is *Gorboduc*—by Thomas Norton and Thomas Sackville—produced at the Inner Temple of the Inns of Court in 1562. (In another two years Shakespeare and Marlowe will be born.) The story of *Gorboduc* is taken from the History of Geoffrey of Monmouth (see Chapter IV) and tells of the quarrel between Ferrex and Porrex, sons of King Gorboduc and Queen Videna, over the division of the kingdom of Britain. Porrex kills Ferrex and Queen Videna kills Porrex. The Duke of Albany (who, with his fellow of Cornwall, suggests *King Lear*) tries to take the country over himself, and civil war breaks out. We shall meet all these ingredients again, many times, especially the murders. What we shall not see again is a certain restraint, whereby violent actions are never shown on the stage but only reported. Later dramatists, including Shakespeare, are to show us, on-stage, all the horrors they can. But Sackville and Norton respect the Senecan tradition, which is to reserve the horror for the language and never for the visible action.

At this point I had better say that there were three ways of being influenced by Seneca. One was to read him (probably at school) in the original; the second was to read certain French plays which acknowledged his influence but watered down his language; the third was to read the Italian plays which called themselves 'Senecan' but were full of horrors enacted on the stage. The third way was the most popular with the Elizabethan dramatists, including Shakespeare. Shakespeare's *Titus Andronicus* is Italianate Seneca at its most gruesome (a recent revival in

61

London made people faint), for it contains mutilation, burying alive, several murders, and the eating of human flesh on-stage.

Blank verse

Seneca is seen even in the medium that Sackville and Norton choose for their dialogue—blank verse. The Earl of Surrey had translated Virgil into this new medium, and this translation had been published five years before *Gorboduc*. It must have seemed both to Surrey and to his followers that verse without rhyme was the best medium for rendering Latin. The first efforts of blank-verse writers certainly resemble the noble music and stately rhythms of the Roman writers hardly at all, but blank verse is a difficult medium, and it took two geniuses—Marlowe and Shakespeare —to show what could be done with it. Here is a sample of pre-Marlovian blank verse from an anonymous play called *Locrine*:

> O gods and stars! damned be the gods and stars
> That did not drown me in fair Thetis' plains!
> Curst be the sea, that with outrageous waves,
> With surging billows did not rive my ships
> Against the rocks of high Cerannia,
> Or swallow me into her wat'ry gulf!
> Would God we had arrived upon the shore
> Where Polyphemus and the Cyclops dwell,
> Or where the bloody Anthropophagi
> With greedy jaws devour the wandering wights!

Poor as that is, it shows a genuine attempt to imitate Seneca, not only in its use of classical imagery, but in the effect of declamation, of 'speaking emotions out loud'. Blank verse is to learn other things too from Seneca —the breaking up of the line between different speakers, the use of repetition, the subtle effects of echo. Here is a line from Seneca (it does not matter if you do not know any Latin; you will still be able to see one of Seneca's tricks):

> —Sceptrone nostro *famulus* est potior tibi?
> —Quo iste *famulus* tradidit *reges* neci.
> —Cur ergo *regi* servit et patitur iugum?

I have italicised the echo-words. The same effect appears again and again in Elizabethan drama:

> I had an Edward, till a Richard kill'd him;
> I had a Harry, till a Richard kill'd him;
> Thou hadst an Edward, till a Richard kill'd him;
> Thou hadst a Richard, till a Richard kill'd him.[1]

---

[1] See T. S. Eliot's essay 'Seneca in Elizabethan Translation' in his *Selected Essays* (Faber and Faber). The book also contains some stimulating essays on the Elizabethan dramatists.

I will not bore you with a catalogue of the Senecan plays produced in the Inns of Court, or in the Universities, or in the noble houses. They all seem to pave the way for the first tragedy capable of holding the public stage—*The Spanish Tragedy* by *Thomas Kyd* (1558–94). This play was popular all through Shakespeare's lifetime (it seemed, indeed, to be pre-ferred by the public to his own, far superior, work), and revivals of it on the modern stage, on the radio and on television, show that it has still a great deal of dramatic vitality.

Thomas Kyd

The story concerns the murder of Horatio—who is in love with the beautiful Belimperia—by agents of his rival in love. Hieronimo, the Knight-Marshal of Spain and father of Horatio, spends the rest of the play contriving revenge. Like Hamlet after him, he delays, talks rather than acts, but, again like Hamlet, he makes use of a play about a murder to effect his vengeful purpose. (Except, of course, that Hamlet still goes on delaying for another two acts.) The play ends in horrors—murder, suicide—and, before the end, Hieronimo performs an act whose horror never loses its absurd appeal—he bites his own tongue out and spits it on to the stage.

The language of the play is curiously memorable, showing that Kyd was no mean verse-writer. The following were catch-phrases for years with the Elizabethans:

> What outcries pluck me from my naked bed,
> And chill my throbbing heart with trembling fear,
> Which never danger yet could daunt before?
> Who calls Hieronimo? Speak, here I am.

And when Hieronimo is distraught with grief we have the following outburst:

> O eyes, no eyes, but fountains fraught with tears!
> O life, no life, but lively form of death!
> O world, no world, but mass of public wrongs,
> Confused and filled with murder and misdeeds!

Kyd is especially important to the student of Shakespeare, for it seems likely that he wrote the earlier version of the Hamlet story upon which Shakespeare was to base his own masterpiece, and certainly a memory of *The Spanish Tragedy* makes Hamlet say:

> I have heard
> That guilty creatures sitting at a play
> Have by the very cunning of the scene
> Been struck so to the soul that presently
> They have proclaim'd their malefactions.

And does not a memory of the distraught Hieronimo perhaps make Hamlet decide to be mad? We must regard Kyd as the father of the popular 'revenge tragedy' of which *Hamlet* is the most notable example.

Early comedy owes something to the Roman comic playwrights, as all Elizabethan tragedy—early and late—owes something to Seneca. *Nicholas Udall* (1505–56) was headmaster successively of Eton and Westminster schools, and he seems to have encouraged the acting, not merely the reading, of the plays of Terence and Plautus among his pupils. His play *Ralph Roister Doister* is, despite its breezy English atmosphere and its galloping rhymed verse, very much under the influence of Plautus. It is arranged into five acts and several scenes, following the Roman pattern, and the main character—Ralph himself—is modelled on the *miles gloriosus*, or boastful soldier, of Plautus. (Shakespeare is to make a great deal out of this braggart type in *Henry IV*.) We also have Mathew Merrygreek, based on the rascally servant found so often in Plautus, and a plot of courtship and misunderstanding which owes something to the Roman master. Associated with *Roister Doister* is *Gammer Gurton's Needle* (published in 1575, and possibly written by a Cambridge scholar, William Stevenson), a farcical tale of an old village woman who loses her needle and, after upsetting the whole village about it, eventually finds it stuck into the trousers of Hodge, her farm-servant. This, like the other play, is pure English country comedy, but it owes something to the Roman comedians in its skilful plot-construction. It contains, incidentally, the finest drinking-song in the English language:

> Back and side go bare, go bare,
>   Both foot and hand go cold,
> But, belly, God send thee good ale enough,
>   Whether it be new or old!

A more sophisticated kind of comedy was developed in the Royal Court itself, in the entertainments given by the Children of St. Paul's and other choir schools before the Queen. (We should note here that the Queen was a genuine patron of drama, encouraging it by liking to witness it, whether in Inns of Court, University, or at the royal revels.) These children (only boys) acted plays written by the first really 'polite' comic dramatist of the period—*John Lyly* (1554?–1606). Lyly started his literary career as the author of a very popular novel called *Euphues*, written in an elaborate prose-style—flowery and full of alliteration—a style since then called Euphuistic. This elaborate prose-style was carried over into the comedies that Lyly wrote; he used verse only in his occasional lyrics. The plays are charming—*Endimion* (a love-affair between the moon and a mortal), *Mother Bombie*, *Midas*, and *Campaspe* which is about the rivalry between Alexander the Great and a painter, Apelles,

Nicholas Udall

John Lyly

for the love of the beautiful captive Campaspe. Here is a specimen of Lyly's prose-style:

> . . . But you love, ah grief! but whom? Campaspe, ah shame! a maid forsooth unknown, unnoble, and who can tell whether immodest? Whose eyes are framed by art to enamour, and whose heart was made by nature to enchant. Ay, but she is beautiful, yea but not therefore chaste. . . . Beauty is like the blackberry which seemeth red, when it is not ripe, resembling precious stones that are polished with honey, which the smoother they look, the sooner they break.

George Peele (1558?–97?) is responsible for one of the most delightful of the pre-Shakespearian comedies—*The Old Wives' Tale* (a title Arnold Bennett, the novelist, was to use three hundred years later). This is one of the earliest attempts at a dramatic satire on those romantic tales of enchantment and chivalry which were already so popular in England. Two brothers are searching for their sister Delia, who is in the hands of the magician Sacrapant, and they themselves are captured by him. But Eumenides, Delia's lover, who gave his last pence to pay for the funeral of a poor man called Jack, finds that Jack's ghost is grateful and, through his superior supernatural gifts, is able to defeat the enchanter. That is the plot, but much of the charm of the play lies in its interludes of song and dance, and odd characters like the giant Huanebango and the mad Venelia. The songs, certainly, are excellent:

George Peele

> Whenas the rye reach to the chin,
> And chopcherry, chopcherry ripe within,
> Strawberries swimming in the cream,
> And schoolboys playing in the stream;
> Then, O then, O then, O my true-love said,
> Till that time come again
> She could not live a maid.

John Milton took the theme of the two brothers and the enchanted sister for his *Comus*. He produced something more poetic, but hardly more dramatic.

The last pre-Shakespearian writer of comedies I will mention is *Robert Greene* (1558?–92), whose best-known play is *Friar Bacon and Friar Bungay*. Here, in the clearly defined main plot and sub-plot and in the use of the clown, we are reminded of Shakespeare's early comedies. The title refers to the magical powers of two friars, who, among other things, produce a kind of television set and create a brazen head which is to tell the secrets of the universe; love interest is provided by Edward, Prince of Wales, who is enamoured of the lovely maid of Fressingfield, sweet Margaret. The play has freshness and charm and humour, but Greene's

Robert Greene

learning tends to intrude over-much. This is how a simple unlearned country girl is made to speak:

> ... Lordly sir, whose conquest is as great
> In conquering love, as Caesar's victories,
> Margaret, as mild and humble in her thoughts
> As was Aspasia unto Cyrus' self,
> Yields thanks. ...

Both Greene and Peele wrote tragedies and histories (Peele wrote an interesting Biblical play about David and Bathsheba), but, as Kyd was greater in the tragic field, and Marlowe greater still, it is more convenient to think of these two as comedy specialists—the complement to the tragedians who belong to the same group, the group known as the 'University Wits'.

The University Wits

The University Wits were, as their group-name proclaims, graduates of Oxford or Cambridge. Men with learning and talent but no money, they could not, like the clerks of the Middle Ages, find a career in the Church. The monasteries had been dissolved by King Henry VIII, leaving the poor scholar who did not wish to take full clerical orders no alternative but to seek secular employment. But the notion of secular employment for men of this type was a new one; the monastery had always been taken for granted previously as the destined home of the penniless scholar. And what secular employment was available in Elizabethan times? Teaching was not an attractive profession, and there were no Civil Service examinations. All that suggested itself was a kind of journalism—pamphleteering, novel-writing, and—perhaps more lucrative—writing plays for the new popular theatres.

So far we have said nothing about these theatres. Men like Sackville and Norton write their plays for the Inns of Court, lucky men like Lyly have their groups of children in the royal schools, their connections in high places. The drama they produce is not popular drama. The University Wits are different; their dramatic fortunes are tied to the theatres of London, and, being men of learning, they produce something better than the old popular morality plays. But what and where were these theatres? I should like you to think of London as a growing and prosperous city, to which streams of visitors flocked, not only from the provinces of England but from the Continent as well. The wandering groups of players would find fair audiences in the inns on the roads that led to London. They would set up their stages in the inn-yards, take good collections of money after their performances, and, finding that the audiences at the inns shifted frequently, consider giving performances daily in the same place—not moving on to fresh inns and fresh audiences, but allowing the fresh audiences to come to them. Here we have the germ of the Elizabethan theatre—a building indistinguishable from an inn in

The building of theatres

A play in a London inn yard in the time of Queen Elizabeth 1st.

architecture, four sides of the building looking into a large yard, the stage at one end of the yard. Tiers of galleries (or verandas), leading originally into inn bedrooms, would provide viewing-places for the 'better sort', while the common people could stand in the yard itself. The old facilities of the inn would be kept, in the way of liquid refreshment, and the very names of these new theatres would suggest their origin as hostelries—The Black Bull, The Swan, The Rose, and so on.

In 1574 the Earl of Leicester obtained a patent for his 'servants' (actors who wore his livery) to perform in public places, either in London or in the provinces. But the City Council immediately banned performances within the City of London itself. Now James Burbage, the chief man of Leicester's company, built a theatre *outside* the city limits, safe from the play-hating Council, and called it the Theatre. This was in 1576. Soon afterwards came another playhouse—the Curtain. In 1587 came the Rose

—built by Philip Henslowe—and in 1594 the Swan. Shakespeare's 'great Globe itself' was built in 1598, out of the timbers of the old Theatre. All these playhouses followed the same architectural lines—the inn-yard surrounded by galleries, the stage which jutted out into the audience and itself had, at the back, two or three tiers of galleries.

We can think of the popular drama of the day as being divided among two great companies of players—the Lord Chamberlain's and the Lord Admiral's; the Lord Chamberlain's (later called the King's Men) operating in their greatest days at the Globe; the Lord Admiral's at the Fortune. These two companies were only nominally the 'servants' of the noble person who lent their titles; they were virtually free agents, protected by their noble patrons from the charge of being vagabonds or 'masterless men'. How could they be either of these if they wore the livery of nobility? Both groups were large, perpetually infused with new blood (as with modern football teams) through transfers of players and through an apprenticeship system which provided a steady flow of boys for the women's parts. All members of the theatrical companies were versatile—they could play tragedy, comedy, they could dance, fence, sing, leap. Two actors were very great—Richard Burbage, son of James Burbage, star of the Lord Chamberlain's Men, first interpreter of all the leading Shakespearian parts; Edward Alleyn, son-in-law of Philip Henslowe, star of the Lord Admiral's Men, creator of Faustus, Tamburlaine, the Jew of Malta—all the Marlowe heroes. Elizabethan England produced a great drama, and it had great actors to interpret it.

Christopher Marlowe

The greatest ornament of the public theatre until Shakespeare was *Christopher Marlowe* (1564–93), born only a few weeks before Shakespeare, but destined to have a working life very much shorter than his. Marlowe was stabbed to death in a 'tavern brawl' in circumstances which we shall never fully understand, although scholars have spent much time in trying to elucidate them. Like all the University Wits, he had a wild reputation—it was believed that he was an atheist, consorted with thieves and ruffians, kept mistresses, fought the police. Yet this reputation may well have been the deliberate disguise of a man whose true nature was not at all wild and irresponsible. It is possible that Marlowe was a secret agent for the Queen's Government, and that the enemies who killed him were the country's enemies before they were his. But the mystery of his short life remains.

Renaissance in England

Marlowe's reputation as a dramatist rests on five plays—*Tamburlaine*, *Doctor Faustus*, *The Jew of Malta*, *Edward II*, and *Dido, Queen of Carthage*. To these five masterpieces might be added *The Massacre at Paris*, a bloodthirsty melodrama now, it seems, little read. In this handful of plays appears the first true voice of the Renaissance, of the period of new learning, new freedom, new enterprise, of the period of worship of Man rather than of God:

That dawn that Marlowe sang into our skies
With mouth of gold and morning in his eyes.

Marlowe sums up the New Age. The old restrictions of the Church and the limitations on knowledge have been destroyed; the world is opening up and the ships are sailing to new lands; wealth is being amassed; the great national aggressors are rising. But, above all, it is the spirit of human freedom, of limitless human power and enterprise that Marlowe's plays convey. Tamburlaine is the great conqueror, the embodiment of tyrannical power; Barabas, the Jew of Malta, stands for monetary power; Faustus represents the most deadly hunger of all, for the power which supreme knowledge can give.

In the part of the Duke of Guise in *The Massacre at Paris* we find the personification of a curious 'dramatic motive' which is to fascinate many Elizabethan playwrights—intrigue and evil almost for their own sakes, a complete lack of any kind of morality, what is sometimes called the 'Machiavellian principle'. The reference is to Niccolo Machiavelli (1469–1527) and his book *The Prince*, a treatise on statecraft which had the aim of bringing about a united Italy through any means which Italian leaders found workable: cruelty, treachery, tyranny were all acceptable so long as they produced, in the end, a strong and united state. It is the 'Machiavellian' note which we hear from the Duke of Guise:

> Now Guise begins those deepe ingendred thoughts
> To burst abroad those neuer dying flames,
> Which cannot be extinguished but by bloud.
> Oft haue I leueld, and at last haue learnd,
> That perill is the cheefest way to happines,
> And resolution honors fairest aime.
> What glory is there in a common good,
> That hanges for euery peasant to atchiue?
> That like I best that flyes beyond my reach.
> Set me to scale the high Peramides,
> And thereon set the Diadem of Fraunce,
> Ile either rend it with my nayles to naught,
> Or mount the top with my aspiring winges,
> Although my downfall be the deepest hell.

It is the note we hear sustained throughout the two parts of *Tamburlaine*. This play is a procession of magnificent scenes, each representing some stage in the rise of Tamburlaine from humble Scythian shepherd to conqueror of the world. Everything is larger than life in *Tamburlaine*. He is not content merely to conquer; he impresses his greatness on the conquered by such acts as slaughtering all the girls of Damascus; using the captive Soldan of Turkey as a footstool and carrying him about in a cage

Tamburlaine

till he beats out his brains against the bars; burning the town in which his mistress, Zenocrate, dies; killing his own son because of his alleged cowardice; harnessing two kings to his chariot and shouting:

> Holla, ye pampered jades of Asia!
> What! can ye draw but twenty miles a day,
> And have so proud a chariot at your heels,
> And such a coachman as great Tamburlaine?

Tamburlaine takes Babylon and has the Governor pierced with arrows (at a performance by the Lord Admiral's Men one of these arrows accidentally killed a child in the audience) and every inhabitant of the town drowned in a lake. This is the modern age with a vengeance, however much Tamburlaine belongs historically to olden times. It is a caricature of our own age, with its Nazi and Communist atrocities, but a caricature made magnificent with Marlowe's rich blank verse. Here is Tamburlaine the braggart:

> The God of war resigns his room to me,
> Meaning to make me General of the world;
> Jove viewing me in arms looks palè and wan,
> Fearing my power should pull him from his throne.

Here is Tamburlaine the bereaved lover:

> Now walk the angels on the walls of heaven,
> As sentinels to warn the immortal souls
> To entertain divine Zenocrate.

Jew of Malta

The Jew of Malta is the story of Barabas, whose wealth is magnificently celebrated in the long opening speech (after Machiavelli has spoken the prologue):

> . . . Bags of fiery opals, sapphires, amethysts,
> Jacinths, hard topaz, grass-green emeralds,
> Beauteous rubies, sparkling diamonds,
> And seld-seen costly stones of so great price,
> As one of them indifferently rated,
> And of a caret of this quantity,
> May serve in peril of calamity
> To ransom great kings from captivity.

Barabas is deprived of all his wealth by the Governor of Malta, who wants it to pay the Turks their tribute, much in arrears. After this Barabas embarks on a long career of revenge, not only on the Governor himself, but on Christians and Muslims generally. He poisons a whole convent of nuns, contrives that the two lovers of his daughter shall kill each other, and finally proposes to slaughter the leaders of the Turks who

have invaded the island and to massacre the Turkish soldiers in a monastery. It is he himself who dies, dropping—through a trick of the
Governor—into a cauldron of boiling oil which he has prepared for his
enemies. His final words are:

> . . . Had I but escaped this stratagem,
> I would have brought confusion on you all,
> Damned Christian dogs and Turkish infidels!
> But now begins the extremity of heat
> To pinch me with intolerable pangs:
> Die, life! Fly, soul! tongue, curse thy fill, and die!

T. S. Eliot, in his essay on Marlowe, points out the use of caricature in
his writing, not for a humorous effect but for an effect of horror. In
Dido, Queen of Carthage there is a description of the taking of Troy which
uses a technique of exaggeration to convey the nightmare violence:

Dido

> I rose,
> And looking from a turret, might behold
> Young infants swimming in their parents' blood,
> Headless carcases piled up in heaps,
> Virgins half-dead dragged by their golden hair
> And with main force flung on a ring of pikes,
> Old men with swords thrust through their aged sides,
> Kneeling with mercy to a Greekish lad
> Who with steel pole-axes dashed out their brains.

There is no caricature, no mingling of the comic and the horrible, in
Doctor Faustus, perhaps Marlowe's greatest play. This is the story of the
learned man who has mastered all arts and all sciences, finds nothing
further in the world to study, and so turns to the supernatural. He con-
jures up Mephistopheles, 'servant to great Lucifer', and through him
concludes a bargain whereby he obtains twenty-four years of absolute
power and pleasure in exchange for his soul. Faustus makes the most of
his time. He brings the glorious past of Greece back to life and even
weds Helen of Troy. These are the wonderful lines he addresses to her:

Faustus

> Was this the face that launched a thousand ships
> And burnt the topless towers of Ilium?
> Sweet Helen, make me immortal with a kiss.
> Her lips suck forth my soul—see, where it flies:
> Come, Helen, come, give me my soul again. . . .
> . . . O thou are fairer than the evening air
> Clad in the beauty of a thousand stars,
> Brighter art thou than flaming Jupiter
> When he appeared to hapless Semele,

> More lovely than the monarch of the sky
> In wanton Arethusa's azured arms,
> And none but thou shalt be my paramour.

And just as remarkable is the long final speech of the play, when Faustus is waiting for the Devil to carry him to hell—his cry 'See where Christ's blood streams in the firmament!' and his ultimate screams as, amid thunder and lightning, he is dragged to the flames by demons:

> My God, my God, look not so fierce on me:
> Adders and serpents, let me breathe awhile:
> Ugly hell, gape not, come not, Lucifer—
> I'll burn my books . . . ah, Mephistophilis.

Despite faults of construction, obvious carelessness and other artistic flaws attendant on youth, Marlowe's achievement is a very important one. He is a great poet and dramatist who, had he not been killed untimely in a tavern in London, might well have become greater even than Shakespeare. And not even Shakespeare could do all that Marlowe could do: the peculiar power gained from caricature; the piled-up magnificence of language; above all, 'Marlowe's mighty line'—these are great individual achievements. There is nobody like Christopher Marlowe.

9. *William Shakespeare*

This chapter should begin and end with the title. For what more can I say about Shakespeare than has already been said? He is the subject of innumerable books, written in all the languages of the world. He has been studied exhaustively. Every line of every one of his plays has been analysed, re-analysed, edited, and re-edited; the scanty details of his life have been examined under countless microscopes; the world has judged him and found him the greatest playwright, perhaps the greatest writer, of all time. This chapter can contain nothing new.

And yet each age, perhaps even each decade, can find some new aspect of a great writer, simply because, being great, no one age, no one person can see all of him. The twentieth-century Shakespeare is different from the nineteenth-century Shakespeare; the Shakespeare of the 1970s is different from the Shakespeare of the 1960s. So it will go on as long as civilisation lasts; and every new aspect of Shakespeare will be as true as any other.

Is Shakespeare's life important to us? Does it matter to us that he was born in Stratford, made a possibly unwise marriage there, migrated to London, amassed a fortune, came back a wealthy citizen, and died— according to tradition—of a fever after a drinking-bout? In a sense it does, for, knowing why Shakespeare wrote his plays, knowing what he wanted out of life, we can attune our view of the plays to his view, understand them better for getting inside the skin of the man who wrote them. It is conceivable that Shakespeare's main aim in life was to become a gentleman and not an artist, that the plays were a means to an end. Shakespeare wanted property—land and houses—and that meant acquiring money; the writing of the plays was primarily a means of getting money. The theatre was as good a means as any of making money, if one happened to be a man of fair education and a certain verbal talent. Shakespeare was such a man. His eye was never on posterity (except perhaps in his poems); it was on the present. It was left to Heming and Condell—two friends of his—to bring out, after his death, the first col-

Shakespeare's aims

Masked ladies in the 'pit' at the old Globe Theatre.

lected edition of his plays; Shakespeare seemed to have little interest in leaving an exact version of his life's work to the unknown future. Nor did Shakespeare seem to think of his plays as literature: he had no interest in the reader in the study, only in the audience in the playhouse. The playhouse was everything to Shakespeare the dramatist, and woe betide us if we forget this fact. Whenever we start to read one of his plays we should erect in our mind's eye a theatre something like Shakespeare's Globe and imagine the play performed there. This will save us from thinking—as the nineteenth-century scholars did—of Hamlet or Macbeth as 'real people' and asking such questions as 'What was Hamlet doing before the action of the play begins?' or 'Was Macbeth's childhood unhappy?' (There was once a very popular book called *The Girlhood of Shakespeare's Heroines.*) This view of Shakespeare's characters as 'real people', who can be separated from the plays in which they appear, is wide of the mark. To Shakespeare, Hamlet was a part for Dick Burbage and Touchstone a part for Armin. What was Hamlet doing before the opening of the play? Probably drinking beer, brushing his hair, dusting his doublet. Hamlet only begins to exist as soon as he is discovered on the stage in Act I Scene ii; before that, he is a rather nervous actor.

Conditions in which Shakespeare worked

Why do so many of Shakespeare's heroines suddenly change into boys' clothes? Because his heroines *were* boys and felt more comfortable (probably acted better too) dressed as boys. Why does the Queen say that Hamlet is 'fat and scant of breath'? Because Burbage, who played the part, probably *was* fat and scant of breath and not fencing very well. Why disguise the fact? Why not admit it to the audience? There was very little of the 'let's pretend' in Shakespeare's theatre. No scenery, no period costumes, no attempt at convincing the audience that they were in ancient Rome, Greece or Britain. *Julius Caesar* and *Coriolanus* proclaimed in their costumes that they were plays about Elizabethan England, or—and this is too subtle for our modern age—plays about Elizabethan England and ancient Rome *at one and the same time*. Similarly the stage could be a real stage and a forest at the same time, a stage and a ship at sea at the same time. The swiftness of Shakespeare's action, his rapid changes of scene, demand—if naturalism is wanted—a medium as fluid as the cinema, and it is in films that Shakespeare has come into his own for many people today.

Shakespeare is cinematic in his swift scene-changes, his swift action. But not in his attitude to language. In the cinema what we see is still more important than what we hear—things have not changed greatly since the days of the early silent films. But words are all-important to Shakespeare—not just, or even primarily, the meaning of words, but the sound of words. Shakespeare wanted to batter or woo or enchant the ears of his audience with language, and in any one of his plays—early or late—

Shakespeare's verbal genius

the word-hoards are opened wide and the gold scattered lavishly. In early plays—*Romeo and Juliet* or *Richard II*, for example—Shakespeare's verbal genius is a lyric one, a musical one. Long speeches, which often hold up the action of the play, weave lovely poetic images, play with words and sounds. In later plays, such as *Antony and Cleopatra* and *King Lear*, language becomes abrupt, compressed, sometimes harsh, and it is often hard to understand. But the words still pour out—there is never any impression of careful slow composition, the leisurely search for the right word. We have it on the evidence of Heming and Condell, and also Ben Jonson, that Shakespeare wrote with great speed and facility, rarely crossing anything out. This explains a certain impatience with language: Shakespeare often cannot wait for the right word to come, and so invents a word of his own.

Attitude to audience

A concern with the *sound* of words implies a concern with the ears that hear the sound. Shakespeare is always greatly aware of his own Elizabethan audience, that mixed bag of aristocrats, wits, gallants, cut-purses, sailors and soldiers on leave, schoolboys and apprentices, which bears a greater resemblance to the modern cinema audience than the modern theatre audience (in Europe, anyway). He tries to establish intimacy with this audience, to bring it into the play, and his soliloquies are not speeches which the actor pretends to be delivering to himself, but intimate communications with the audience. It was, anyway, difficult to pretend that the audience was not there: the daylight blazed on the audience, the audience surrounded three sides of the stage, some of the audience even sat on the stage. The modern actor, cut off from his audience by footlights and darkness, can pretend that they are rows of cabbages, not people at all. Not so the Elizabethan actor: he had to establish contact with auditors who were critical, sometimes rowdy, certainly always daylit flesh-and-blood, not abstractions hidden by darkness. This audience had to be given what it wanted, and, being a mixed bag, it wanted a variety of things—action and blood for the unlettered, fine phrases and wit for the gallants, thought and debate and learning for the more scholarly, subtle humour for the refined, boisterous clowning for the unrefined, love-interest for the ladies, song and dance for everybody. Shakespeare gives all these things; no other dramatist has given anything like as much.

Collaboration and competition

Before we take a bird's-eye view of Shakespeare's work, we had better remind ourselves that it is not always easy or even possible to say of the Elizabethan drama, 'This man wrote that; that man wrote this.' Collaboration was common, and Shakespeare probably worked with Beaumont and Fletcher as well as other notable writers. Moreover, he occasionally took an existing play (such as the original *Hamlet* probably written by Kyd) and re-fashioned it, always certainly improving it. This re-fashioning was more congenial to him than the invention of new plots; in fact, he normally prefers to take somebody else's plot or dig out a story from a history book or a popular pamphlet—his interest is more in the *telling* of the story than the story itself. However, of the plays I shall mention now, Shakespeare is certainly the author, either wholly or mostly.

Shakespeare's poetic (as opposed to dramatic) fame began with two long poems—*Venus and Adonis* and *The Rape of Lucrece*—and with the first of the Sonnets which he continued writing alongside his plays. In his early London days he had, as patron and friend, the Earl of South-ampton, and so his knowledge of the great, of such power-seekers as the Earl of Essex and the whole busy world of court intrigue and politics, is not wholly second-hand. Among his first plays are the three parts of *Henry VI*—a pageant of history with a patriotic flavour which, as Shake-speare well knew, was a factor unifying all the diverse elements of his audience. This was the time when national pride was greatest—the Armada defeated, the English navy the strongest of Europe, the country itself unified under a powerful monarch. The popularity of these plays was such as to excite antagonism in at least one fellow-dramatist—Robert Greene, whose posthumous *A Groatsworth of Wit Bought with a Million of Repentance* introduces a parodic form of Shakespeare's name—'Shake-scene'—in a context of bitter envy. For the provision of new plays for the London theatres had been the responsibility, self-elected, of men with Oxford and Cambridge degrees—University Wits, learned poets like Greene, Peele, Marlowe. Here was a newcomer from the pro-vinces, with no more than a grammar-school education, who was beating the masters of arts at their own game. Greene saw in Shakespeare a *Johannes Factotum* or jack-of-all-trades—a clever and ruthless oppor-tunist who gave the public what it wanted, not what it ought to have. If there was an appetite for the pornography of violence, Shakespeare was well able to satisfy it, providing in *Titus Andronicus* a remarkable mixture of rape, torture, massacre, and even cannibalism. If the farce of mistaken identity was required, Shakespeare could, with his *Comedy of Errors*, out-do Plautus and Terence in mad complication. For those Roman comedi-ans had been content to gain their laughs from the theme of twins who, separated from birth, suddenly turned up in the same place unknown to each other. Shakespeare was not satisfied, as they had been, with one set of twins: he had to make their servants twins too. He was essentially an outdoer, a writer who liked to go further than his predecessors, whether in intrigue, violence, or sheer lyric beauty.

The lyrical Shakespeare first manifests himself in a series of romantic comedies of which the earliest—*Love's Labour's Lost*—was conceivably written for an aristocratic audience, aimed indeed directly at the Earl of Southampton's circle. It is full of high-flown language in the manner of John Lyly, it makes subtle references to the court of Henry IV of France, there is an attack—undoubtedly meant to please Southampton—on that

Early romantic comedies

man so adept at making enemies, Sir Walter Raleigh. It was certainly not a play for the sausage-chewers of the public theatres. To balance its polished exquisitries, Shakespeare wrote *The Taming of the Shrew*, whose comparative crudities are tempered by being presented as a play within a play. Christopher Sly, a drunken tinker, is the victim of a practical joke which has him believe that he is a lord who has lost his memory, and the interlude of wife-taming is presented before him. It is hard not to feel that Shakespeare has put something of himself in the part of Sly—a Warwickshire tinker (or tinkerer with plays) a sly man who is taking the place in the world of drama of poor dead Christopher Marlowe, a lowly provincial who has become the friend and protégé of a noble lord. The play that Sly sees is set in Padua, and Shakespeare is beginning to show some second-hand knowledge of north-eastern Italy—perhaps knowledge gained from the Italian John Florio, secretary to the Earl of Southampton. *The Two Gentlemen of Verona*—which has the first of the exquisite incidental songs, 'Who is Sylvia?'—is flooded with Italian sunlight, which we may think of as London-bottled Chianti, and the Italian ambience (or specifically the Venetian ambience) is to haunt Shakespeare's next productions.

Romeo and Juliet, with another Verona setting, is a remarkable lyrical tragedy, in which Shakespeare, with his opportunist eyes wide open, tries to produce something to please every section of his multi-layered public audience—fights, low comedy, philosophical truisms (for the men of the Inns of Court to write down in their notebooks), young love star-crossed, untimely death. There is even, underlying the tale he took from *Topicality* a popular poem, that streak of topicality which is usually to be found in even the remotest-seeming dramatic subject of Shakespeare's—a notorious and murderous quarrel between two English families, the Longs and the Danvers brothers, the latter friends of Southampton who, despite the issue of warrants for their arrest, arranged for them to escape to France. There is the same topicality in *The Merchant of Venice*, which, though following Marlowe's *The Jew of Malta* in its conventional anti-semitism, exploits the particular feelings aroused by the allegation (on the part of the Earl of Essex, Southampton's friend and hero) that Queen Elizabeth's Jewish physician Lopez was a Spanish spy. Lopez was hanged, drawn and quartered; Shylock, whose sole crime is usury, is too complex for easy condemnation.

A Midsummer Night's Dream has a mad sunlit, or moonlit, setting which combines mythical Athens with Shakespeare's own Warwickshire. Written for the nuptials, one supposes, of the Lady Elizabeth Vere (whom Southampton had been ordered by his godfather Lord Burleigh to marry, though he preferred to refuse and pay a fine of five thousand pounds) and the Earl of Derby, it extends the fairy music of Mercutio's Queen Mab speech in *Romeo and Juliet* into a whole play. It also blames the bad summer and harvest of the year 1594 on the dissension of the King and Queen of the fairies, and, in the Pyramus rhodomontade of Bottom the weaver, satirises the elocutionary technique of Edward Alleyn, chief tragedian of the Lord Admiral's Men. Shakespeare was by now a shareholder in the Lord Chamberlain's Men and resident playwright of the Theatre in Shoreditch. He was beginning to do well.

With *Richard II* Shakespeare returned to English history and the serial *Histories* composition of a dramatic epic on the troubled era that was to resolve itself gloriously in the establishment of the Tudor dynasty. *Richard III* had come, apparently, on the hot heels of the *Henry VI* trilogy and, despite its melodramatic power, must be regarded as a product of an apprentice phase; *Richard II* was lyrical, subtle and, again, topical. Shakespeare undoubtedly learned from Marlowe's *Edward II* how to put together an historical play that should be more than a mere pageant of violence, but in the theme of the weak monarch and the usurping strong noble (Henry Bolingbroke deposes Richard II and turns himself into Henry IV) the followers of the Earl of Essex saw a tract for the times. Elizabeth was, so many thought, becoming senile; in the absence of a declared heir to the throne should not the rule go to that great popular hero—soldier and flower of chivalry—Robert Devereux, Earl of Essex? Whether Shakespeare deliberately intended his *Richard II* as a work of propaganda we cannot know, but we do know that the play was soon to be regarded as inflammatory and, indeed, was used as an act of inflammation when a special performance of it preceded the Essex rebellion in 1601.

King John, which appeared in 1596, is an interlude in the great procession of plays about the Plantagenets, and perhaps intended primarily —apart from its entertainment value—as a comment on the bad times. The Spanish were causing trouble again, the French had allowed them to take Calais, and the play is full of fickle France and defiant England. There are also evident references to the death of Shakespeare's son Hamnet, which took place in that year:

> Grief fills the room up of my absent child,
> Lies in his bed, walks up and down with me,
> Puts on his pretty looks, repeats his words,
> Remembers me of all his gracious parts,
> Stuffs out his vacant garments with his form.

It was a painful year for Shakespeare, and a certain failure of inspiration makes this play the worst, probably, of his maturity, but the year ended with his being confirmed in the rank of gentleman, complete with coat of arms, and his making arrangements to purchase New Place, the finest house in Stratford. From then on the plays breathe maturity and confidence.

The two *Henry IV* plays are direct sequels of *Richard II*, but they are more than mere histories. The character of Sir John Falstaff, who holds up the action gloriously, is, as L. C. Knights put it, the meat surrounded by dry historical bread. A character of huge popularity, he was to appear again—it is believed by the Queen's own request—in *The Merry Wives of Windsor*, where he is much diminished by being shown ridiculously in love, or lust. Lechery does not suit Falstaff, and he has played out his wit in a more congenial setting. *Henry V*, the most swingeingly patriotic of all the plays, one may think of as perhaps opening up the new Globe Theatre in 1599. Although the theme was the conquest of France, Shakespeare undoubtedly had in mind the impending conquest of Ireland—a conquest unfulfilled, alas—by the Earl of Essex. The Chorus of *Henry V*, who reminds us that the new theatre is a 'wooden O', makes a direct reference to him:

> Were now the general of our gracious empress—
> As in good time he may—from Ireland coming,
> Bringing rebellion broachèd on his sword,
> How many would the peaceful City quit
> To welcome him!

But, with the shamed return of unvictorious Essex, these patriotic enlargements turned sour, and, indeed, English history became a dangerous thing to present upon the stage: it was too easy to find, in any aspect of England's past, seditious parallels to the present. History from now on had to be remote and foreign—*Julius Caesar*, *Coriolanus*, and any other tales of ancient Rome Shakespeare could filch from Suetonius and Plutarch.

More comedies

But first there was a new vein of comedy to tap, along with a new approach to that essential element in Elizabethan comedy—the clown. Will Kemp, with his leers, trippings and lewd improvisations, had been the highly popular funny man of the Lord Chamberlain's Men, but now Shakespeare was conceiving of a more subtle, complex clown, one who could sing sad songs and stick to the script. Kemp left the company, and Robin Armin took his place. For him Shakespeare wrote the parts of Touchstone in *As You Like It* and Feste in *Twelfth Night*. *As You Like It* is a fine pastoral comedy with a melancholy character called Jaques—Shakespeare's attempt at outdoing Chapman, who had created a notable black-suited melancholic called Dowceser—who recites a speech that makes a direct reference to the motto of the Globe Theatre, woven on its flag under the representation of Hercules carrying the world on his shoulders: *Totus mundus agit histrionem*, loosely translated as 'All the world's a stage'. *Twelfth Night*, a strangely melancholy tapestry, despite hard-drinking Sir Toby Belch and the foolish Sir Andrew Aguecheek, has lost topicalities (lost to all but the probing scholar of court-life) in its references to the disgraced Mistress Mary Fitton, called Mall, and Sir William Knollys, Controller of the Queen's Household, who, though married and old, fell in love with her. *Mall voglio*—I want Mall; the character of Malvoglio homes intimately to the court for which the play was written as an entertainment suitable for the last day of Christmas.

Julius Caesar and *Troilus and Cressida*—the one a dark tragedy of Roman history, the other a dark comedy of Greek myth—seem to reflect Shakespeare's own perturbations about the troubled times in which the rebellion of the Earl of Essex, disgraced at court but still the flower of chivalry to many, was preparing itself. Shakespeare's concern is with the need for order to be maintained in the state—'Take but degree away, / untune that string,/ And hark! what discord follows . . .' If *Troilus and Cressida* failed as a play (and there is evidence that it had only one performance), it was because it preached too much about order and the need to maintain degree. When the Earl of Essex revolted and tried to smash the order of the English commonweal, Shakespeare gave up political preaching. He was silent for a whole year, or very nearly, and then he summed up the whole of the dying Elizabethan age—the conflict between inherited mediaeval thought and the new scepticism, the inherent sickness of the world—in *Hamlet*. It is perhaps this one play, of all the plays ever written, that the world would least willingly be without, and it ushers in a period of Shakespeare's maturity which is marked by disillusion and hopelessness.

That great phase belongs to the Jacobean period, not the Elizabethan. Queen Elizabeth I died in 1603, and James VI of Scotland united two kingdoms as James I of England. The Lord Chamberlain's Men became the King's Men, and Shakespeare became a Groom of the Royal Bedchamber. None of the euphoria of this promotion, and his undoubted establishment as greatest poet of his time, is found reflected in his work, even in the comedies. *All's Well that Ends Well* and *Measure for Measure* are not meant primarily for laughs. *Macbeth*, which, with its Scottish setting, honours a Scottish king, is, on one level, a compendium of things that interested James I—his own ancestry, the prevalence of witchcraft—but, on another, it is a very bitter vision of life: 'Out, out, brief candle.' *King Lear* and *Timon of Athens* are near-hysterical denunciations of ingratitude (what ingratitude had the poet himself had recently to suffer?). *Coriolanus* has, in its title role, a man who despises the mob, perhaps as Shakespeare was learning to despise it. *Antony and Cleopatra* soars above mere history and finds the one reality—though bitterly destroyed by the world—in a human love built on corruption and irresponsibility.

Disillusion

Shakespeare half-retired to his great house in Stratford in 1610, and, finding comfort in his daughters Judith and Susannah, reflects something of the redemptive power of an innocent female soul in the last great

The late comedies

comedies. *The Winter's Tale*, *Pericles* (perhaps not so great and perhaps only half Shakespeare's work) and *The Tempest* are in a new and delicious vein of lyricism; the tragic bitterness has been purged, the magician buries his staff and awaits his serene end. In 1613 the Globe Playhouse was burned to the ground during the first performance of *Henry VIII*, which Shakespeare seems to have written in collaboration with John Fletcher, one of the coming young men. Another Globe was to be built, but it would not concern the living Shakespeare. He had put so much of himself into the life of that 'wooden O' that its destruction must have been like the destruction of a faculty or a limb. Although he still had three years to live, the end of the great Globe marks the end of his career. It was, to put it mildly, one of the most astonishing literary careers in all history.

Wherein chiefly lies Shakespeare's greatness? It would seem that it lies in a consistency of achievement. Many men who wrote plays in his lifetime produced single works of great excellence, but none achieved the same consistency of excellence as, from about 1593 on, he showed in play after play. He could do as well in tragedy as the tragic specialists, and—in astonishing works like *Hamlet*—far better. He could match the comic specialists and, moreover, was able to do strange and great things in fields which hardly anyone else touched—'dark' comedy like *Measure for Measure*, the exalted vision of *The Tempest*. It is an all-round dramatic excellence, and it is served by a supreme gift of language. We remember a few characters from other playwrights—superb creations like the Duchess of Malfi or Tamburlaine or De Flores or Volpone—but nobody gives us so vast a gallery of living personages as Shakespeare. He encloses the playwrights of his time; he is twenty men in one, and he is also himself, enigmatic but curiously sympathetic. His greatness was summed up by Dumas: 'Next to God, Shakespeare has created most.' We may well leave it at that.

10. Other Elizabethan Dramatists

When we study Shakespeare at school, we have a vague picture of him as not merely dominating the Elizabethan theatre, but standing alone. This is because plays by his contemporaries are so rarely set for examinations below the University or University Entrance level. It should be the task of a history like this to correct the impression of Shakespeare's 'uniqueness' and to show the richness of the Elizabethan theatre generally. The trouble is that the richness is so incredible, the men of talent so many, and space so short, that only the most superficial impression of the dramatic achievements of that age can be given. I shall attempt to do little more than mention plays that are worthy to stand by plays of Shakespeare, and to give the names of their authors.

Shakespeare's greatest contemporary (after Marlowe) was Ben Jonson (1574–1637). Jonson's aims were different from those of his friend: indeed, so different, that we feel from Jonson's writings about Shakespeare that he did not fully appreciate, or even like, the works of his senior. Shakespeare followed no rules and had no dramatic theory; Jonson was a classicist, whose masters were the ancients, and whose every play was composed on an established ancient pattern. Jonson's plays generally obey the rules of 'unity': the action takes less than a day and the scene never moves from the initial setting—Venice in *Volpone*, a London house in *The Alchemist*. Moreover, Jonson had a theory of dramatic character already out-of-date in his own day. While Shakespeare sees human beings as strange mixtures, walking masses of conflict and contradiction, unpredictable, always surprising, Jonson sees them as very simple and almost mechanical combinations of four elements. This was a mediaeval idea: the human soul was made out of 'humours' —sanguine, choleric, phlegmatic, melancholic—which, mixed in various proportions, gave different human 'types'. Jonson's characters are all 'humours', and his comedy *Every Man in His Humour* seems to be little more than a demonstration of the theory. In each character one quality predominates: amorousness, cowardice, avarice, irascibility, boastful-ness. We seem in many ways to be close to the moralities with their personifications of virtue and vice; the character, once established, never changes—indeed, any hint of complexity or capacity for change would destroy the self-contained worlds that Jonson builds.

But Jonson, despite the limitations that theory imposes on him, is a very great playwright. His tragedies have little appeal (for tragedy one needs conflict and capacity for change: the appeal of Macbeth is precisely the warring within himself, the gradual corruption of his nature) but his comedies are admirable. *Volpone* and *The Alchemist* both have the same theme—the rogue and his assistant who get fat and rich on the credulity of the stupid. In *Volpone*, the old fox who gives his name to the title pretends to be very rich and very ill: lying on his pretended death-bed he informs every one of his visitors that he, and he only, shall inherit Volpone's wealth. Needless to say, each visitor brings substantial presents so that Volpone shall not change his mind. *The Alchemist* deals with two rogues who pretend to have discovered the magic formula for turning base metal to gold. They receive dupe after dupe, take money and goods from them, and become involved in a series of rollicking comic situations which are often far less 'knock-about', more keenly satirical than anything in Shakespeare's comedies. Romance is outside Jonson's scope, but he has a wonderful lyrical gift that owes a lot to Marlowe, and his love-scenes have a sensuousness of language which always seems to be under control—unlike some of Shakespeare, where the very flow and flood of language seems to have the poet in its power. Here is Volpone the lover:

> Why droops my Celia?
> Thou hast, in place of a base husband, found
> A worthy lover: use thy fortune well,
> With secrecy and pleasure. See, behold,
> What thou art queen of; not in expectation,
> As I feed others: but possess'd and crown'd.
> See here a rope of pearl; and each more orient
> Than that the brave Egyptian queen caroused:
> Dissolve and drink them. See, a carbuncle
> May put out both the eyes of our St. Mark;
> A diamond, would have bought Lollia Paulina,
> When she came in like star-light, hid with jewels,
> That were the spoils of provinces; take these,
> And wear, and lose them: yet remains an ear-ring
> To purchase them again, and this whole state.

Jonson is the great dramatist of 'realism'. He does not, like Shakespeare, turn his back on Elizabethan London and visit strange places like Illyria or the Forest of Arden; he is concerned with making his comedy out of the situations of his own time: he is always contemporary in his themes and settings. But he can be fanciful as well as realistic, as his masques show. (The masque was the later version of the interlude: an elaborate but short piece with music, dance, gods, goddesses, and abstractions, played in the great houses on great occasions.) And Jonson is the greatest purely lyric poet of the early seventeenth century, the founder of a whole school of poets—the 'Tribe of Ben'. This is, perhaps, the most popular song in the language:

> Drink to me only with thine eyes,
>   And I will pledge with mine . . .

And the following seems to contain the very essence of Ben Jonson the poet: colour, light, form.

> Have you seen but a bright lily grow
>   Before rude hands have touch'd it?
> Have you mark'd but the fall of the snow
>   Before the soil hath smutch'd it?
> Have you felt the wool of beaver,
>   Or swan's down ever?
> Or have smelt o' the bud o' the brier,
>   Or the nard in the fire?
> Or have tasted the bag of the bee?
> O so white, O so soft, O so sweet is she!

Jonson's gift, like Shakespeare's, is primarily a verbal one, but it is coupled with sharp observation, a keen sense of satire, and a strong concern with form.

Jonson is not the only dramatist to present us with a living picture of the London of his time. Francis Beaumont (1584–1616) and John Fletcher (1579–1625) paint in gentler colours, but their *Knight of the Burning Pestle* is as compelling a view of middle-class London as *The Alchemist*. These two playwrights worked together for several years, achieving a common style, so that it is hard in any given play to separate Beaumont's contribution from Fletcher's. They learned a great deal from Shakespeare, especially in the field of romantic comedy, but lacked Shakespeare's genius and Shakespeare's delicacy of touch. Their treatment of amorous themes, for instance, often leaves a nasty taste in the mouth; in *A King and No King*, incestuous love between brother and sister occurs quite casually, with no attempt to probe the moral issues of such guilty love. But *The Knight of the Burning Pestle* is wholesome and charming. It stands in the shadow of Cervantes' *Don Quixote* and satirises the middle-class taste for books on knight-errantry. At the start of the play a London grocer and his wife climb on to the stage and insist that their apprentice Ralph be given a part. After some argument, Ralph is

Beaumont and Fletcher

allowed to play a Grocer Errant, carrying a shield with a Burning Pestle painted on it. He has the same sort of absurd adventures as Don Quixote himself, and his story of dream-chivalry sets off another plot—the story of the apprentice Jasper who strives for the hand of his master's daughter Luce. The most delightful episodes of the play, however, are the comments made by the London grocer and his wife, who represent—in language, taste, and morality—the growing middle-class of the age—the middle-class which, a century later, is to begin its dictation of literary standards.

Other Elizabethan comedies

Associated with this play is *The Shoemaker's Holiday* by Thomas Dekker (1570?–1632), another comedy about London and the middle-class. The hero is Simon Eyre, 'the mad shoemaker', who fears no man, is loud-mouthed but lovable and eventually becomes Lord Mayor of London. He strides through the play with his catchphrases—'Avaunt, avoid, Mephistophilus!' (to his wife) and 'Prince am I none yet am I princely born'—calling for his apprentices' breakfasts, giving his men beer, the model employer, the individualist, the middle-class English eccentric. Dekker, best known for his poem 'Golden slumbers kiss your eyes', was a typical poor journalist of the age, the author of many pamphlets, the collaborator in many plays, and of his dramatic works perhaps only *The Shoemaker's Holiday*, *The Honest Whore*, and *Old Fortunatus* are now remembered. *The Shoemaker's Holiday* is typical of his good humour, his liveliness, and his sympathy with the lower orders of society.

Of other comedies one can only mention names—*The Roaring Girl*, *A Chaste Maid in Cheapside*, *A Trick to Catch the Old One*, *The Spanish Gipsy*, and others by Thomas Middleton (1570–1627), mostly in collaboration with other authors; *Eastward Ho!* by George Chapman (1559?–1634?), Ben Jonson and John Marston (1575?–1634)—the play which gave offence to James I by its satirical references to the Scots and led to imprisonment for all three authors; *The Fair Maid of the West* (an admirable picture of the bustling life of Elizabethan Bristol) by Thomas Heywood (died 1650); not to mention the other comedies of Jonson and Beaumont and Fletcher. To cover Elizabethan comedy adequately would require a whole shelf of volumes.

Webster

The greatest tragic dramatist after Shakespeare was undoubtedly John Webster (1580?–1638). He collaborated in comedies with Dekker and others, but his two great tragedies, *The White Devil* and *The Duchess of Malfi*, seem to be entirely his own work. It is hard to convey the greatness of these without much quotation. Webster, like Jonson and Shakespeare, has a strong verbal gift; he is a remarkable poet able to convey a situation or a state of mind in the fewest possible words. But he approaches Shakespeare in his ability to create character, and the tortured, haunted creatures of his two tragedies, once known, can never leave the memory. *The White Devil* concerns the Duke of Brachiano (*sic*) and his illicit love for

Vittoria Corombona, wife of Camillo. Vittoria's brother Flamineo arranges for Camillo to be killed, and for the Duke's seduction of Vittoria. Flamineo also kills his virtuous brother Marcello after a violent quarrel. For his part, the Duke kills his wife Isabella. Revenge inevitably follows—the Duke poisoned by Isabella's brother, Vittoria and Flamineo murdered. This plot sounds unpromising—sheer blood and thunder, like an early Senecan play—but Webster's psychology and language raise it to the level of high seriousness. Flamineo is truly evil—not a painted devil but a real one—and his final lines bring a shudder:

> My life was a black charnel. I have caught
> An everlasting cold; I have lost my voice
> Most irrecoverably. Farewell, glorious villains . . .

Webster's lyrical gift is best heard in the funeral-song of Marcello, intoned by his distracted mother:

> Call for the robin-redbreast and the wren,
> Since o'er shady groves they hover,
> And with leaves and flowers do cover
> The friendless bodies of unburied men.
> Call unto his funeral dole
> The ant, the field-mouse, and the mole
> To rear him hillocks that shall keep him warm,
> And (when gay tombs are robb'd) sustain no harm;
> But keep the wolf far thence, that's foe to men,
> For with his nails he'll dig them up again.

The Duchess of Malfi is another tale of many murders. Its climax comes when the Duchess of the title undergoes mental torture from her brother and his hired villain and is then strangled with her two children. After that follow vengeful murders, madness, and sublime and terrible poetry. Here is the guilty Cardinal; he enters reading a book:

> I am puzzled in a question about hell:
> He says, in hell there's one material fire,
> And yet it shall not burn all men alike.
> Lay him by. How tedious is a guilty conscience!
> When I look into the fish-ponds in my garden,
> Methinks I see a thing arm'd with a rake,
> That seems to strike at me.

Nothing is more pathetic in all drama than the line of the damnable Ferdinand, the murdering brother, looking on the corpse of his sister:

> Cover her face; mine eyes dazzle: she died young.

Bear-baiting was a popular pastime in Elizabethan England.

Webster, despite his small output, is very great. Both his tragedies are visions of hell displaying a verbal power and an imagination that Shakespeare only could touch. And not even Shakespeare could see evil with the terrible clarity of vision that is Webster's peculiar gift.

John Ford (1586–1639?) has something of the same sharpness of vision and the same sort of taste for horrors. His tragedy *'Tis Pity She's a Whore* deals—like Beaumont and Fletcher's *A King and No King*—with incest. But while Beaumont and Fletcher seem not to have the courage of their convictions, having it revealed towards the end of the play that the brother and sister in love with each other are not really brother and sister, Ford faces all the moral implications of genuine incestuous passion and produces a most moving play. Here is Giovanni, the brother, speaking to his sister:

Ford

> Kiss me. If ever aftertimes should hear
> Of our fast-knit affections, though perhaps
> The laws of conscience and of civil use
> May justly blame us, yet when they but know
> Our loves, that love will wipe away that rigour,
> Which would in other incests be abhorr'd.
> Give me your hand: how sweetly life doth run
> In these well-coloured veins! how constantly
> These palms do promise health! but I could chide
> With Nature for this cunning flattery—
> Kiss me again—forgive me.

A few lines later he stabs her: it is the only way out of the monstrous situation they find themselves in, to kill her and then himself to die.

Another dramatist who 'supped full with horrors' was Cyril Tourneur (1575?–1626), whose two important plays are *The Revenger's Tragedy* and *The Atheist's Tragedy*. In these, especially the first, there is evidence of a strong taste for the perverse and the unnecessarily horrible in the audiences of the post-Shakespearian theatre: Tourneur is evidently trying to feed a public appetite almost as cruel as that of the Romans under Nero. (One should not forget, incidentally, that this liking for blood and pleasure in cruelty was always there in the Elizabethan age, an age of bear-baiting, public beheadings, burnings, and hangings, traitors' heads stuck high on the City gates.) Tourneur's hero Vindice has his revenge on the Duke, who poisoned Vindice's betrothed for refusing to yield her honour to him, and this revenge is a terrible one. The Duke, by a trick, is made to kiss the poisoned skull of Vindice's late mistress, and, while his lips are burning away and he is screaming for help, Vindice stamps on him. The agony is prolonged, and the Duke's line 'Is there a hell besides this, villains?' elicits not a little sympathy from us. There are more horrors and deaths to come—fewer, it is true, than in

Tourneur

Titus Andronicus, but the shudder comes not from the events themselves so much as from the spirit, the attitude, and the language. It is the sophistication of these late tragedies that makes them so frightening. The early revenge plays are so crudely written that they are as little terrifying as puppet-shows; writers like Tourneur and Webster can give us a whole inferno in a single line, and the vision of evil they conjure up in their skilful verse is almost too terrible to look at.

Thomas
Middleton

And so to Thomas Middleton, whose tragedy *The Changeling* is his greatest play. This is about Beatrice-Joanna, ordered to marry de Piracquo by her father, but really in love with Alsemero. In order to avoid this hateful marriage she employs De Flores—a man whom she hates but who she knows is passionately in love with her—to murder de Piracquo. She enters this scheme light-heartedly, and, when De Flores has performed the act of murder, offers him money: to her it is just another transaction, like buying jewels or horses. But De Flores wants no money, no goods, he wants *her*. Beatrice-Joanna is shocked, her virtue outraged:

> Why, 'tis impossible thou canst be so wicked,
> Or shelter such a cunning cruelty,
> To make his death the murderer of my honour!
> Thy language is so bold and vicious,
> I cannot see which way I can forgive it
> With any modesty.

Yet, as the play progresses, she learns that she is tied to De Flores; the complicity in the murder has made them one soul, as well as one flesh. At the end, she has changed from an innocent but irresponsible woman to a creature with a moral sense learned from her own crime. She had the crime committed to gain Alsemero, but it is not he she gains, it is the man she loathed, the man about whom she finally says:

> Beneath the stars, upon yon meteor
> Ever hung my fate, 'mongst things corruptible.

While De Flores cries:

> I loved this woman in spite of her heart;
> Her love I earned out of Piracquo's murder . . .
> Yes, and her honour's prize
> Was my reward; I thank life for nothing
> But that pleasure; it was so sweet to me,
> That I have drunk up all, left none behind
> For any man to pledge me.

This is a great play.

Thomas
Heywood

To Thomas Heywood we owe the remarkable *A Woman Killed with Kindness*, the story (unlike the others so far mentioned, set in England) of an unfaithful wife whose husband, discovering the infidelity, does not seek revenge in the normal passionate way of husbands, but indeed kills her with kindness. He sends her to live in a comfortable country house, but she is not allowed to see either her husband or her children again. And so she dies, slowly, having ample solitude and leisure to feel remorse and grow fatally ill of it. At the end her husband comes to her death-bed and forgives her. It is a touching play, full of fine lines, and one of the few Elizabethan tragedies to have a setting in contemporary England instead of an unreal timeless Italy.

Finally, of the tragic dramatists, we must mention briefly George Chapman and his two plays about Bussy D'Ambois. Chapman is known best as the translator of Homer, as the poet who spoke out 'loud and bold' and made young John Keats feel like 'some watcher of the skies when a new planet swims into his ken'. He came late to the writing of plays, collaborating, as we have seen, with other dramatists in various comic productions, but *Bussy D'Ambois* and *The Revenge of Bussy D'Ambois* are his own work. The hero of both plays is a fiery gallant, quarrelsome, and amorous, whom not even death can put down, for, murdered at the end of the first play, he appears as a ghost in the second, urging his brother to encompass his revenge on various members of the French court. The plays have a tremendous sweep and power, and again a great gift of language is in evidence. Bussy's huge ranting speeches, recalling Tamburlaine but possessing a greater maturity of phrasing and rhythm, were unfairly described by Dryden as 'dwarfish thought, dressed up in gigantic words, repetition in abundance, looseness of expression and gross hyperboles'. Even such a condemnation as that indicates to us that there is at least nothing tame about Chapman!

George Chapman

We have been using the term Elizabethan Drama for many pages now, perhaps giving an impression that all these plays—and the many others unmentioned—were written and performed in the reign of Queen Elizabeth I. This, of course, is not so; the great age of drama lasted also throughout the reign of James I and only began to peter out in Charles I's time, as the Civil War approached. The theatres were closed by the Puritans in 1642 (we shall hear more about the Puritans in a later chapter) and this date has sometimes been taken as marking the end of a great period of art—a period which, it has been alleged, might have lasted much longer if the Puritans had not performed this puritanical act. But the fact is that the fire of the great drama burned so intensely that it could not last very long, and long before the closure of the theatres it was already losing inspiration, taste, and skill. The last important name is that of Philip Massinger (1584–1639). (Other names—such as that of James Shirley (1596–1666)—we shall have to ignore: the scope of our brief history cannot take them in.)

Philip Massinger

Massinger is almost an exact contemporary of John Ford. Ford's work, however, seems to belong to the true Elizabethan 'blood-and-thunder' tradition: it always sounds and reads as if it were much earlier than Massinger. Massinger's work could not well have been produced at an earlier period. Ford shows the imprint of Shakespeare's influence, while Massinger's is a development of Ben Jonson's example. Massinger is Ben Jonson without blood, without fireworks. His finest play is a comedy, *A New Way to Pay Old Debts*, which, despite its skill in construction and language, is to Ben Jonson as black-and-white is to technicolor. The chief character is the monstrously mean, power-and-gold-loving, cruel, atheistical Sir Giles Overreach (the last great character of Elizabethan drama), who despises the whole world, gets pleasure from the tears of women and children, and only wants his daughter to marry a lord so that he can be in a position to insult the aristocracy more effectively. His speeches are powerful, but we have none of the magnificence of Ben Jonson, in whom the light of his master Marlowe still burns. With Massinger poetry begins to disappear from the stage: a dimension has been removed from the drama, and soon we shall need the beginnings of a new dramatic tradition, able to approach life in a new 'non-Elizabethan' way. We shall need new influences, even a new kind of stage. So the Puritans, who had warred against the theatres for so long, who had been ridiculed by the playwrights but had the last laugh, were, in shutting the theatres, not stopping a wild party at its height. They were merely closing the stable-door after the horse had left.

11. *Tudor Poetry and Prose*

The Great Glory of the Tudor period—or, to be more accurate, the age of the last Tudor and the first Stuarts—is the Drama. For that reason we have spent quite a long time considering it. But the other forms of literature were flourishing as well, and our task now is to survey briefly what happened in the fields of poetry and prose during the time of the great dramatists.

Let us imagine that Shakespeare himself, in 1616, is sitting quietly in his parlour in Stratford, drinking a little ale and looking back, not at his own achievements or those of his fellow-dramatists but at the books— books for reading, not acting—which created most of a stir in his lifetime or in his father's lifetime.

In the field of prose, translation seems to come first. A prose literature can only grow by taking nourishment, and this nourishment can only be obtained from foreign sources. Thus translations from the Greek, Latin, French, and Italian make up much of the first Tudor prose, and, of course, pre-eminent among all Tudor translations is one from the Hebrew as well as the Greek—the English Bible. The influence of those versions of the Bible made before 1611 is quite evident in Shakespeare's plays—he must have read Tyndale or Coverdale, or heard them read in church—though perhaps Shakespeare is the least 'religious' of English writers: Christianity in its formal sense rarely appears in his plays, though he is much concerned with moral problems, and some of his speeches—like Portia's great one in *The Merchant of Venice*—are almost Christian sermons.

Translation

Contemporary with the great Tyndale was Sir Thomas More (1480– 1535), one of the precursors of the Renaissance, the New Learning—a man of bold imagination and vision. He can be mentioned in connection with Shakespeare, for it seems that a play on his life—of which fragments have recently come to light—was probably written by Shakespeare. More's most imaginative work was written in Latin—*Utopia*, which is Greek for 'nowhere', a book which depicts an imaginary island where

Sir Thomas More

everything is nearly perfect. We still use the word Utopia to describe the paradise that every politician promises, the ideal world which men can build on reason, charity, and proper social organisation. We have recently come to distrust the vision of a perfect state that is realisable—we have had too many disappointments in the present century—and perhaps the last of the 'Utopiographers' was H. G. Wells. But More's point is contained in his title: his perfect island does not exist and never can—it is nowhere.

Translations   Secular translations of the Elizabethan age include Sir Thomas North's version of the *Lives* of Plutarch, made in 1579, and Philemon Holland's rendering of the *Lives of the Twelve Caesars* by Suetonius, made in 1606. Shakespeare was devoted to the former, for he frequently borrowed his plots from those terse biographies of the great Greeks and Romans, and he was not averse to 'lifting' whole sentences and paragraphs from North. The famous description of Cleopatra on the Nile in *Antony and Cleopatra* is little more than a skilful versifying of North's own words. The Elizabethans were interested in biography, especially of the ancients, and to this was allied an interest in history, especially of their own country. We may note here that Sir Thomas More was a pioneer in the field of historical writing, and his *Life and Reign of Edward V* is a model of clear, objective documentation. The historian who provided Shakespeare with material for his historical plays was Raphael Holinshed (died 1580?), whose *Chronicle* he used again and again.

An important Elizabethan translation from the French was Florio's rendering of the *Essais* of Montaigne. The Essay is a prose-form that has oppressed all of us, all over the world, in classroom and examination-hall. So well-established is it, that we tend to think it has existed from the beginning of time. Actually Michel Eyquem de Montaigne (1533–92) was its inventor, and he conceived of it as a brief—or, occasionally, not so brief—loose composition in which he could informally chat of subjects that interested him. Montaigne was one of the first 'modern men', a man with no strong religious beliefs but great tolerance and kindness, a strong intellectual curiosity but an awareness of the limitations of reason and science. In essay after essay we are faced with the question '*Que sais-je?*'— 'What do I know?' Montaigne was a sceptic, coming at a time when scepticism was necessary as a foundation for modern science. It is certain that Shakespeare's Hamlet has read a good deal of Montaigne, as have the characters who argue about a perfect island in *The Tempest*. (Here we have a hint of the interest shown by intellectual Europe in More's *Utopia*.) Florio, who was the secretary of the Earl of Southampton, renders Montaigne into fluid English prose, catching the gentleness, the humour, and the charm of the great Frenchman's personality.

Bacon   The first English essayist was Sir Francis Bacon (1561–1626)—the man who, according to certain fanatics, wrote Shakespeare's plays among other things. Bacon's big Latin works lie outside our scope (he wrote in Latin because he believed that English would not last), but we may mention that in his *Novum Organum* he lays the foundations for modern scientific study. The *Essays*, however, have kept his name alive more than any of his weightier achievements. These are brief, pithy observations on a variety of subjects—death, revenge, reading, gardens, education, and so on—and we get the impression of ideas rapidly jotted down, ideas which have no place in a big philosophical work but, nevertheless, are worth recording. These essays are simple, strong, admirably clear and concise, and many statements are as memorable as lines of poetry. We can never forget these openings: 'Men fear death as children fear to go in the dark'; 'Revenge is a kind of wild justice'; 'God Almighty first planted a garden'; '"What is truth?" said jesting Pilate and would not stay for an answer' (the Bible again).

One book that Shakespeare never lived to read (although John Ford did, and was much influenced by it) was *The Anatomy of Melancholy* by Robert Burton (1577–1640). It is a great pity that the work appeared so shortly after the death of Shakespeare (only five years), for one is tantalised by the thought of what use Shakespeare would have made of it. The work is a treatise on that mental ailment which we would now call neurosis or depression, the disease that Hamlet suffers from. Every age has its pet malady (the twentieth century has had *angst*, or anxiety, just as the Middle Ages had *accidia*), and Elizabethan melancholy seems to have been characterised by inability to make up one's mind, perform necessary actions, or get any pleasure out of life. Sometimes melancholy leads to suicide (Hamlet contemplates it), but usually the melancholy man thinks too much about suicide ever to get down to committing it. *The Anatomy of Melancholy* is a huge work—over half-a-million words—and full of the most fascinating stories, incredible scraps of learning, astonishing quotations from old writers. The section on Love Melancholy is especially to be recommended. (There is a very good Everyman's Library edition in three volumes: Love Melancholy comes in the last.)

Anatomy of Melancholy

Shakespeare was probably not greatly interested in the religious controversies of the day, and it is doubtful whether he would have been impressed by the *Book of Martyrs* by John Foxe (1516–87), a lurid and bitter account of the deaths of Protestants at the hands of Catholic persecutors. This book was for a long time second only to the Bible as required English Protestant reading; it is a furious, passionate book, long-winded at times, but often moving. The really great religious book of the age is the *Laws of Ecclesiastical Polity* by Richard Hooker (1554–1600), an attempt to show how the Church of England could be so organised that the Catholic–Protestant struggle would be resolved once for all: the Church should take the middle way, absorbing from Catholicism and Protestantism the best qualities of each. Hooker's prose-style

Religious works

Religious persecution as shown in Foxe's Book of Martyrs.

Queen Elizabeth dancing at Court.

is as much a noble compromise as the Church he dreams of: mid-way between the solemn style of Latin and the homely, earthy style of spoken English.

Spoken English—that is the key to understanding the peculiar virtues of Elizabethan prose. The Elizabethans addressed themselves to the ear rather than the eye, and this explains the sensation of warmth and intimacy we get from even the most scholarly Elizabethan writing. A hundred years later, as we shall see, prose became more scientific, less concerned with making human contact through suggesting common speech, and, although literature thus gained through a greater precision, it lost through discarding homely, intimate qualities. The popular but minor prose writings of Elizabeth's day—prose for entertainment—bubble with life: we have the impression that the author is talking directly to us, words rushing out like a river, non-stop. It is the modulations of a voice that we hear, not the scratchings of a pen. These minor books seem to be written rapidly, without undue care—sheer cheap journalism churned out to pay the rent—but even the cheapest pamphlet has a vitality that we have long ceased to look for in our modern journalistic prose.

Elizabethan prose

The prose stories of the Elizabethan age are interesting. In them we see the beginnings of what, very soon, is to be our most popular literary form—the Novel. A great Spaniard died, as we know, on the same day as Shakespeare—Miguel de Cervantes, creator of *Don Quixote*. This, perhaps, is the first true novel. We expect a novel to be fairly long (think of Tolstoy, Dickens, Scott), and *Don Quixote* is so long that those of us who succeed in reading it once rarely find time to read it twice. The first English novels are more like long short stories, and the writers of long novels—people like Smollett and Fielding and Dickens—are not likely to learn much from them from the point of view of construction. But as stories they are good, and, though incident is more important than character, yet they contain a robust flavour which reminds us of *Tom Jones* and *Oliver Twist*. Certain novels of the ancient world were translated during Shakespeare's lifetime—particularly *Daphnis and Chloe* and *The Golden Ass*. Also that curious work by Petronius—the *Satyricon*—was read a good deal in the original Latin. These probably influenced men like Nashe and Deloney to create rather improper tales full of incident, crime, love, and other still popular ingredients. I heartily recommend Nashe's *The Unfortunate Traveller*—a lurid tale full of astonishing dialogue and description and the strangest adventures. Nashe had a short life (1567–1601), but it was undoubtedly crowded with 'low-life' experiences, and most of these are recounted—blown-up, it is true, exaggerated like the details of a nightmare—in this tale of a rogue in the army of Henry VIII. The horrors that drew spectators to *The Spanish Tragedy* or *Titus Andronicus*, or to the baiting by dogs of the bear Sackerson in Paris

Garden, or to public executions, find their way into the last chapters of the novel, with their gruesome descriptions of torture and death. Thomas Deloney (1543–1600) gives us a more homely story in *Jack of Newbury*, which is all about life in the weaving trade, and *The Gentle Craft* is a robust and vivid tale of shoemakers (compare it with *The Shoemaker's Holiday* by Dekker). Other novels were more aristocratic, more refined. John Lyly's *Euphues* we have already mentioned—high-flown, elaborate, wordy, learned, and just a little boring. Sir Philip Sidney (1554–86)—soldier, poet, scholar—wrote *Arcadia*, which is a long fantastic tale of aristocrats shipwrecked on an ideal island, an island full of the highest principles, the most knightly courtesy, the most beautiful ladies. It is the sort of dream which any courtier, aware of the squalor of London and the corruption of the court, might well conceive, and, once again, we are reminded of *Utopia*.

The Elizabethan age is full of odd racy brilliant books about all the subjects under the sun—recipes, cures for the plague, the London underworld, how to cheat at cards, what flowers to grow, weird adventures in strange lands, murders in Italy, accounts of the Great Frost, books of devotion and prayer with titles like 'The Most Spiritual Snuff-box to Make the Most Devout Souls Sneeze'. The astonishing thing about so many of them is their vitality: there is so little of the slack, sickly prose that we find in popular magazines today. Elizabethan prose was healthy, and even the near-illiterate seemed able to write it well.

Spenser

What poets did Shakespeare prize above all others? First, undoubtedly, Edmund Spenser (1552–99). Spenser is the first writer of verse to 'sum up' the aspirations and dreams of the Elizabethan age. He loves the English language—unlike such men as Bacon, who have no real confidence in it—and tries to do for it what Homer did for Greek and Virgil for Latin. He wants to write important works which shall speak of the glories of the Elizabethan age as Virgil's *Aeneid* spoke of the glories of the Rome of Augustus. Spenser's major work is *The Faerie Queene*, which, though unfinished at Spenser's death, is still a monumental poem far too long for many modern readers. It tells of the human virtues—love, faith, friendship, and so on—in the form of allegory, giving to each virtue a special knight or protector, and presenting in Gloriana (the Fairy Queen herself) the glory which comes from possession of virtue. Gloriana is also Queen Elizabeth, to whom Spenser addresses himself, and the whole poem is suffused with genuine devotion to Queen and country. Spenser is at one with both the people of England and the Court of England: he knows the traditions and superstitions of the common folk, he can use their earthy speech (he uses it consistently in *The Shepherd's Calendar*), but he is filled also with the sophistication of the aristocratic, and *The Faerie Queene* is full of noble ideals, patriotism, polite learning, and chivalry. What Spenser bequeathed to poets to come was a stanza of his own invention, called after him the Spenserian Stanza, which you will find much used in poets like Shelley, Keats, Tennyson—romantic poets who sought inspiration in the dreamy music of Spenser. The individual music of this stanza strikes up at the very beginning of *The Faerie Queene*:

> A gentle knight was pricking on the plain,
> Yclad in mighty arms and silver shield,
> Wherein old dints of deep wounds did remain,
> The cruel marks of many a bloody field;
> Yet arms till that time did he never wield:
> His angry steed did chide his foaming bit,
> As much disdaining to the curb to yield:
> Full jolly knight he seemed, and fair did sit,
> As one for knightly jousts and fierce encounters fit.

A lovely poem of Spenser's is his *Epithalamion*, or 'marriage-song', written by him for his own bride. Spenser gains his melodious effects not by compression, as Shakespeare does, using as few words as possible, but by deliberate extension, so that a Spenser poem only yields its music after many lines. Here is part of the *Epithalamion*:

> Now all is done; bring home the bride again,
> Bring home the triumph of our victory;
> Bring home with you the glory of her gain,
> With joyance bring her and with jollity.
> Never had man more joyful day than this,
> Whom heaven would heap with bliss.
> Make feast therefore now all this live-long day,
> This day for ever to me holy is;
> Pour out the wine without restraint or stay,
> Pour not by cups, but by the bellyful,
> Pour out to all that wull,
> And sprinkle all the posts and walls with wine,
> That they may sweat, and drunken be withal.
> Crown ye god Bacchus with a coronal,
> And Hymen also crown with wreaths of vine,
> And let the Graces dance unto the rest;
> For they can do it best:
> The whiles the maidens do their carol sing,
> To which the woods shall answer, and their echo ring.

It would seem that all Elizabethan poets learned a great deal from Spenser. He was in love with words, especially their melodious arrangement, and showed his brother-poets—even those who wrote for the stage—how to get the maximum musical effect from the simplest of words.

Donne

At the other end of the scale is John Donne (1573–1631). Where Spenser is gentle ('mild', Wordsworth called him), Donne is fiery; where Spenser is smooth, Donne is rough. For a long time Donne's poetry was thought nothing of, and it is only in the twentieth century that he has come into his own (though Coleridge and Charles Lamb admired him). Shakespeare himself has some of Donne's qualities—qualities of harshness, toughness, knotty involved thoughtfulness. In fact, I often think that Shakespeare is a 'synthesis' of Spenser and Donne—capable of the sweetness of the one and the sourness of the other, sometimes not only in a single play but even in a single speech.

Donne had two sides to his character. He started off as 'Jack Donne', the soldier, lover, drinker, writer of passionate amorous verses. He ended as Doctor John Donne, Dean of St. Paul's, great preacher of sermons, devoutest of men. And yet the two extremes were in him all his life. As the passionate lover he was always analytic, thoughtful, trying to dissect and explain his passion almost scientifically. As the divine, he approached God with the passion he had formerly shown to women: he addresses Christ with the fierceness of a lover. Just as his character seems made up of opposites, so does his verse. When he is deepest in love with living flesh it is then that he sees the skeleton beneath it. When his passion is most physical he expresses it most intellectually. Even when dying he cannot help comparing his body to a map over which the physicians, like cosmographers, discuss the 'North-west passage' to death. He reflects that, in all flat maps, east becomes west, and so the sinking of the sun becomes its rising; thus death is only another term for life: after death comes the resurrection. His poems show a brain that works as hard as an engine. In him, as in Shakespeare, thought goes on all the time, getting mixed up with emotion and sensation, and producing strange and wonderful results. In his work there is a kind of violence of expression that we do not find in Spenser, so that he startles us by beginning a love-poem:

For God's sake hold your tongue and let me love!

Or he will take the strangest images and produce something like this:

Go and catch a falling-star,
  Get with child a mandrake root,
Tell me where all past dreams are
  Or who cleft the devil's foot.
Teach me to hear mermaids singing
  Or to keep off envy's stinging,
    And find
      What wind
Serves to advance an honest mind.

He is impatient of convention and invents many new verse-forms of his own. In his images, the stranger the comparison the better he likes it. ('Oh, my America!' he cries to his mistress, 'my new-found land!') He is always startling, always invigorating, and always curiously modern. When we read him we do not feel that it is the work of a man long dead: with his doubts and confusions and harshness and strange ideas he seems to be a product of the Atomic Age. John Dryden, and, after Dryden, Doctor Johnson, called him a 'metaphysical poet', meaning a poet who liked ideas as much as feelings, and the name has stuck. After him came a number of poets who filled their work with strange images, some of them quite fantastic. We shall discuss these followers of Donne in another chapter.

Shakespeare, in his closing days, might reflect on the great wealth of lyrical poetry that had appeared in his lifetime, and perhaps look back with affection at two 'pioneer-poets' of the early Tudor days—Sir Thomas Wyatt (1503–42) and the Earl of Surrey (1517–47). If these poets had not lived, Shakespeare might never have written any sonnets and never written his plays in blank verse. Surrey was the first to use blank verse—ten syllables to a line, five stresses, no rhyme—as the most suitable medium for translating Virgil. You see again how important translation is in the Tudor age. Wyatt wrote the first English sonnets.

The sonnet

The sonnet had been accepted for a long time in Italy as the most suitable for a love-poem. The mediaeval poet Petrarch had used the sonnet consistently to address his beloved Laura. With Petrarch the sonnet had fourteen lines and was divided into two parts—the octave, containing eight lines; the sestet, containing six lines. The octave expressed the first half of an idea, the sestet the second half; the octave posed the question, the sestet gave the answer; the octave expressed a theme, the sestet contradicted it. With the Italians, the rhyme-scheme was strict: octave—a b b a; a b b a; sestet—c d e, c d e or c d c, d c d, or any other combination of two or three rhymes. Such a verse-form is easy to manage in Italian, because Italian has many rhyming words. If I choose the word *affetto*, other words immediately rush into my head, all perfect rhymes: *stretto, letto, petto, allegretto*, and so on. But English is much more limited, has far fewer perfect rhymes. English poets found it hard to stick to the Italian (or Petrarchan) form, and so invented rhyme-combinations of their own, the only condition being that there should be fourteen lines. Shakespeare's own sonnets are written in a comparatively simple form:

> Let me not to the marriage of true minds
> Admit impediments. Love is not love
> Which alters when it alteration finds
> Or bends with the remover to remove:

> O, no! it is an ever-fixed mark,
>> That looks on tempests and is never shaken;
> It is the star to every wandering bark
>> Whose worth's unknown, although his height be taken.
>
> Love's not Time's fool, though rosy lips and cheeks
>> Within his bending sickle's compass come;
> Love alters not with his brief hours and weeks,
>> But bears it out even to the edge of doom.
>
> If this be error, and upon me prov'd,
> I never writ, nor no man ever lov'd.

Shakespeare took the sonnet-form farther than the Italians: he used it not solely for description of the loved one, for protestations of passion, and so on, but also for the expression of ideas. His contemporaries—Sir Philip Sidney, Samuel Daniel, Spenser, and Michael Drayton (whose fine sonnet beginning 'Since there's no help, come let us kiss and part' is perhaps the greatest Elizabethan sonnet outside Shakespeare) were content to deal with love in its more conventional aspects. You can spend a useful hour or so looking through the *Oxford Book of English Verse*, in which you will find specimens from all these writers, and others.

John Donne, inevitably, used the sonnet-form not for love-poetry (despite the title of his volume of love-poems—*Songs and Sonnets*) but for passionate religious poetry. His *Holy Sonnets* are written in a combination of the Italian form and the Shakespearian. They have arresting openings —'Batter my heart, three-person'd God . . .'; 'Death, be not proud, though some have callèd thee Mighty and dreadful, for thou art not so.' In them we are a long way from the delicate amorous world of Petrarch and Laura. '. . . And Death shall be no more; Death, *thou* shalt die!'

Shakespeare might reflect that he himself had added a good deal to the poetic riches of the age. He had written, not only sonnets, but two powerful narrative poems—*Venus and Adonis* and *The Rape of Lucrece*. He had seen the flowering of songs of all kinds—England had indeed become a nest of singing birds—and he had, in his plays, contributed lovely lyrics —sad, gay, amorous, or pure nonsense. All over the land people were singing, and the words were as worth hearing as the tunes. He had seen and heard the flowering of the word in England; he had seen English rise from the position of a minor peasant dialect to that of a major literary language. And all this in a very few years.

12. The age of Milton: End of a Period

After the death of Shakespeare great changes took place in English life and thought. With the removal of the threat of Catholic Spain—one of whose missions had been to re-impose Catholicism on Protestant England—a certain division began to show itself strongly: England began to split into two warring camps. This division had, under Queen Elizabeth I, not seemed very dangerous, but under Charles I it grew and led to Civil War. Briefly speaking, we may say that the division was between the old way of life and the new. On the one hand was the conservative element of the country—those who derived their wealth from the land, from old estates, and who supported the reigning monarch and accepted the established religion of England. On the other hand were those whose livelihood came from trade, who belonged to the towns, who wanted a greater share in the government of the country, and who thought that the Reformation of religion in England had not gone far enough. In other words, the split in the country was a threefold one—economic, political, religious—but it resolved itself into a simple issue of 'party': the great political parties of England emerged out of the struggle—the Tories and the Whigs. The new men of England, the men who gained their wealth from trade, were inclined to a sort of religious belief very different from the established faith of England. They were for the most part *Puritans*: they wanted a purer kind of Christianity than the Reformation had brought to the country. They wanted a Christianity so pure that it would admit of no toleration, no joy, no colour, no charity even; an austere religion which frowned on easy pleasure and punished vice in the sternest possible way. The Protestantism of the Established Church derived a good deal from the German Luther, whose 'reforms' did not move too far away from traditional Christianity; but the Puritans followed John Calvin of Geneva, who taught that free will did not exist and that men were predestined from the beginning of time to go to either heaven or hell. This doctrine, implying that your deeds or misdeeds could make little difference to your ultimate destination, led to the con-

Civil War

Puritanism

trolling of people's morals from without rather than within—in other words, people must be *made* to be good by a sort of government of holy men. Under Calvinism there is no real division into Church and State, each with separate powers: Church and State become one, and England after the Civil War has a government 'of saints' on the Geneva pattern. One pleasure only seems open to Calvinists, and that is the making of money. Traditional Christianity condemned the lending of money on interest; Calvinism allowed it. And so we can see the bond between the new men of trade and the religion they practised, and the bond between their religion and their politics.

The reign of Charles I is a struggle for power on the part of the English Parliament, which mostly represents the new men—the 'Roundheads'—and a vain attempt on the King's part to resist this new force. War comes, and the Parliamentary side wins. These Puritans, as might be expected, were not gentle victors: they executed the King, declared a republic which soon became a dictatorship under Cromwell, and imposed on England a way of life such as it had never known before. The Old Testament became the book of the law, pleasure was regarded as sinful, moral crimes were savagely punished. It was a way of life perhaps foreign to the English character. Certainly it did not last, and 1660 saw the restoration of the monarchy and an attempt to return to the old way. But England could never be the same again, and 1660 virtually starts a new era—an era in which the old land-owning class sinks and the new middle-class rises, an era too in which the English character seems to have become subtly changed. A sense of guilt seems to permeate all pleasure, and this has continued to the present day. The English Sunday—everything closed and nowhere to go except church—was, till very recently, one of the many living monuments to Puritan rule. Another perhaps, is the Englishman's peculiar restraint—the coldness that repels so many Africans and Asians, an unwillingness to 'let oneself go'.

The literature we shall discuss briefly in this chapter, then, must be seen against this background of struggle and change. In the seventeenth century, even literature takes sides: we find Cavalier poets as well as Roundhead poets. Of the Puritans, Milton is the greatest—both in verse and prose—and he dwarfs the writers of the opposing camp so completely that we are right to call this age his age. But the seventeenth century strikes one, curiously, as a century of 'charming' rather than great work (except for the gigantic Milton), and sweetness and grace predominate surprisingly in a period of such bloody struggle. We are limited to prose and to non-dramatic poetry: the Puritans, having tried throughout Elizabeth's reign to close the playhouses permanently, had their will at last in 1642. From then on drama became an underground activity—memories of odd fragments of Elizabethan plays, performed out of sight of the Cromwellian police. True, Milton wrote a drama, but that was when Charles II was on the throne, and, anyway, Milton never intended it for performance. So for this chapter the stage is silent.

There were two main influences on the poetry of the time (I refer, of course, to poetry other than that of John Milton) and those were the influences of John Donne and Ben Jonson. They were, on the whole, good influences—Donne encouraging imagination and a certain intellectual vitality; Jonson inducing a sense of form and careful craftsmanship. Very frequently the two influences are found together in the work of one poet, as, for instance, in Andrew Marvell and Thomas Carew, and thence we get a peculiar poetic flavour only to be associated with this century, not to be found elsewhere at all.

Ben Jonson

Ben Jonson followed the ancients, as we have seen, and he took as his examples poets like Horace (who talked of the 'labour of the file', the paring and shaping and cutting and refining of a poem) and Virgil, whose average daily poetic output was one line of perfect verse. But he also took from the Roman writers their peculiar pagan spirit: 'this life is short, after death there is only a long sleep, let us be happy while we may'. This simple, most un-Puritanical philosophy is summed up in the phrase *Carpe diem*: 'pluck the day like a flower'. That is Horace's phrase; another Roman poet, Catullus, talked of death as *una nox dormienda*—one long night to be slept through—and then asked his mistress Lesbia to give him a hundred kisses, then a thousand, then another hundred. . . .

Robert Herrick

Robert Herrick (1591–1674) follows Ben Jonson closely—both in form and in pagan philosophy. He is a lover of pleasure, a singer of the beauty of women and of flowers, a praiser of wine. His poems—*Hesperides*—are full of the transience of human joy, the brevity of human life, which he compares to a flower:

> Fair daffodils, we weep to see
>   You haste away so soon;
> As yet the early-rising sun
>   Has not attain'd his noon.
>   Stay, stay
>   Until the hasting day
>   Has run
>   But to the evensong;
> And, having pray'd together, we
>   Will go with you along.

There is nothing in all poetry more exquisite than *Corinna's Going a-Maying*, where young love is invited to take pleasure in the spring—which is beautifully evoked—and is told at the end:

> Our life is short, and our days run
> As fast away as does the sun.

> And, as a vapour or a drop of rain,
> Once lost, can ne'er be found again;
> So when or you or I are made
> A fable, song, or fleeting shade,
> All love, all liking, all delight
> Lies drowned with us in endless night.
> Then, while time serves, and we are but decaying,
> Come, my Corinna, come, let's go a-Maying.

Andrew Marvell   Andrew Marvell (1621–78) has this same theme of the brevity of life in his fine poem *To His Coy Mistress*. Here we have all the elegance and delicacy of Ben Jonson, but we also hear the 'metaphysical' voice of John Donne. The subject is simple: if we had all the time in the world, dear lady, I should be quite willing to wait until you were ready to give me your love; but, unfortunately, time is short, and I suggest that we take advantage of the present and start our love affair immediately. This is presented with great wit, eloquence, and the sort of fantastic exaggeration that Donne made fashionable:

> Had we but world enough, and time,
> This coyness, Lady, were no crime,
> We would sit down, and think which way
> To walk and pass our long love's day.
> Thou by the Indian Ganges' side
> Shouldst rubies find: I by the tide
> Of Humber would complain. I would
> Love you ten years before the Flood,
> And you should, if you please, refuse
> Till the Conversion of the Jews.
> My vegetable love should grow
> Vaster than empires and more slow . . .

After a recital of the vast stretches of time Marvell would give to each of the lady's charms, we suddenly hear a new threatening note:

> But at my back I always hear
> Time's winged chariot hurrying near;
> And yonder all before us lie
> Deserts of vast eternity . . .

It is the seriousness lying beneath the wit and fancy that is so characteristic of these Metaphysical Poets. But here we hear not merely the voice of the seventeenth century but of the pagan Roman poets too: it is genuine horror at the thought of the endless night that comes after this brief sunlit span. Marvell catches it better than any other poet of the age.

Marvell, strangely enough, was a Puritan—an admirer of Cromwell, a devout reader of the Bible, a supporter of the joyless régime whose spirit is so unlike that of his verse. But human beings, and especially Englishmen, are contradictory creatures: whatever Marvell's public face was like, his private voice—as revealed in his poems—is bright, humorous, tolerant, above all civilised. He is a lover of gardens:

> What wondrous life in this I lead!
> Ripe apples drop about my head;
> The luscious clusters of the vine
> Upon my mouth do crush their wine;
> The nectarine and curious peach
> Into my hands themselves do reach;
> Stumbling on melons, as I pass,
> Ensnar'd with flow'rs, I fall on grass.

But even in a poem so sensuous, so full of the simplest of pleasures, we come up against intellectual profundity:

> Meanwhile the mind from pleasure less,
> Withdraws into its happiness;
> The mind, that ocean where each kind
> Does straight its own resemblance find;
> Yet it creates, transcending these,
> Far other worlds, and other seas;
> Annihilating all that's made
> To a green thought in a green shade.

There is always an element of surprise. In the fine Ode (written in the metre of Horace) which praises Cromwell so extravagantly we find a noble reference to the martyred Charles I:

> He nothing common did or mean
> Upon that memorable scene,
> But with his keener eye
> The axe's edge did try.

In fact, Marvell, with his many facets—wit, seriousness, intellectuality, sensuousness, force, and compassion—is, next to Milton, the most important poet of the period. And, Milton not excepted, he is certainly the most attractive.

Other C17 poets

The other secular poetry of the age is best read in anthologies. We have courtly poets like Thomas Carew (1598?–1639), the precursor of the Cavalier poets—Suckling (1609–42), Lovelace (1618–58), John Cleveland (1613–58) and others. Carew is the first to acknowledge, in a long *Elegy*, his debt to Donne, but generally it is the tone of Ben Jonson that we chiefly catch:

> Ask me no more where Jove bestows,
> When June is past, the fading rose;
> For in your beauty's orient deep
> These flowers, as in their causes, sleep. . . .
>
> Ask me no more whither doth haste
> The nightingale when May is past;
> For in your sweet dividing throat
> She winters and keeps warm her note . . .

Lovelace   Woman is the main subject of these poets—woman unkind, woman kind, woman despised, woman always seen through a witty film of exaggeration, suggesting that the poet is not really sincere. But sincerity rings through the poems of Richard Lovelace, a symbol of the Cavalier gallantry of the age, a man who lost all for the Royalist cause, twice imprisoned, finally ruined. Going to the wars, he says to his mistress:

> Tell me not, Sweet, I am unkind,
>   That from the nunnery
> Of thy chaste breast and quiet mind
>   To war and arms I fly.
>
> True, a new mistress now I chase,
>   The first foe in the field;
> And with a stronger faith embrace
>   A sword, a horse, a shield.
>
> Yet this inconstancy is such
>   As thou too shalt adore;
> I could not love thee, Dear, so much,
>   Loved I not Honour more.

And all the world still remembers his brave words from prison:

> Stone walls do not a prison make,
>   Nor iron bars a cage;
> Minds innocent and quiet take
>   That for an hermitage;
> If I have freedom in my love
>   And in my soul am free,
> Angels alone, that soar above
>   Enjoy such liberty.

Religious verse   The age produced interesting religious verse, verse much indebted to Donne but showing also Jonson's concern with sound craftsmanship. All the Christian sects were evincing a fervour and passion which found expression in many literary forms—sermons and homilies as well as poems. Catholicism was a fighting force on the Continent, trying to win

back souls from Protestantism; Puritanism was white-hot in its zeal; the
Anglican Church, attacked by both sides, was producing militant
preachers and writers. Of the Anglican poets, George Herbert (1593–   *George Herbert*
1633) was the greatest. He is ingenious and skilful, capable of wit and
also passion and even drama. His poem *The Collar* catches some of the
tones of the Elizabethan dramatists in its irregular rhymed verse. This
presents the poet himself striving to leave his faith as too great a burden,
seeking the world and all its pleasures as giving more tangible good.
But at the end comes the voice of his true nature and a fine dramatic
surprise:

> Away! take heed;
> I will abroad.
> Call in thy death's-head there, tie up thy fears;
> He that forbears
> To suit and serve his need
> Deserves his load.
> But as I rav'd and grew more fierce and wild
> At every word,
> Methought I heard one calling, 'Child';
> And I replied, 'My Lord.'

Poetry in which the poet seems to be recounting direct experience of the
supernatural is often called 'mystical', 'mysticism' being the term used
for the belief that certain minds can establish immediate contact with
God. All religions have their mystics and their mystical poetry. In
Christian mystical poetry the divine being is presented not as a mere
abstraction, a mere piece of religious doctrine, but as a real and living
person. The relationship between the poet and the vision of God is
almost that of bride and bridegroom, and the language is often the language of human love (as in some of Donne's *Holy Sonnets*). Herbert's
mysticism is gentle and homely: Christ appears as the mildest of lovers:

> Love bade me welcome; yet my soul drew back,
> Guilty of dust and sin.
> But quick-eyed Love, observing me grow slack
> From my first entrance in,
> Drew nearer to me, sweetly questioning
> If I lack'd anything.
>
> 'A guest,' I answered, 'worthy to be here:'
> Love said, 'You shall be he.'
> 'I, the unkind, ungrateful? Ah, my dear,
> I cannot look on Thee.'
> Love took my hand, and smiling did reply,
> 'Who made the eyes but I?'

> 'Truth, Lord; but I have marr'd them: let my shame
>   Go where it doth deserve.'
> 'And know you not,' says Love, 'Who bore the blame?'
>   'My dear, then I will serve.'
> 'You must sit down,' says Love, 'and taste my meat.'
>   So I did sit and eat.

Vaughan   Of other Anglican poets, Henry Vaughan (1622–95) comes next to Herbert, not because of great power of language or thought of feeling, but because he is curiously memorable:

> My soul, there is a country
>   Far beyond the stars,
> Where stands a wingèd sentry
>   All skilful in the wars . . .

Or his lines on the dead:

> They are all gone into the world of light!
>   And I alone sit lingering here;
> Their very memory is fair and bright,
>   And my sad thoughts doth clear.

The Puritan faith found its greatest voice in Milton, but it is interesting to note that John Donne's influence found its way over the Atlantic, to appear in the verse of at least one of the Puritan Pilgrim Fathers, Edward Taylor:

> Who laced and filleted the earth so fine
> With rivers like green ribbons smaragdine?
> Who made the seas its selvedge, and its locks
> Like a quilt ball within a silver box?
> Who spread its canopy? Or curtains spun?
> Who in this bowling-alley bowled the sun?[1]

Crashaw   Of Catholic poets we shall mention only Richard Crashaw (1612–49). He started off as an Anglican and an admirer of Herbert's poetry, but later he became a Catholic and worked in Rome. There he came under the influence of Italian and Spanish mystical poets, some of whose exotic richness he brings into his verse. Crashaw is, in many ways, one of the most un-English of English poets, and his richness and extravagance are too much for some tastes. But the skill of his work cannot be denied, even when his metaphysical fancies appal the reader. Here we see the metaphysical mind at its most grotesque (the poet is writing on Mary

---

[1] Quoted in Marcus Cunliffe, *The Literature of the United States.*

Magdalen and her perpetual tears of repentance):

> 'Twas his well-pointed dart
> That digged these wells, and dressed this wine;
> And taught the wounded heart
> The way into these weeping eyn.
>> Vain loves avaunt! Bold hands forbear!
>> The lamb hath dipped his white foot here.
>
> And now where'er he strays,
> Among the Galilean mountains,
> Or more unwelcome ways,
> He's followed by two faithful fountains;
>> Two walking baths; two weeping motions;
>> Portable and compendious oceans.

These last images (remember that he is describing Mary Magdalen's eyes) suggest that kind of architecture and sculpture sometimes called *baroque*—the raw material twisted, as it were, into shapes for which it was not really intended—stone suggesting flowing draperies, a poetic metaphor taken much too far. The baroque is really a kind of elaboration approaching—and sometimes reaching—the absurd.

But Crashaw is capable of dignified simplicity, as his lines on the Nativity show:

> Welcome, all wonders in one sight!
>> Eternity shut in a span.
> Summer in winter. Day in night.
>> Heaven in earth, and God in man.
> Great little one! Whose all-embracing birth
> Lifts earth to heaven, stoops heaven to earth.

The prose writings of the age show, to some extent, the same preoccupations as the poetry. Sir Thomas Browne (1605–82), the Norwich physician, had the same fantastic humour as the Metaphysical poets and that interest in religion which, with the Puritans, was to be almost exclusive of all other literary topics. Browne's most interesting work is the *Religio Medici* ('The Religion of a Doctor'), which is somewhat ornate and rambling, closer to poetry than to prose in its rhythms and images, but nevertheless reveals a complex and curious mind, a mind in many ways ahead of its time. Browne confesses that he is 'naturally inclined to that which misguided zeal terms superstition'; in other words he has a religious temperament that, despite his Anglicanism, is capable of embracing any belief so long as it requires more faith than reason. He seems to enjoy the practice of faith, seems to ask religion to produce more and more mysteries so that his faith may be tested to the uttermost, saying with the Church father Tertullian: 'I believe because it is impossible.'

Browne

There is something of the mystic about Browne, which comes out in such works as *The Garden of Cyrus*, where he finds a holy and inexplicable mystery about the number five, which he tries to establish as a kind of pattern—a *quincunx*—in everything in the universe. We soon cease to attend to his meaning and become quite content to listen to his sleepy rich music—'. . . But the quincunx of heaven [the constellation known as the Hyades] runs low, and 'tis time to close the five ports of know-ledge. . . . To keep our eyes open longer were but to act our Antipodes. The huntsmen are up in America, and they are already past their first sleep in Persia. . . .'

Other religious writers

Other writers—writers with an exclusively religious content—are Jeremy Taylor (1613–67) and Thomas Traherne (1634?–1704) (whose works were only published fifty years ago)—Traherne the mystic with his vision of Heaven ('orient and immortal wheat stretched from everlasting to everlasting') and Taylor the writer of excellently clear and very modern prose, a man with a profound knowledge of the human heart, and one of the most forceful and yet homely expositors of the Anglican faith that English literature possesses. To the Anglican prose-writers George Herbert also belongs, on the strength of his *The Country Parson*, which gives a charming picture of the life of a typical Anglican clergyman of the time (a picture which, to some extent, still applies in our own age).

Translation of prose

The most important work of translation was done by Sir Thomas Urquhart (1611–60), an English version of *Gargantua and Pantagruel* by François Rabelais (1490?–1553). Rabelais is a great figure in French literature—one of the fathers of the Renaissance, one of the greatest humorists of all time. True, his humour is a little too strong for some stomachs—'Rabelaisian' always implies a kind of joke that cannot be told to ladies—but there is such a strong wind of vitality and love of living blowing through his book, that one cannot really be offended by even his most disgusting jests. The work is a loosely knit novel about the adventures of the two giants who give their names to the title, and it contains also Rabelais' philosophy of life—'Do as you please'—and his symbol of life—the Holy Bottle. The vigour of Urquhart's translation (which really captures the Rabelaisian spirit) can be seen from the following:

(The cake-bakers of Lerné are having a quarrel with the cake-bakers of Gargantua's country.)

. . . The bunsellers or cakemakers . . . did injure them most outrageously, calling them brattling gabblers, licorous gluttons, freckled bittors, mangy rascals, drunken roysters, sly knaves, drowsy loiterers, slapsauce fellows, slabberdegullion druggels, lubbardly louts, cozening foxes, ruffian rogues, paultry customers, sycophant-varlets, drawlatch hoydens, flouting milksops, jeering companions, staring clowns, forlorn snakes, ninny lobcocks, scurvy sneaksbies, fondling fops, base loons, saucy coxcombs, idle lusks, scoffing braggards, noddy meacocks, blockish grutnols, doddipol joltheads, jobbernol goosecaps, foolish loggerheads, flutch calf-lollies, grouthead gnat-snappers, lob-dotterels, gaping changelings, codshead loobies, woodcock slangams, ninnie-hammer fly-catchers, noddie-peak simpletons, and other suchlike defamatory epithets.

There, I think, you have enough material to season any quarrel.

Two other names in the field of seventeenth-century prose are Izaak Walton (1593–1683) and Thomas Fuller (1608–61). Walton is best-known for his charming treatise on fishing—*The Compleat Angler*—which breathes the fragrance of the English countryside, is full of good advice and splendid fish-recipes, and is interlaced with old songs. He is also responsible for a series of biographies—the Lives of Donne, George Herbert, Richard Hooker, and Sir Henry Wotton—which give us intimate pictures of the two poets, the divine, and the ambassador. Thomas Fuller is also a biographer, but his *Worthies of England* inclines to gossip about great men—anecdotes rather than carefully documented life-stories. But we all love gossip, and this gossip is fascinating.

And so we come to John Milton (1608–74), who has been towering over us like a mountain while we explored the houses of the village which lie in its shadow. Supreme in verse, as well as in prose, he is also perhaps the first great literary personality of England—it is Milton himself who shines through all his writings, it is Milton who is the hero of his epic-poem and his tragedy, it is Milton who seems bigger than the Puritanism he expounds in his prose-works. He is too big for us to treat adequately here: all we can do is to say what he wrote, and discuss briefly his philosophy and his general significance.

Milton

Milton came of a London family with a certain amount of money, and Milton never had to earn his own living. He had leisure that Shakespeare never had, and was able, by hard study, to equip himself with more learning than any previous great poet. His father was a composer of music (his works are sometimes played today) and Milton himself was blessed with a musical ear. In fact, he was destined by physical endowment and eventual physical loss to be a poet of the ear rather than the eye. After a lifetime of overworking already weak sight, he went blind, and his greatest work was written after this calamity struck him. But even in his early works it is the music of the language that strikes us first—a music like nothing ever heard before, suggesting the deep and grave tones of the instrument which Milton himself played—the organ. Milton's exquisite ear and command over the sheer sound of language is manifested not only in his English poems, but in those he wrote in Latin and Italian as well: Italian scholars were astonished at his skill in weaving melodies in their own language; his Latin poems might have been written by a Roman.

Musicality

In Milton's earliest poems we meet the distinctive Miltonic person-ality—pure, austere, not to be seduced by either wine or women, in complete control of his learning and his poetic medium. At twenty he wrote the Ode '*On the Morning of Christ's Nativity*', in which he is not content, like Crashaw, merely to praise the new-born heavenly child, but must describe Christ's victory—while yet in his cradle—over the false gods:

> Peor, and Baalim,
> Forsake their Temples dim,
>   With that twice-batter'd god of Palestine,
> And mooned Ashtaroth,
> Heav'ns Queen and Mother both,
>   Now sits not girt with Tapers holy shine,
> The Lybic Hammon shrinks his horn,
> In vain the Tyrian maids their wounded Thammuz mourn.

Fully to understand all these references would require a page of notes: Milton's learning is much in evidence. But there is also something that Milton is to exploit throughout his poetic career—the sheer magic of the sound of a catalogue of strange names. And he also knows how to exploit the rhythm of the difficult stanza-form he has chosen:

> The old Dragon under ground
> In straiter limits bound,
>   Not half so far casts his usurpèd sway,
> And wrath to see his Kingdom fail,
> Swinges the scaly horror of his folded tail.

In the last line, image and rhythm are made one: we *see* the scaly horror, hear it and almost feel it.

This poem was written while Milton was still at Cambridge University (where his physical beauty and flowing hair earned him the name 'the lady of Christ's'—Christ's being his college). Between 1632 and 1638 Milton lived in retirement in the country, reading and writing, pro-ducing works like *L'Allegro* and *Il Penseroso* ('The Cheerful Man' and 'The Melancholy Man'), which show his descriptive gifts and, again, his

Milton's highly individual music. Also we learn much of Milton's temperament.
temperament He pictures himself seeking joy in country life, watching the harvesters at work, drinking ale and listening to old stories, going to the theatre—but it is a joy essentially solitary: it is a lonely man looking in at life from the outside. *Il Penseroso*, with its celebration of the pleasures of solitude and contemplation, depicts the real Milton much more adequately:

> But let my due feet never fail
> To walk the studious cloisters pale,

And love the high embowèd roof,
With antique pillars massy proof,
And storied windows richly dight,
Casting a dim religious light.
There let the pealing organ blow
To the full-voic'd choir below,
In service high, and anthems clear,
As may with sweetness, through mine ear,
Dissolve me into ecstasies,
And bring all Heav'n before mine eyes . . .

As Dr. Johnson said, there is no mirth in Milton's melancholy, but plenty of melancholy in his mirth. Milton was destined to be the man alone, sufficient unto himself, finding no pleasure in the gay world about him.

Belonging to this period of country retreat are the masque *Comus* and the elegy *Lycidas*. *Comus* was written to celebrate the appointment (in 1634) of the Earl of Bridgewater as Lord President of Wales—a sort of morality play for amateur performance, presenting the usual morality theme of virtue triumphing over vice. The simple story owes something to Peele's *Old Wives' Tale*, telling as it does of a virtuous lady imprisoned by an enchanter, the search of her two brothers, the intervention of a good spirit to aid them, the final defeat of the magician Comus. The masque is completely undramatic—there is too much talking and arguing, too little action, but the verse is superbly contrived, there are some lovely songs, and again we see a good deal of the man Milton. Comus tells his fair prisoner of the pleasures of the senses, and the lady herself counters with praise of austere virtue: the lady is Milton in disguise; the temptations of Comus are the temptations that he, as a born artist, must have often felt; the victory is the victory of Milton's own solitary and pure temperament. There is a coldness in this masque, despite all its beauties, the coldness of a temperament born to be aloof from the delights of the world. *Lycidas*—one of the most astonishing literary performances the world has ever seen—is a poem on the death of Edward King, a fellow-undergraduate whom, it seems, Milton did not know very well but whose untimely loss he was asked, along with other poets, to mourn. Here, in the midst of the lamentations, comes a warning of the political and religious strife to come. St. Peter is made to appear to add his voice to the mythological mourning, and he is made to compare the promising pure young Lycidas with the grasping shepherds of a corrupted English Church:

What recks it them? What need they? They are sped:
And when they list, their lean and flashy songs
Grate on their scrannel pipes of wretched straw.

Englands Miraculous Preſervation Emblematically Deſcribed, Erected
for a perpetuall *MONVMENT* to Poſterity.

A satirical example of Puritan propaganda.

> The hungry sheep look up and are not fed,
> But swoln with wind, and the rank mist they draw,
> Rot inwardly, and foul contagion spread:
> Besides what the grim Wolf with privy paw
> Daily devours apace, and nothing said;
> But that two-handed engine at the door
> Stands ready to smite once, and smite no more.

It is a prophecy and a warning: the Church is corrupt, the Wolf of
Catholicism is abroad, the double engine—political and religious—of
the new men is ready to strike: war is coming.

At the end of his period of country quiet, Milton began to feel that he
was destined for some great work; he knew that he had in him the
qualities of a great epic poet, and he contemplated various themes for a

work which should compare with Homer's *Iliad* or Virgil's *Aeneid*—
among them that myth which will never cease to fascinate English
writers, the myth of King Arthur. But Milton was not yet ready to start
so tremendous an undertaking. He had to study more, see the world,
and so he went to spend sixteen months in Italy. But, while he was
away, the great struggle began at home, and Milton returned to give his
genius not to poetry but to the Puritan cause. For twenty years Milton
produced only sonnets and political and religious books; the epic had to
wait. But the sonnets, though a minor achievement only, showed what
could be done with a medium that had traditionally been fit only for
conventional love-sentiments. Milton, as Wordsworth said, turned the
sonnet into a trumpet. Never had poetry known such eloquent indignation as that which Milton turned on the slaughterers of the
Waldensians in Piedmont:

> Avenge, O Lord, thy slaughtered saints, whose bones
>   Lie scattered on the Alpine mountains cold,
>   Ev'n them who kept thy truth so pure of old,
> When all our fathers worshipped stocks and stones;
> Forget not: in thy book record their groans
>   Who were thy sheep, and in their ancient fold
>   Slain by the bloody Piedmontese that rolled
> Mother with infant down the rocks. Their moans
> The vales redoubled to the hills, and they
>   To heav'n. Their martyred blood and ashes sow
> O'er all the Italian fields, where still doth sway
>   The triple Tyrant; that from these may grow
> An hundredfold, who, having learnt thy way,
>   Early may fly the Babylonian woe.

(Milton, it may be noted, uses the Italian or Petrarchan form of the
sonnet. The repetition of rhymes in 'o' gives this poem the dirge-like
quality of a tolling bell.)

But during the period of the Civil War and the Commonwealth—   *Propaganda*
when the new state of England was exciting adverse criticism on the
Continent—Milton gave himself almost wholly to prose propaganda. He
defended the Commonwealth in his Latin works—*Defence of the British
People* and the *Second Defence*; he wrote a reply to *Eikon Basilike* ('The
Kingly Image'), the book which was trying to elevate Charles I into a
martyr, and called it *Eikonoklastes* ('The Image-Breaker'). He was ready
to attack his own government where he thought it was limiting freedom
of thought, and his *Areopagitica* is an eloquent defence of a free press, a
stormy onslaught on censorship. But theological matters also concerned
him, and his unfortunate first marriage led to his works on Divorce, in
which he cites the Bible as the authority for abolishing the existing

marriage-laws. Here we see Milton the egocentric, the proud self-centred man around whom the universe revolves. What Milton wants, God also must want; if Milton's marriage is a failure, the marriage-laws must be altered; if Milton despises woman, woman must be inherently despicable. Milton is never wrong, according to Milton.

Paradise Lost

Milton was able to return to the full-time composition of poetry only in 1660, when the monarchy was restored, and, with the death of the Commonwealth, his public tasks were over. In 1652 he had lost his sight —a fact which he records stoically in his most famous sonnet—and from now on his world became a dim world of remembered images, of sounds not colour, a highly personal self-centred world, the world of *Paradise Lost*. This great epic records the greatest event known to the Hebraico-Christian peoples: the Fall of Satan and the consequent Fall of Man. Milton's sightless world enables him to paint the dim vastness of Hell much more tellingly than the clear-visioned Italian poet Dante, but it makes the real world—as represented in the Garden of Eden—seem unreal and artificial, the trees and flowers and beasts seen through the medium of books and memory, not actually, as with the living eye of Shakespeare. Milton is the hero of the poem, consciously in the flowing-haired Adam, to whom woman, the lesser creature, looks up submissively; unconsciously in the magnificent Satan, the fearless rebel thrown out of the well-ordered sunlit heaven which is really the new England of Charles II. Satan does emerge as the real hero of *Paradise Lost*: as Blake shrewdly said, 'Milton was of the devil's party without knowing it.' For this poem Milton created a new kind of English and a new kind of blank verse: both highly artificial, both a world away from the English of everyday speech. This, of course, was necessary for his subject, which was far above the everyday world of human passions and actions, but it served to slow the development of English poetry as a *natural* medium of expression; it encouraged a mode of utterance in which rhythms and constructions and even vocabulary veered to Latin rather than Anglo-Saxon English. Milton's sentences are long, like Latin sentences; he inverts the order of words, like a Latin author; he has to talk about 'elephants endorsed with towers' instead of 'elephants with towers on their backs'; these same elephants must 'wreathe their lithe probosces', not their trunks. But there is no denying the magnificence that glows in this highly individual and artificial style:

> Now came still Evening on, and Twilight gray
> Had in her sober Livery all things clad;
> Silence accompanied, for Beast and Bird,
> They to their grassy Couch, these to their Nests
> Were slunk, all but the wakeful Nightingale;
> She all night long her amorous descant sung;

Silence was pleas'd: now glow'd the Firmament
With living Saphirs: Hesperus, that led
The starry Host, rode brightest, till the Moon
Rising in clouded Majesty, at length
Apparent Queen unveil'd her peerless light,
And o'er the dark her Silver Mantle threw.

Paradise Lost is a religious epic, and its subject matter makes it the common theological property of Jews and Muslims, as well as Christians. *Paradise Regained*, a shorter poem, deals with Christ's temptation in the desert, his resistance to Satan's temptation balancing Eve's yielding to that same temptation in *Paradise Lost*, and its appeal is essentially Christian. It is a smaller poem in technique and vision as well as length. Milton's final great achievement is his tragedy *Samson Agonistes*, which again has Milton himself as its hero. The play follows classical Greek procedure, with its choruses, its messenger, its reports preferred to direct action, and its long monologues. Here we see the blinded Samson–Milton, betrayed by Dalila (Milton's first wife, who came from the Philistine or Royalist camp) 'at the mill with slaves', a ruined giant made a show for a Philistine holiday. He laments his fall and his blindness ('O dark dark dark amid the blaze of noon'); in speech after speech his greatness is recalled; his humiliation is lamented or gloated over; but at the end he is triumphant. He pulls down the temple of the Philistines on the heads of his enemies, himself dies in the ruins, and the chorus is left to make a tranquil conclusion (there is nothing to mourn; Samson has behaved like Samson).

Samson Agonistes

It is a fitting epiloque to the career of a great poet. Even in his last days Milton is still experimenting with verse and language, producing new tones and rhythms. And, in the new cynical, bright but corrupt England of Charles II, *Samson Agonistes* stands as a monument to an age whose literary glories, moral aspirations, genuinely heroic spirit can never be even remotely approached in the centuries to come. Milton is the last man of the old; now we must take a deep breath and dive into the new.

13. The Age of Dryden

Restoration
From the political point of view, 1660 does not really start a new era. Charles II came to the throne from exile; James II, his brother, went from the throne to exile—the years from 1660 to 1688 show us a cynical Stuart and a fanatical Stuart playing out the end of the Stuart dynasty. The 'Glorious Revolution' of 1688 drove away a king who was trying, too late for English history, to play the all-powerful monarch; after that date a compromise begins. It is a compromise between the fanatical republicanism of the Puritans and the fanatical absolutism of the two ill-fated Stuarts; it brings about a limited monarchy (a royal ruler with comparatively little power) and a parliamentary system which works slowly towards true democracy. It means also the gradual rise of the middle-class, who are soon to dictate religious forms, moral standards, and artistic taste. But, in the Restoration period, this is yet to come. 1660 brings in an unheroic, cynical age, distrustful of deep convictions, whether in life or in literature.

The main characteristic of the new literature may be summed up in the phrase 'From the head, not the heart.' The literature of the past had been passionate, concerned with the relationship between God and man, man and woman, man and man as seen from the viewpoint of feeling and imagination. But in the Restoration period, feeling and imagination were mistrusted: feeling implied strong convictions, and strong convictions had produced a Civil War and the harsh rule of the Commonwealth; imagination suggested the mad, the wild, the uncouth, the fanatical. It was best to live a calm civilised life governed by reason. Such a life is best lived in the town, and the town is the true centre of culture; the country estates are impoverished, and little of interest is going on there; the country itself is barbaric. And so the themes of the new literature are town themes—politics, the doings of polite society, the intellectual topics of men who talk in clubs and coffee-houses. We may expect no more Shakespearian nature-pieces, no poems smelling of flowers or telling of shepherds and milkmaids. The human brain has taken over and is in complete control: good manners replace passion, wit replaces eloquence; the heart is not worn on the sleeve nor, seemingly, anywhere else. The literature of the Restoration is neither moved nor moving.

John Dryden is the first great name of the new, as John Milton was the last great name of the old. But the way had been paved for Dryden by a number of writers who linked the two ages. Abraham Cowley (1618–67) started off as a follower of John Donne and ended up as a poet of cool reason, very much the intellectual who thought the brain, not the heart, had all the answers. Edward Waller (1608–87) was another poet who, so Dryden believed, showed the Restoration poets how to use rhyme, especially in the *heroic couplet*, and set a standard of grace and refinement. John Denham (1615–69) was extravagantly admired and imitated, and in many ways his *Cooper's Hill*—in language and metre—anticipated the style of Dryden and, later, Pope. Nobody cares to read these poets nowadays: one finds it hard to understand the high praises of men like Dryden and Dr. Johnson. But they did their work: they ushered in John Dryden. Dryden (1631–1700) is the one writer of the age who, brilliant in all forms, encloses and sums up its qualities.

Milton was, in his poetry at least, aloof from his age, immersed in myth and religion. Dryden was just the opposite: he identifies himself with official opinion and, in some ways, regards himself as the chronicler of the age. Thus, before the Restoration, he wrote an elegy on Cromwell; when Charles II came back from exile, he celebrated the event in *Astraea Redux*; when 1666 brought plague, fire, and victory over the Dutch fleet, he wrote *Annus Mirabilis* ('The Wonderful Year'). Dryden's conversion to Catholicism coincides with James II's attempt to make England once more a Catholic country (although, to his credit, it must be said that Dryden did not turn away from his faith in 1688, when a Protestant king came over from Holland: he suffered somewhat for this). There are few poems by Dryden which are not inspired by current happenings or controversies: the measure of his greatness is that the poems still interest us long after the events are forgotten. *Absalom and Achitophel*, for instance, deals with the Monmouth rebellion. Charles II had no legitimate children, and the Whig party was frightened of the prospect of his Catholic brother's succeeding him. This inspired the Earl of Shaftesbury to encourage the Duke of Monmouth—an illegitimate son of the King—to seize power. The attempt was a failure. Dryden recorded the whole history in *Absalom and Achitophel*, presenting it in Biblical terms: Absalom was Monmouth; King David was King Charles, 'the curst Achitophel' was Shaftesbury, the Jews were the English, Jerusalem was London, and so on. It is a brilliant satire, full of memorable lines, bristling with wit:

> In pious times, ere priestcraft did begin,
> Before polygamy was made a sin;

> When man on many multiplied his kind,
> Ere one to one was cursedly confined;
> When nature prompted, and no law denied
> Promiscuous use of concubine and bride;
> Then Israel's monarch, after heav'n's own heart,
> His vigorous warmth did variously impart
> On wives and slaves, and, wide as his command,
> Scattered his maker's image through the land.

And the character of Zimri—even though we may forget that Zimri was Buckingham—shows Dryden's ability to hit off an eternal type:

> Stiff in opinions, always in the wrong,
> Was everything by starts, and nothing long;
> But, in the course of one revolving moon,
> Was chymist, fiddler, statesman and buffoon.

And here is Achitophel himself:

> For close designs and crooked counsels fit,
> Sagacious, bold and turbulent of wit,
> Restless, unfixed in principles and place,
> In power unpleased, impatient of disgrace;
> A fiery soul which, working out its way,
> Fretted the pigmy body to decay
> And o'er-informed the tenement of clay.
> A daring pilot in extremity,
> Pleased with the danger, when the waves went high,
> He sought the storms; but, for a calm unfit,
> Would steer too nigh the sands to boast his wit.
> Great wits are sure to madness near allied,
> And thin partitions do their bounds divide . . .

Here we see the perfection of the heroic couplet in its first stage (Pope is to make something slightly different out of it). It is a limited form, tending to statements which are complete in two rhymed lines, a world away from the long blank-verse paragraphs of John Milton. It is ideal for
Satire   satire, however, and one of the small glories of the Restoration period and the century that followed is the perfection of this medium as an instrument for argument, philosophical exposition and (often cruel) wit.

Satire was one of the most typical products of the Restoration period. The function of the satire is supposed to be the ridicule of human manners as a corrective to them, but it was almost always used in this age as a scourge to one's enemies—personal or political. Dryden is not above attacking his poetical rival, Shadwell, in *MacFlecknoe*:

> The midwife placed her hand on his thick skull,
> With this prophetic blessing: *Be thou dull.*

And Samuel Butler, in his *Hudibras*, slams away, hard and long, at the Puritans. Butler (1612–80) looks back, in the form he uses, to the *Satires* of John Donne, in respect of deliberate roughness if not of metre. Here he describes his Presbyterian hero:

> He knew the seat of Paradise,
> Could tell in what degree it lies:
> And, as he was disposed, could prove it,
> Below the moon, or else above it:
> What Adam dreamt of when his bride
> Came from her closet in his side:
> Whether the Devil tempted her
> By a High Dutch interpreter:
> If either of them had a navel;
> Who first made music malleable:
> Whether the Serpent at the fall
> Had cloven feet, or none at all,
> All this without a gloss or comment,
> He would unriddle in a moment
> In proper terms, such as men smatter
> When they throw out and miss the matter.

This tale of Sir Hudibras, the fat and quarrelsome knight, and his squire Ralph, out in search of adventure, reminds us of Cervantes, but also of Rabelais in its occasional coarseness. It is uneven, somewhat formless, but very vigorous, and it has given the term Hudibrastic—applied to any rough satire—to the language.

Andrew Marvell turned to satire in his later days, attacking the private life of the court, public scandals, and the foreign policy of Charles II. Indeed, there was plenty to attack, but a certain warmth appears in Marvell, a moral warmth, and good satire is essentially cold: it is the head calmly criticising, the heart deliberately subdued. Once the satirist becomes angry or indignant, he loses control: good satire is always in full control of the situation. John Wilmot, Earl of Rochester (1647–80) had the makings of an important satirist. His *Satire Against Mankind*, as the title implies, has a far wider scope than the purely political satire of the day. Most of his writing shows that the heart has been excluded from the body's commonwealth: we see the workings of a brilliant brain, we are aware of a strong sensuality, and there is no 'buffer' between them. Many of Rochester's poems are scurrilous, but his wit is great and his facility in verse remarkable.

Lyrical verse

Of the purely lyrical verse of the time, Dryden's contribution stands supreme. The *Song for Saint Cecilia's Day* and *Alexander's Feast* both celebrate the power of music in lines which ask for musical setting (and indeed the former was set excellently by Henry Purcell in the seventeenth

century, and both by Handel in the eighteenth). The catalogue of musical
instruments in the *Song* contains lines like the following:

> The trumpet's loud clangour
> Excites us to arms,
> With shrill notes of anger,
> And mortal alarms.
> The double double double beat
> Of the thundering drum
> Cries Hark! the foes come;
> Charge, charge, 'tis too late to retreat!

I particularly like the sly ironical touch of the last line: an heroic age
would never have dared to sing about retreating, but Dryden is realistic,
not heroic. The final lines of the *Song* have great strength:

> So when the last and dreadful hour
> This crumbling pageant shall devour,
> The trumpet shall be heard on high,
> The dead shall live, the living die,
> And Music shall untune the sky!

Dryden's *Ode* to the memory of Anne Killigrew is also remarkable. It has
a passion unusual for the age, a genuine sincerity, and yet is capable of
the intellectual, even the witty, concept:

> O wretched we! why were we hurried down
>   This lubric and adulterate age
> (Nay, added fat pollutions of our own),
>   To increase the streaming ordures of the stage?

(There the Dryden of the satires is speaking.)

> When rattling bones together fly
> From the four corners of the sky;
> When sinews o'er the skeletons are spread,
> Those cloth'd with flesh, and life inspires the dead;
> The sacred poets first shall hear the sound,
>   And foremost from the tomb shall bound,
> For they are cover'd with the lightest ground.

It would take too long to enumerate all the other lyrical poets of the
age. Of most of them we can say that we admire form and grace and correctness, but we detect insincerity. We are beginning to get certain stock
expressions—'every killing dart from thee'; 'languish in resistless fires';
'bleeding hearts'; 'O turn away those cruel eyes', and so on. Love poetry
is becoming—what it had been before in the Middle Ages—something
of a game which any aristocratic gentleman (or lady) can play. The great

curse of the eighteenth century is, as we shall see, 'poetic diction', and authors like Etherege, Sedley, Aphra Behn, Otway, the Duke of Buckingham, and Oldham are the founders of it.

Being an intellectual age, the Restoration period was most interested in theory—especially in literary theory. Dryden again comes first. He gives us, in essays, prefaces, dramatic prologues, and epilogues, his considered opinions on the literary art, and can be regarded as the first of the English literary critics. Criticism forms an important part of a nation's literary heritage. We revere Coleridge's criticism as much as his poetry, and the same may be said of T. S. Eliot in our own day. The great critic has a philosophy of literature: he is clear in his own mind as to the function of literature, and he knows the conditions under which this function can best be fulfilled. He praises and condemns not as most of us do, saying 'I don't like this, but I like that'; he has clear reasons for finding an author important or unimportant, and these reasons are related to his philosophy. He finds connections between authors who, at first sight, seem to have little to do with each other, and out of these connections he is able to build up the image of a 'tradition'. Dryden's philosophy is clearly stated, particularly in the *Essay on Satire* and the *Essay of Dramatic Poesy*. He proclaims himself a 'classicist'. The purpose of literature is to give a picture of truth, to imitate nature in the manner of the ancient Greeks and Romans. The ancients are the best models, and it is safe for the beginner to imitate them. Literature must primarily satisfy the reason. Literature must obey rules, and the rules that Dryden lays down for dramatic composition go back to Ben Jonson in their insistence on the unities. Blank verse suggests disorder, so Dryden insists on rhyme, even in drama (though, in his last plays, he went back to blank verse). Dryden's theory of literature is a 'civilised' one; it has no room for eccentricity or too much individuality, it wants conformity to the standards of the age. Shakespeare's plays do not fit well into the classical pattern—too wild, lawless, individual—and it is not surprising that Shakespeare is either revised by Restoration writers, 'tidied-up', so to speak, or not performed at all.

Dryden's skill at exposition of ideas is shown both in prose and verse. His essays on his own religious beliefs—*Religio Laici* and *The Hind and the Panther*—show the way to Pope's philosophical poem, the *Essay on Man*: the heroic couplet is admirable for the orderly, epigrammatic unfolding of a philosophy. But Dryden's prose-style not merely fits into his own period: it looks forward to the modern age.

The Elizabethans wrote entertaining and vigorous prose, but it was not really suitable for scientific or philosophical argument. (That is one of the reasons for Bacon's writing his scientific works in Latin, which is at least clear and logical.) Elizabethan prose is too close to the heart and the senses: the words bubble out in slang and metaphor and ornament, and any argument is quickly lost in a forest of bright colours. With the emphasis on the head rather than the heart in Dryden's time, it became at last possible to produce a 'cold' kind of prose suitable for the development of a scientific argument. Dryden's prose is logical; he is never carried away by the sound of words or the lure of a metaphor or simile, but is able to cling to the thread of his discourse.

The Restoration period marks the beginning of the scientific age. This *Science* age had already been prepared by Bacon and others, who insisted on rational argument and observation of nature as a prelude to the production of theories. Some scientific experimentation had been going on between his day and the Restoration, but not always with official approval (secret experiments suggested magic; chemistry smacked of alchemy). But with the return of Charles II from France in 1660, science became fashionable: Charles had become interested in anatomy on the Continent, members of his court developed similar interests, and it seemed quite natural for a charter to be given to a Royal Society for the advancement of scientific knowledge in 1662. This Royal Society was a meeting-ground for scientists of all kinds, but also laymen with an amateur interest in science were not debarred from membership: Dryden himself, as well as Abraham Cowley, was interested, and one can see fruitful potentialities in the contact between literary men and scientists—certainly the development of 'rational' prose is partly a consequence of this spreading of scientific interest.

An interest in science usually goes with an interest in philosophy (in- *Philosophy* deed, it was perhaps impossible for a mind of this period to separate the two). By philosophy we mean an inquiry into the nature of reality, an attempt to answer such questions as 'What do we mean when we say that a thing *exists*?' or 'What definite *certainty* can we find behind a universe of such diversity and change?' Philosophers, like scientists, want to build up a system; but their system attempts to go much farther than that of science. The scientist makes a limited enquiry in terms of his own subject: the chemist is only concerned with the constitution of matter, the psychologist with the nature of mind; but the philosopher desires a system which can take in the *whole* of experience. Descartes, in France, had started off the big seventeenth-century enquiries. He had begun by doubting—systematically and deliberately—the existence of everything. But then to doubt, there must be a doubter, and Descartes had concluded that he himself, the doubter, must exist: *Cogito ergo sum*—'I think, therefore I am'. On that basis he built up his system. Such enquiries required courage: they meant accepting no assumptions, not even the assumption that God exists. Such courage, and such ability to throw off long-accepted assumptions were difficult even for a great scientist like Sir Isaac Newton (1642–1727), who was prepared to base one of his scientific works on the assumption that the earth had been created in 4004 B.C.

Newton did not really have the philosophical mind: he was brilliant in his own field, and his discoveries were remarkable, but he points the big difference between science and philosophy—science consists of particular observations and particular conclusions (such as the law of gravity); philosophy is speculation of the most general kind, the big enquiry which comes after the small scientific conclusions.

Hobbes

Thomas Hobbes (1588–1678) is the greatest of the Restoration speculators. The work for which he is best known, *Leviathan*, was published in 1651, but his general spirit belongs to the later age. He is a materialist, believing that sensations, and hence ideas, which are derived from sensations, are the result of matter in motion. Motion is the big unifying force, the cause of all existence, and man reacts to external motions with motions of his own—appetites, which are directed towards self-preservation. Man is fundamentally a selfish animal, and out of his selfishness come 'contention, enmity and war'. The life of man is 'solitary, poor, nasty, brutish and short', unless he is willing to adopt 'articles of peace'. These articles involve the setting up of a 'commonwealth', and the granting of absolute power to a ruler or body of rulers. This rule is unified, and cannot be divided between, for instance, a king and a parliament; the rule is absolute, but the subject can refuse to obey if the ruler does not perform the task for which he was appointed—namely, to keep order and thus preserve the life of the individual. The impact of Hobbes's philosophy on his own time can well be imagined: it was thought that it inspired Cromwell to consider becoming king, and, later, provided a justification for James II's desire for absolute rule. It is interesting to

Locke

compare Hobbes with John Locke (1632–1704), whose views on Government were quite opposed to those of *Leviathan*: he published his two *Treatises of Government* in 1690, two years after James II had been deposed, and stressed the importance of the *contract* in government: supreme power rests in the people, not the monarch, and the people can 'remove or alter the legislative when they find the legislative act contrary to the trust reposed in them'. Hobbes believed that the ruler of a state was not responsible to the people, but only to God (to keep order does not necessarily mean to govern the people as they want to be governed); Locke points to the modern democratic way which the Revolution of 1688 presaged—the contract between governed and governor, and the right of the governed to take action when the governor breaks faith.

To read either of these two philosophers is to become aware of the huge changes of thought that had taken place between the death of Shakespeare and the deposition of James II. We seem to be reading somebody who very nearly belongs to our age; to turn back to the prose-writings of Elizabethan thinkers is genuinely like plunging back to an alien period whose thought-processes are quite different from our own.

History

Discussing philosophy we are only on the verge of literature. As we remember, a writer whose main concern is to impart information is not producing literature, and hence he should lie outside our scope. The philosophers are influential, however—they are part of the background of literature. As for the historians, they are still part of literature itself: history has not yet become a science, and writers of history are almost fulfilling the function of the novelist—bringing an age to life, delineating character, for they regard history not as a matter of 'movements' and 'trends' but as a pattern of events produced by human personalities. The Earl of Clarendon stands out with his *History of the Rebellion and Civil Wars in England*, as does Gilbert Burnet with *The History of My Own Times*. Clarendon (1608–74) gives us admirable portraits of seventeenth-century personalities—both Royalist and Roundhead—and his study of Cromwell, for instance, strives hard to be impartial:

> ... In a word, as he had all the wickedness against which damnation is denounced and for which Hell fire is prepared, so he had some virtues, which have caused the memory of some men in all ages to be celebrated, and he will be looked upon by posterity as a brave, bad man.

It is interesting to compare the portrait of the Duke of Buckingham given by Burnet (1643–1715) with Dryden's in *Absalom and Achitophel*:

> ... He had no principles of religion, virtue, or friendship. Pleasure, frolic, or extravagant diversion was all that he laid to heart. He was true to nothing, for he was not true to himself. He had no steadiness nor conduct: he could keep no secret, nor execute any design without spoiling it.

As can be seen, this was an age interested in the dissection of character. To it belong not only the histories but also a great number of brief biographies, such as the *Short Lives* of John Aubrey (1626–97), in which, for example, we learn that John Milton

> ... had a very good memory; but I believe that his excellent method of thinking and disposing did much help his memory.
>
> Of a very cheerful humour.
>
> He was very healthy, and free from all diseases, seldom took any physic ... and only towards his later end he was visited with the gout—spring and fall; he would be cheerful even in his gout-fits: and sing.

The Renaissance—the awakening of interest in Man—manifested itself in the Elizabethan age in terms not of distinct human personalities but of huge mythical types—Tamburlaine, Hamlet. The later seventeenth century is interested in the minutest details of historical personalities, and, by a natural transition, writers become interested in themselves. So with Abraham Cowley we get the beginnings of the highly personal essay which is to come to full flower in Lamb and Hazlitt and E. V. Lucas. Cowley writes on himself:

It is a hard and nice subject for a man to write of himself, it grates his own heart to say any thing of disparagement, and the reader's ears to hear any thing of praise from him. There is no danger from me of offending him in this kind; neither my mind, nor my body, nor my fortune, allows me any materials for that vanity.

Diarists

But those fascinating writers on themselves, the diarists of the Restoration period, did not need to worry about grating anyone's ears. John Evelyn (1620–1706) and Samuel Pepys (1632–1704) wrote for themselves alone, keeping minute accounts of their daily transactions, recording history in terms of its immediate impact on their own personalities. Pepys, in particular, is fascinating. He kept his diary in code which was not deciphered till 1825; in that year, a historical personage who had appeared previously only as a grave civil servant and President of the Royal Society, suddenly sprang into life as a human being: every intimate detail of his life was revealed, and the events of the years 1660–69 shown fresh and living as never before. Pepys provides us with a door leading straight into the Restoration—all its personalities emerge, its political problems, its customs, its very smell. Pepys' Diary is not literature, but it makes the same sort of impact as literature—revelation of a personality, of the thought-processes and tastes of an age, all with an astonishing sharpness.

Religious writers

Our final concern is with those writers who do not properly belong to the new currents of thoughts and style. Puritanism, of course, had not completely died in this new cynical age—Milton was its greatest voice, as we have seen—and that new religious sect known as the Quakers preserved its strength, despite derision and even persecution. Fox is the great personality of the Quakers, and his Journal, published in 1649, is an important religious, if not literary, monument. But religious fervour found, after Milton, its finest artistic expression in the writings of a man with little education but a strong literary gift—John Bunyan (1628–88). Bunyan knew only one book really well—the Bible, and his style is based on it, as well as his imagery. His *Pilgrim's Progress* is still read widely, and is known to people who have never even heard of Dryden. It is a simple enough story, very traditional in its use of allegory and personification, suggesting plays like *Everyman* in its delineation of life as a journey beset

Bunyan

with pitfalls, an arduous pilgrimage to the next world. It is the story of Christian travelling to the Eternal City, having been warned that the town in which he and his family live—the City of Destruction—is to be destroyed by fire. His family will not go with him, so he goes alone. He travels through the Slough of Despond, the Valley of Humiliation, the Valley of the Shadow of Death, and so on. He sees his companion, Faithful, put to death in Vanity Fair. He meets characters with names like Mr. Worldly Wiseman, Giant Despair, the fiend Apollyon, and others, and, after many adventures, reaches his goal. His story takes up the first part of the book; the second part tells of the journey of Christiana—his wife—and their children to the same celestial destination. Despite the purely Christian—and Puritan—nature of the allegory, *Pilgrim's Progress* can be, and is, read for the sake of its narrative skill, its humour, its intensity of observation and description; and its religious moral can pass over the reader's head. Its popularity as a pure fairy-story is shown by the fact that it has been translated into over a hundred languages. Bunyan had a natural story-telling gift, and the story of his own conversion from sinfulness to godliness—*Grace Abounding*—is one of the most interesting autobiographies of all time.

So much for the verse and prose of 'Good King Charles's Golden Days' (the title, incidentally, of a play by Bernard Shaw which will give you a painless history lesson on the Restoration) and the less golden days of his brother. It is now our task to see what was happening in the theatre.

14. The New Drama

The plays of the Restoration period and, for that matter, the whole of the eighteenth century, cannot be compared for importance and interest with the drama of the Elizabethan and Jacobean ages. For that reason I shall attempt to put the new drama in its place, and devote one chapter only to the dramatic writing of nearly a hundred and fifty years. This is not unfair. Every age seems to choose one literary form to specialise in: with the Elizabethans it was obviously the drama; with the twentieth century it is the novel; in the 'age of reason' we are now concerned with, genius mainly chose the moral or satirical essay—in prose or verse. The attitude of the age towards the drama was—although this was not realised fully—fundamentally frivolous: it was able to produce a handful of comedies that still please, but it failed almost completely in tragedy. Its plays seem to specialise in the knowing laugh, the heroic posture that does not convince, or the sentimental tear. Serious analysis of human motive and conduct was reserved to other literary forms.

The re-birth The Puritans closed the theatres in 1642, and thus destroyed a tradition of play-making and play-acting which could never be recovered. When the King—three months after his return from exile—granted patents to Thomas Killigrew (1612–83) and Sir William Davenant (1606–68) to start dramatic companies, English drama had to begin all over again, inventing new techniques, appealing to a new kind of taste. The dates of the two founders of the Restoration theatre show that they had a link with the last drama of the great age, and indeed Davenant claimed to be the illegitimate son of Shakespeare. But the needs of the Restoration audiences were different from those of the earlier period, and the actual physical circumstances of the drama had changed. London had only two dramatic companies now, and only two theatres—one for the King's

The theatres Players, one for the Duke's Players. They were indoor theatres (picking up the fashion that was already growing in the later days of Shakespeare) and they tended to be bigger, less intimate than the old Globe and Fortune. Davenant had had some experience of producing masques in Charles I's reign, and his taste lay in the direction of elaborate staging, the use of many 'machines'—effects tending to the spectacular more than the intimate. Inigo Jones, the architect, had shown what wonderful things could be done on the stage in the masques of Ben Jonson—how lighting and swift changes of scene could strike wonder more than the subtler effects of poetry. Davenant himself had been granted permission in 1656 to put on *The Siege of Rhodes* at Rutland House, and this play had relied more on song and spectacle than on poetry and plot. Indeed, it has been called the first English opera, and the 'operatic' is one of the qualities we see, certainly, in the new tragedies, many of whose conventions suggest music rather than speech. In the new theatres, the Elizabethan platform-stage—the stage that jutted right into the audience—was incorporated, but it gradually grew shallower and shallower, and the action was thrust back, away from the audience behind the picture-frame which we call the proscenium-arch. The modern stage began in this period, and any school-stage will show us what we lost: instead of the old big platform in front of the proscenium, we have a tiny 'apron' on which acting is practically impossible; everything takes place behind the proscenium, and there is no personal contact between actors and audience. We have lost the old intimacy of the Elizabethan theatre.

Another Restoration innovation was the introduction of women players—such as Mrs. Nell Gwynn, Mrs. Bracegirdle, and Mrs. Barry (*Mrs.* did not then necessarily mean a married woman). At last a more realistic sexual atmosphere was possible on the stage. Elizabethan audiences knew that Shakespeare's Cleopatra, for instance, was really a boy-actor dressed as a woman, and this gave only a *poetic* amorousness to the love-scenes with Antony. But the 'realistic' thrill was provided in the Restoration period because there *really* were two sexes on the stage. We nowadays take actresses for granted; in Restoration days they were excitingly novel.

Women

The Puritans killed that theatre-going habit which had formerly been diffused among all classes of society. From 1660 on, theatre-going becomes a monopoly of now one class, now another, but never again do we find a drama which is intended to appeal to *everybody*. We shall find it hard in our own day to point to one dramatist who has in mind a mixed audience of intellectuals, lovers of low comedy, suburban housewives who 'want a good cry', people who get a thrill from divorce and adultery, and those who delight in poetry. We have no Shakespeare today partly because we do not have Shakespeare's audience: 1660 ushers in a long era (still going on) of *specialist* drama. Restoration audiences had narrow tastes: they wanted smartness, humour, sex, but little else. They certainly did not want to be moved too much or made to think. And so Shakespeare and Ben Jonson are almost completely absent from the new theatres. Here are some comments by Samuel Pepys on certain Shakespeare revivals:

1662—. . . saw *Romeo and Juliet* (Shakespeare) the first time it was ever acted, a play the worst that ever I heard in my life. *Midsummer Nights Dream* (Shakespeare), which I had never seen before, nor shall ever again, for it is the most insipid, ridiculous play that ever I saw in my life.

1663—*Twelfth Night* (Shakespeare), a silly play, and not related at all to the name or day.

Restoration comedy

Shakespeare was too rich for this new age; he had too much poetry, too much complexity. The new tradition of language was a French one (perfect correctness and perfect lucidity), just as the new manners and attitude to love were French. (We must not forget that Charles and his court had spent their exile in France, at the splendid but dissolute court of Louis XIV, the 'Sun-king'.) And so dramas by Beaumont and Fletcher held the stage, plays that required no thought and in which poetry never got in the way of immediate understanding. Also their rather cynical exploitation of amorous themes appealed to an age in which neither love nor marriage was sacred.

When the new dramatists began to appear, they specialised for the most part in comedy which mirrored the manners of the day and in which the main ingredients were lust, cuckoldry, intrigue, covered by a smart veneer of wit. The senior Restoration comedian was George Etherege (1634–91), best known for *Love in a Tub* and *She Would if She Could,* and in him the dissolute and cynical qualities have hardly yet appeared: *Love in a Tub* (which owes something to the great Frenchman Molière) is serio-comic, and a plot about love-rivalry, in heroic couplets, alternates with a prose plot which is quite farcical. *She Would if She Could* is closer to that tradition which we think of as peculiarly 'Restoration'—it is about the pleasures of London town, with its dissipations, love-affairs, intrigues. It deals with the adventures of Sir Oliver and Lady Cockwood, up from the country to have a good time in London—she to pursue men, he to get drunk—and the confusions which follow. It is in the plays of William Wycherley (1640–1716) that we get the real cynicism, the real turning upside-down of morality. *The Country Wife* is witty but coarse, relying on the theme of jealousy, and having as a main character a man called Horner who has spread the rumour that he is impotent, the better to cuckold various husbands. ('Cuckoldry' is an old theme, of course: it becomes wearisome even in Shakespeare, where husbands are always worrying about whether they have been made to 'wear the horns'.) *The Plain Dealer* (perhaps based on Molière's *Le Misanthrope*) is a fierce satire on human faith and trust, in which Manly, the sea-captain, has lost confidence in everybody except his friend and the woman he loves. But it is these very two who let him down most badly. (Shakespeare makes hatred of mankind a tragic theme in his *Timon of Athens*; it is typical of the Restoration period that it can be treated more or less lightly.)

John Vanbrugh (1664–1726)—as can be seen from his dates—was born within the Restoration period, and his plays come at the end of the century. (So many so-called Restoration dramatists belong to the reign of William and Mary or of Queen Anne.) *The Relapse* is a continuation of a play by Colley Cibber (1671–1757) called *Love's Last Shift*, but far superior in style and characterisation to Cibber's work. There are two plots, one dealing with the relapse from virtue (hence the title and sub-title—*Virtue in Danger*) of Loveless, formerly a rake but now a respectably married man, on a visit from the country to London; the other is more genuinely comic and leaves less of a nasty taste in the mouth—a complicated intrigue involving Sir Tunbelly Clumsey and Lord Foppington (a typical young man about town, or 'beau') and other late seventeenth-century types. Vanbrugh's *The Provok'd Wife* is a comedy with the expected ingredients—a cowardly drunken wife-beater called Sir John Brute, his wife—really provoked—who nearly allows herself to be made love to by Constant, the jealous Lady Fancyfull, and so on.

Apart from Dryden perhaps the most talented of the new playwrights was William Congreve (1670–1729)—and there are critics who say that not even Dryden can compare with him. His comedies deal with the world of fashion, courtship, seduction, but they are so beautifully composed, so witty, that one of them—*The Way of the World*—still holds the English stage, and the character of Millamant is one of the classic female roles. Here is a sample of Congreve's polished prose (from a speech by Mrs. Marwood):

> . . . 'Tis an unhappy circumstance of life, that love should ever die before us; and that the man so often should out-live the lover. But say what you will, 'tis better to be left, than never to have been loved. To pass our youth in dull indifference, to refuse the sweets of life because they once must leave us, is as preposterous as to wish to have been born old, because we one day must be old. For my part, my youth may wear and waste, but it shall never rust in my possession.

His other comedies are *The Double Dealer, The Old Bachelor,* and *Love for Love.* They sparkle and race along, despite the complicated plots and the crowds of characters. One would like to have seen them with the great Thomas Betterton and the charming Mrs. Bracegirdle lending their talents to their first productions. (The great acting of the present day can be recorded on film and sound-track, and handed down to the future: we can only read with envy the contemporary reports which praise the acting ability of these two, and, for that matter, Burbage before and Garrick after.)

Congreve wrote a tragedy called *The Mourning Bride*. The story would make little appeal to a modern audience, and the villainous King Manuel —who gets beheaded by mistake—and the virtuous Almeria, his daughter, are curiously unreal when compared with the tragic creations of Shakespeare. But the play contains two lines, often misquoted, which many people have attributed to Shakespeare:

> Music has charms to sooth a savage breast,

and the second line of the following couplet:

> Heaven has no rage, like love to hatred turned,
> Nor hell a fury like a woman scorned.

The new drama produced little that was important in the tragic field. Dryden himself had something of the heart of the matter in him. His *Conquest of Granada*, with its rhymed couplets and its raving and ranting, was perhaps not an outstanding production, and it perhaps deserved to be satirised in Buckingham's skit *The Rehearsal*. But the later blank-verse tragedies—*All for Love* (based on Shakespeare's *Antony and Cleopatra*) and *Don Sebastian*—are readable and actable still, despite the conventional 'love versus honour' theme and the somewhat unreal psychology. Dryden wrote comedies too (adding to 'the streaming ordures of the stage'), one of which is memorable—*Marriage à la Mode*. This has a 'quadrangular' theme—husband no longer loves wife; husband's friend does not love fiancée; husband becomes attracted to fiancée, husband's friend to wife; husband decides there must be something attractive in wife after all, if other man can woo her so ardently; husband's friend feels the same about fiancée; husband returns to wife; husband's friend marries fiancée. Neat, witty, very competent.

Of other playwrights working in the Restoration period proper, one must mention Thomas Otway (1652–85), whose *Venice Preserved* is perhaps his finest work. This is a genuine pathetic tragedy, much closer to anything of the Elizabethan age than even Dryden's *All for Love*. It has a closely-knit story based on a plot against the state of Venice and a plan to kill all the senators. The heroine, Belvidera, shows genuine passion and evokes genuine pity, and her final madness and death are managed with great dramatic skill. But the Restoration period, despite its love of heroic couplets, was not an heroic age, and tragedy of a high order did not come easily to its poets. The characteristic achievement is the witty, immoral comedy of manners, and—as we have seen—the composers of these are few. During this new age, ascendancy in the drama had passed from England to France, and the great dramatic names are Molière, for comedy, and Racine and Corneille for tragedy. The influence of these writers on English dramatists was considerable, but there was now no man like Shakespeare, who could readily be influenced by foreign authors but always produce something far greater than they. Molière's achievement alone is worth all the works of our Restoration dramatists put together.

With the turn of the century, English drama declines still further. A man called Collier attacked 'the immorality and profaneness of the English stage' in 1698, and there was a general movement to clean up comedy and to appeal to middle-class sentiments and taste. Comedy became less witty, less shocking and—inevitably—much duller. George Farquhar (1678–1707) wrote a couple of charming plays—*The Recruiting Officer* and *The Beaux' Stratagem*—but there is little sophistication and wit, little of the talent shown by Congreve. At the beginning of the eighteenth century, opera seems likely to steal much of the limelight from drama, and we have the beginning of that idolisation of foreign music which, till recently, killed musical enterprise in England. Italian opera, Italian singers, thrilled the evenings of the upper classes, and drama had to look for support to business-men and their families.

Decline of drama

Beginnings of opera

And so comes a new standard in drama, less subtle, less intellectual, less poetical than anything ever known before. George Lillo (1693–1739), in plays like *The London Merchant* and *The Gamester*, provoked sentimental tears and stood solidly for middle-class morality. Nicholas Rowe (1674–1718) wrote tragedies—*The Fair Penitent* and *Jane Shore*—which laid the pathetic stress on woman's suffering. The first of these two plays has the now proverbial 'gay Lothario', and the fair Calista, who is killed when her fiancée finds her kissing another man. (The great Garrick and Mrs. Siddons played these two leading roles.) *Jane Shore* is about the beautiful woman who fascinated King Edward IV but was accused of witchcraft by Richard III and so, disgraced and driven from high society, died in rags. The stress is on easy tears in these two plays, not on the catharsis we have noted in nobler tragedies.

Both Joseph Addison (1672–1719) and Dr. Samuel Johnson (1709–84) tried their hands at tragedy. Johnson's *Irene* was a resounding failure, put on the stage by Johnson's old pupil Garrick out of kindness, but proving itself completely undramatic—long, long moral lectures instead of true dialogue. Addison's *Cato* shows French influence strongly in its lengthy speeches—almost like operatic recitative—but has a certain English robustness, shown in its choice of theme: the Roman Cato, a republican, refuses to surrender to the tyrannical Caesar, and takes his own life rather than live under a dictator.

But for the most part sentimentality holds sway—in the comedies of Richard Steele (1672–1729) for example, which are a sort of propaganda for middle-class virtue, a dramatic presentation of the kind of lesson in goodness of heart which was taught in the *Tatler* and the *Spectator*. (We shall hear more of both Steele and Addison and their journalistic work in the next chapter.) Sentimentality reaches its tearfullest and most embarrassing in the plays of Richard Cumberland (1732–1811). Drama had, in fact, become so feeble and anaemic that a blood-transfusion was urgently needed. And it was left to two Irishmen to give this transfusion.

Prisoners exercising at Newgate prison.

Oliver Goldsmith (1730–74) and Richard Brinsley Sheridan (1751–1816) revived the spirit of the Restoration comedy—witty, but purged of coarseness. There is in Goldsmith a thoroughly wholesome humour, a compassionate more than a satirical attitude to his characters, and a solid sense of the stage. In *The Good-natured Man*, young Mr. Honeywood—who stupidly gives away his money to people who pretend to be 'deserving poor' and thus cannot pay his bills—is treated with a kind of affection, and learns the error of his ways by comparatively gentle means. *She Stoops to Conquer* is based, or so it is believed, on an actual incident of Goldsmith's youth—the mistaking of a private house for an inn. This comedy of errors is delightful—comedy, song, and love-scenes and such characters as Hardcastle and Tony Lumpkin make it sparkle engagingly, and throughout one is aware of a tolerance and a humanity that the Restoration comedians hardly found possible. Sheridan's achievement, however, is greater than Goldsmith's. *The Rivals* (written when Sheridan was only twenty-two) introduces the famous Mrs. Malaprop (who mixes up her long words and makes a fool of herself) and the romantic Lydia Languish, as well as the red-hot choleric Sir Lucius O'Trigger. The plot is very skilfully managed, and the dialogue has an easy flow amazing in a playwright so inexperienced. *The School for Scandal* is, of course, one of the classics of the stage: revival after revival, both professional and amateur, show its humour and shrewdness unimpaired by time. Sir Benjamin Backbite, Lady Sneerwell, and Mrs. Candour—the scandal-mongers—are mercilessly portrayed, and the other characters have, collectively, a variety and, individually, a depth which is unmatched in any other English comedy of the century. Sheridan's third comedy, *The Critic*, is a farcical satire on the pretensions of contemporary tragedy, and it is still brilliantly funny.

Burlesque comedy was a fine corrective to the sentimental excesses of the stage. Henry Fielding (1707–54), better known as a great novelist, started his literary career as a dramatist, ending it at the age of thirty because of an unfortunate happening. He wrote a satire called *Pasquin*, following it with another called *The Historical Register for 1736*, in which he attacked Walpole, the Prime Minister, so vigorously that Walpole closed all theatres except the one at Covent Garden and the one at Drury Lane, and also brought in stage censorship. From then on Fielding abandoned the stage and took to the novel. But he had achieved one admirable burlesque—*The Life and Death of Tom Thumb the Great*—in his brief dramatic career.

Finally we must mention one of the gayest (appropriately, considering the name of its author) and most original stageworks of the age. This was *The Beggar's Opera*, by John Gay (1685–1732), an English answer to the spate of Italian opera that was beginning to flow into London. The setting is deliberately unromantic—Newgate prison—and the charac-

Goldsmith

Sheridan

ters are thoroughly low-life, including as they do Macheath the highway-man and Peachum, the receiver of stolen goods. The lyrics—set to traditional tunes—are delightful, and the success of its first production (said to have made Gay rich and Rich, the producer, gay) has been steadily repeated in our own century. A film has been made of it, and the German playwright, Berthold Brecht, brought it up to date in *The Three-penny Opera*.

So the arid stretch of eighteenth-century drama is relieved by a few cheerful oases. But the desert remains, and we must look elsewhere for the real literary riches of this Age of Reason.

15. Poetry in the Age of Reason

The eighteenth century is sometimes called England's Augustan Age. The reference is to that period of Roman history when the Emperor Augustus ruled, and when the Roman Empire enjoyed great power, prosperity, and stability. Eighteenth-century England had all these things too: trade flourished, an empire was growing, two formidable rivals—Holland and France—had been soundly trounced, there was no more trouble between King and Parliament. The middle-class was firmly established and the Whig party dominated the century, but the middle-class, through marriages into the aristocracy, was drawing in something of aristocratic culture. It was not an age of conflict, but of balance. The rule of reason seemed possible, progress was no empty myth, and with some satisfaction men looked back to that sunlit Roman age where order and taste ruled, wherein they saw clearly reflected an image of their own achievement.

In art, the spirit of the period was 'classical'. This is not an easy term to define, but its implications are clear: social conventions are more important than individual convictions, reason is more important than emotion, form is more important than content. Despite the calm surface of order that ruled the eighteenth century, the opposite of the 'classical' was slowly being prepared, to burst out at the time of the French Revolution. This opposite we call 'romantic', and we associate it with the individual rebelling against society—against accepted good taste and good manners—and with an unwillingness to accept conventional artistic forms. The Romantic is much concerned with himself, highly emotional, and generally impatient of the restrictions which a stable society demands.

One expression that, nowadays, is sometimes heard in criticism of eighteenth-century literature is 'dissociation of sensibility'. That is a hard expression, but it can be explained simply as follows: the 'healthy' human soul exhibits a perfect balance between intellect, emotion, and body. There is a time for reason, a time for deep feeling, a time for yield-

Classicism

ing to the demands of the senses; but no one faculty ever gets the better of the others for long. In Shakespeare which faculty rules? Is Shakespeare a writer from the brain, the heart, or the senses? The answer is, from all three; all three are in perfect balance, and, moreover, are capable of *fusion*, so that in a Shakespeare speech or sonnet we seem to be listening to thought and feeling and physical passion at one and the same time. In John Donne, too, we get this fusion: in a love-poem of his we find all the human faculties working hard together—his physical passion for his mistress, his affection for her, are presented in conjunction with a busily analytical brain trying to explain love and relate it to the rest of experience. Now, in the eighteenth century, reason and emotion no longer work together. Emotion is kept down, made into an inferior. Emotion sometimes resents this and then decides to break out and have a kind of drunken spree. But, having forgotten how to behave, emotion rarely makes a good job of expressing itself: unchecked by taste, it gives us works of 'sentimentality'; determined to get away from the 'town' atmosphere, it broods on the abnormal, the wild and the rugged and produces, for instance, the 'Gothic' novels; trying to express itself, it cannot find the right language and, using instead the language of reason, produces something tasteless or even absurd. So, if, in eighteenth-century literature, we are told to expect the bright coinage of reason, it is as well to remember that every coin has two sides.

Pope

The greatest poet of the period is Alexander Pope (1688–1744). In many ways he sums up the eighteenth century: son of a prosperous merchant, he lacks neither money nor leisure—the aristocratic refinement of his work has a middle-class basis. But, though the voice of the age, he is in many ways outside it. A Catholic, he could not go either to a public school or a university (Protestant England was strict about this); elegant and strong in his work, he was weak, dwarfish, and ugly in himself. If he had been a Romantic writer, he might have gone off into exile, weeping with self-pity, cursing God and society. But, being a classical poet, he accepted the world as it was, participated in the life of society, and worked off any resentment he may have felt about two accidents of birth into satire, or allowed it to melt into philosophical acceptance. Pope is essentially the singer of order in the universe ('a mighty maze, but not without a plan') and of order in society. We can expect his works, then, to be philosophical, or critical and satirical (as we have seen in the Restoration period, the man who is vitally concerned with society spends much of his time nagging at the flaws in it).

Pope began to write verse very early—

As yet a child, nor yet a fool to fame,
I lisped in numbers, for the numbers came.

His *Ode to Solitude* and his *Pastorals* belong to his early 'teens, and the *Essay on Criticism* was produced at twenty. The views he presents in this last work are the very stuff of classicism—critically, as well as formally, Pope is Dryden's heir. He preaches correctness in literary composition, the filing and polishing of phrases and lines until perfection is reached. And he makes wise—if obvious—remarks like the following:

> A little learning is a dangerous thing;
> Drink deep, or taste not, the Pierian spring.
> There shallow draughts intoxicate the brain,
> But drinking largely sobers us again.

In fact, we can look for little originality of thought in Pope. His aim is perfection in the expression of the obvious:

> True wit is nature to advantage dress'd—
> What oft was thought but ne'er so well express'd.

The *Essay on Man*, produced when Pope was fifty-one, hardly seems to show any advance on the formal virtues of the earlier essay. Pope seems early to have attained perfection in the narrow field of the heroic couplet, and Pope is indeed the only English writer of whom the word 'perfection' can be used. This shows both the limitations and the peculiar strength of the Augustan view of art: the greatest artists are rarely perfect because they are always attempting *too much*, they are trying to venture into new worlds which they cannot fully understand, they are always experimenting with new ways of using language. The Augustans wanted to be completely in control of what they already knew; experiment might mean failure, so they avoided experiment. Hence the tendency to repeat the same effects over and over again—nearly always to use the heroic couplet, to exploit the same rhythms, the same phrases, the same similies. Hence that *petrifaction* of language which we call 'eighteenth-century poetic diction', in which women are always nymphs, fishes always members of the 'finny tribe', meadows always verdant, lips always ruby, love always equipped with darts.

Essay on Man

This *Essay on Man* owes, in its content, a great deal to the philosophies of Viscount Bolingbroke (1678–1751) and the Earl of Shaftesbury (1671–1713) (the latter not to be confused with Dryden's Achitophel). Bolingbroke was a Deist, that is to say, a man who accepted the notion of God as a purely rational idea and rejected much of the miraculous, much of what appealed purely to faith, in Christianity. This Deism is, of course, typical of an age which tried to reduce everything—even religion—to reason. Shaftesbury preached rationalism and tolerance and worked out a system of morality which was founded on a conviction we should now find it hard to accept—namely, that man is fundamentally good, desires the happiness of others, and can distinguish instinctively between good and evil, the beautiful and the ugly. This idea looks forward to the Romantic era and its belief in the value of instinct, the veneration of the untaught savage (as in Rousseau) and of the child in Wordsworth (*Ode on Intimations of Immortality*). A rational age has the seeds of Romanticism in it: once reason is accepted as the prime faculty, man hardly needs external laws to tell him about right and wrong. Hence laws and religions become unnecessary, and anarchy—the essence of Romanticism—begins to appear.

Pope's *Essay on Man* must seem too simple in its fundamental premises for us to take seriously as philosophy. But as a collection of pithy couplets, summing up admirably the rational notions of the day, it is superb. Some of the lines have become proverbial:

> An honest man's the noblest work of God.

> Hope springs eternal in the human breast:
> Man never *is*, but always *to be* blest.

And, rather wistfully, we must approve the good sense of—

> Know then thyself; presume not God to scan:
> The proper study of mankind is man.

Rape of the Lock   To many lovers of Pope's work, the most delightful poem is *The Rape of the Lock*, a story of the theft of a curl from the hair of a young lady of fashion. This is told in that absurdly dignified style known as *mock-heroic*, in which the joke lies in the disparity between the trivial subject and the high-flown language. But Pope not only entertains; he has some sharp jabs at the society of his time:

> Meanwhile, declining from the noon of day,
> The sun obliquely shoots his burning ray;
> The hungry judges soon the sentence sign,
> And wretches hang that jurymen may dine;
> The merchant from the Exchange returns in peace,
> And the long labours of the toilet cease.

Pope's gift of sharp satire is at its scintillating best in the *Moral Essays*, the *Epistles and Satires* and the *Imitations of Horace*. In these latter poems the two Augustan ages meet; Pope translates Horace's satires but modernises them completely, so that ancient Rome becomes contemporary London, and the abuses of the two societies—seventeen hundred years apart—somehow become identical. But Pope shows his own weaknesses when he attempts poems of passion, such as the *Elegy to the Memory of an Un-*

fortunate Young Lady, which, though sincerely conceived, does not sound sincere:

> What beck'ning ghost, along the moonlight shade
> Invites my steps and points to yonder glade?
> 'Tis she!—but why that bleeding bosom gor'd,
> Why dimly gleams the visionary sword?
> O, ever beauteous, ever friendly! tell
> Is it, in heav'n, a crime to love too well?

Here we see the inability of the language of the brain to express feeling. It all sounds forced, artificial, a little too neat to be true. Pope is best when he refuses to feel any generous emotion, when he flashes his rapier in attacks on his enemies or his inferiors. (*The Dunciad* is a scathing onslaught on the minor poets of the day, unjust in many ways, but astonishingly vigorous.)

As a translator, Pope interpreted Homer for the Age of Reason, as Dryden before him had interpreted Virgil. Pope became wealthy as well as famous with the translation of the *Iliad* (the translation of the *Odyssey* is not all his own work). This is a remarkable performance, but we can sympathise with the critic who said that it was very pretty, but not Homer. All the Homeric heroes seem to be wearing silk stockings and periwigs; their language is too refined, and the heroic couplet does not convey the free and sometimes stormy music of the original. But every age must produce its own translators, whose appeal must not be expected to carry over into another age: nowadays we get our Homer from translations which make it seem almost like a modern novel. Pope's *Iliad* tells us little about Homer, but plenty about the Age of Reason.

The influence of Pope lies heavy on the age. For an eighteenth-century poet to take up the heroic couplet meant also taking up Pope's diction, rhythms, his epigrams, his wit. Though some poets had enough individuality to bring fresh tones and attempt fresh themes, we are always aware of the authoritative figure of Pope somewhere in the background. Oliver Goldsmith (1730–74) produced two long poems in heroic couplets —*The Traveller* and *The Deserted Village*, the second of which is perhaps the most popular of all eighteenth-century poems. There are few English people who cannot quote one or two of its lines, such as:

Pope's influence, followers and successors

> Ill fares the land, to hast'ning ills a prey,
> Where wealth accumulates, and men decay.

Or the description of the village parson:

> A man he was to all the country dear,
> And passing rich with forty pounds a year;
> Remote from towns he ran his godly race,
> Nor e'er had changed, nor wished to change his place.

Or the schoolmaster:

> In arguing, too, the parson own'd his skill,
> For e'en though vanquished, he could argue still.

Goldsmith has a gentler humour than Pope, and a quality of compassion which reveals itself in his lament over the decay of English village life. But he finds it hard to bring us that direct, immediate quality of particular observation in his country descriptions: we are still a long way from Shakespeare and Herrick on the one side, Keats and Shelley on the other:

> Along thy glades, a solitary guest,
> The hollow-sounding bittern guards its nest;
> Amidst thy desert walks the lapwing flies,
> And tires their echoes with unvaried cries.
> Sunk are thy bowers in shapeless ruin all,
> And the long grass o'ertops the mould'ring wall . . .

It is always *the* bittern, *the* lapwing, *the* bashful virgin, *the* matron, *the* swain: always a general idea, never a particular image. And again we have the artificial poetic diction in 'dear lovely bowers', 'gazing rustics', 'the glassy brooks', 'mantling bliss' (which means beer!). But Goldsmith did at least turn away from the town to the country, and in his attempt to express the romantic pleasures of rural life, as well as in his generosity of feeling, he looks forward to a later period. It is useful to associate with Goldsmith a perhaps more important poet, George Crabbe (1754–1832). Crabbe has become well-known in our day as the

Crabbe

author of the gruesome poem about the sadistic fisherman, Peter Grimes, which was turned into a successful opera by Montagu Slater and Benjamin Britten. Crabbe's *The Village* and *The Borough* showed that country life was not idyllic, not a romantic dream, and he bitterly attacked the complacency with which town-dwellers viewed the lot of humble farmers, fishermen, agricultural labourers, painting vividly the squalor and poverty of their lives. He provides an answer to Goldsmith:

> . . . Cast by Fortune on a frowning coast,
> Which neither groves nor happy valleys boast;
> Where other cares than those the muse relates,
> And other shepherds dwell with other mates;
> By such examples taught, I paint the Cot
> As truth will paint it, and as Bards will not.

Another of the followers of Pope, of the exploiters of the rhythms of the heroic couplet, is Dr. Samuel Johnson (1709–84), whose two satires, *London* and *The Vanity of Human Wishes*, modernised the Roman poet Juvenal as Pope had modernised Horace. Johnson's achievement in prose, and his bulky personality, have tended to overshadow his gifts as a poet, although T. S. Eliot attempted to show that these gifts are considerable. We hear a forceful personality in lines like these (from *London*):

> Has heaven reserv'd, in pity to the poor,
> No pathless waste, or undiscover'd shore?
> No secret island in the boundless main?
> No peaceful desert yet unclaim'd by Spain?

And:

> This mournful truth is everywhere confess'd,
> SLOW RISES WORTH, BY POVERTY DEPRESS'D!

It is the note of personal suffering that makes Johnson's early poems impressive. We do not feel that we are reading mere poetical exercises in the style of Pope, but listening to the real voice of grievance.

Of the poets who turned from the heroic couplet and sought other forms, we must mention first James Thomson (1700–48), a Scotsman who looked for fame in London. Like Crabbe after him, Thomson wrote about the country, but, unlike Crabbe, he found more inspiration in Milton's blank verse than in Pope's couplets. *The Seasons* is a minute description of the changing countryside, under snow, spring rain, or summer sunlight, but it is not quite a Romantic poem—nowhere does it approach Keats in the *Ode to Autumn* or *Fancy*. The descriptions are too general, suggesting abstract thought more than concrete observation, and some of the words used are as conventional as anything in Pope:

Thomson

> At length the finish'd garden to the view
> Its vistas opens and its alleys green.
> Snatched through the verdant maze, the hurried eye
> Distracted wanders; now the bowery walk
> Of covert close, where scarce a speck of day
> Falls on the lengthened gloom, protracted sweeps;
> Now meets the bending sky, the river now
> Dimpling along, the breezy ruffled lake,
> The forest darkening round, the glittering spire,
> The ethereal mountain, and the distant main. . . .

Thomson attempted the Spenserian stanza in *The Castle of Indolence*. The theme implies both mediaeval allegory and the more modern love of personification which begins with *The Faerie Queene*. Pilgrims are enticed by the magician Indolence into a castle full of sensual joys. Losing all initiative, and becoming diseased with self-indulgence, the inhabitants of the castle (among whom are presented, in the true eighteenth-century manner, certain real persons of the age) are thrown to rot into a dungeon. But two knights—not quite Spenserian—called Arms and Industry come along to storm the castle, capture Indolence, and free the prisoners.

Thomson manages the difficult stanza-form with skill, and is the prophet of its revival with Scott, Byron, Shelley, and Keats.

Gray

Thomas Gray (1716–71) is best known for his *Elegy in a Country Church-yard*, which uses the *heroic quatrain* of Dryden's *Annus Mirabilis*. This poem is too well known and too well loved to require description or analysis here, but we should note that Gray has the same classical concern with perfection of form as Pope. The line 'The ploughman homeward plods his weary way' is said to have caused Gray hours of trouble (this may be mere legend, but it is significant legend): how should it be written? 'The ploughman homeward . . .' 'The homeward ploughman . . .' 'Homeward the ploughman . . .' 'The weary ploughman . . .' 'Weary, the ploughman . . .' Gray did, in fact, expend great trouble on the polishing of his verse, and the *Elegy*'s easy flow is the result of hard work more than inspiration. In every stanza we meet lines that have become part of the English language, sounding almost Shakespearian in their familiarity, but Gray had nothing of the swiftness and fluency of the great Elizabethan. Every effect was worked for, and Gray deserves his success. The poem is loved perhaps chiefly because it appeals to that mood of self-pity which is always ready to rise in all of us. 'The short and simple annals of the poor' and 'Full many a flower is born to blush unseen' will bring tears to the eyes of the toughest and least poetical of men, because they feel that, given the chance, they could have risen high in the world. They have not risen high, and here is a poet to lament it and to comfort them by saying that it does not matter: 'The paths of glory lead but to the grave.' But to create a poem whose formal perfection cannot be questioned, and, at the same time, whose popular appeal can never die, is no small achievement. When General Wolfe said he would rather have written the *Elegy* than taken Quebec, he knew what he was saying: his sense of values was not at fault. A poem like the *Elegy* is a small miracle. Gray, moving towards Romanticism, attempts in other poems a greater freedom of form, and chooses themes that suggest wildness and anarchy, as for instance in the Pindaric Ode *The Bard*. The Pindaric Ode was a form which gave eighteenth-century poets the maximum of freedom, while suggesting—because Pindar was a Greek poet—the classical with its overtones of design and restraint. Yet, in practice, the Pindaric Ode was so free as to allow any rhyme-scheme, any length of line, any rhythm. Dryden had used the Pindaric form in the two odes on music; Gray was perhaps the best of his successors. But *The Bard*, because of the artificiality of its language, somehow falls flat. There is too much of 'Pale Grief, and Pleasing Pain, With Horror, Tyrant of the throbbing breast' and '. . . yon sanguine cloud . . . has quench'd the Orb of day'—poetic diction at its worst. And in the famous *Ode on a Distant Prospect of Eton College* (with its memorable conclusion about '. . . where ignorance is bliss 'Tis folly to be wise') we have ludicrous descriptions of schoolboys 'cleaving, with pliant arm, the glassy wave' and 'chasing the rolling circle's speed' and 'urging the flying ball'. Again, it is the language of abstract ideas trying to perform the tasks of descriptive language.

William Collins (1721–59) is much more of a Romantic than Gray. His *Persian Eclogues*—striving to be mysteriously oriental—are a failure, but his *Ode to Evening*, which attempts honestly to convey the impressions of certain natural scenes as observed by the poet, is very nearly a triumphant success. It is still obviously an eighteenth-century poem: Collins uses what seems to be a revolutionary stanza-form (two long lines, two short lines, no rhyme) but on closer inspection it is seen to be the form of Horace's Odes—thoroughly classical:

> If aught of oaten stop, or pastoral song,
> May hope, chaste Eve, to soothe thy modest ear,
>   Like thy own solemn springs,
>   Thy springs and dying gales. . . .

It is eighteenth-century too in its *generalising* approach to the subject: we are presented with homage to evening in general, the idea of evening, not—as it would be in Wordsworth or Keats—a particular evening, vividly realised and described. But it is Romantic, suggesting even Shelley, in such lines as:

> While sallow Autumn fills thy lap with leaves,
> Or winter, yelling through the troublous air,
>   Affrights thy shrinking train,
>   And rudely rends thy robes. . . .

The poem is essentially a musical achievement, a magical invocation. But how tame and eighteenth-century-at-its-worst is the ending:

> So long, regardful of thy quiet rule,
> Shall Fancy, Friendship, Science, rose-lipp'd Health
>   Thy gentlest influence own,
>   And hymn thy favourite name!

William Cowper (1731–1800) achieved a larger bulk of verse than either Gray or Collins, and he lived long enough to emancipate himself almost completely from the domination of the couplet and conventional poetic diction. He is a poet of Nature, and, in his long blank-verse work *The Task*, he comes fairly close to Wordsworth in his insistence that Nature is the great friend and healer, that the town—far from being an Augustan paradise—is fundamentally wicked. Cowper, however, does not make a religion out of Nature. He is deeply Christian and, with surprise, we discover in him something of the old Puritan spirit of Bunyan—

fear of damnation looms large in his life, and sometimes finds outlet in his verse. But the God of *The Task* is gentle:

> In his side he bore,
> And in his hands and feet, the cruel scars.
> With gentle force soliciting the darts,
> He drew them forth, and heal'd, and bade me live.

Cowper is capable of sentimentality. One feels, in poems like *On the Receipt of My Mother's Picture*, that the personal element is over-done: that the reader is forced to look at some purely domestic scene which is not really his business. And also in *My Mary* there are too many personal tears which should not be wept in public:

> And should my future lot be cast
> With much resemblance of the past,
> Thy worn-out heart will break at last—
> My Mary!

Burns

Meanwhile, in Scotland, a young peasant was creating a Romantic Revolution on his own. This was Robert Burns (1759–96), perhaps the first real poetic rebel of the century. He revolted, in his personal life, against the restraints of conventional morality and the repressive Presbyterian religion of Scotland: he drank too much, loved not wisely but too well, died too young. He shows himself capable of writing masterfully in two distinct styles—the polite style of England, using heroic couplets and Spenserian stanza and the idiom of Pope; the rougher and more earthy style of his own land, with a dialect that is almost unintelligible to many Englishmen, but is brisk and vigorous and—after so many years of conventional poetic diction—extremely refreshing. There is nothing hypocritical about Burns. He sings about the things he likes—including drink and women—with gusto and without shame. He has a strong sense of humour (seen at its best in *Tam O'Shanter*), and a sympathy with the downtrodden, whether man or beast, which enables him to write a perfectly serious *Ode* to a mouse:

> But, mousie, thou art no thy lane
> In proving foresight may be vain:
> The best-laid schemes o' mice and men
> > Gang aft a-gley,
> An' lea'e us nought but grief an' pain
> > For promised joy.

Precursors of Romanticism

Of the other poetical movements leading to Romanticism we must speak very briefly. A new interest in old poetry was aroused by Percy's *Reliques of Ancient English Poetry,* published in 1765. (The title-page, with its pattern of a harp leaning against a blasted tree, with a background of ruins, is a perfect symbol of the growing appreciation of the 'quaintness' of the past.) This volume opened up the world of the ballads, with their wild and concise vigour, to the periwigged snuff-takers and powdered ladies. Two literary fabrications are noteworthy: James Macpherson (1736–96), a Scottish schoolmaster, pretended to have discovered some ancient poems written by a fictitious Gaelic bard called Ossian, and he published prose 'translations' of them; Thomas Chatterton (1752–70) pretended to have discovered a mediaeval poet called Rowley, and the mock-mediaeval poems that Chatterton published deceived many people, even the learned. Chatterton really was a remarkable poet, and his suicide at the age of eighteen robbed the world of a rare talent. Both the Ossian and the Rowley fabrications are interesting comments on the way in which certain minds were trying to escape from the hard sunlight of the Age of Reason, trying to get back to a remoter, more magical world. Certainly, both Macpherson and Chatterton helped to prepare the way for the Romantic Revolution.

Certain eccentrics make their appearance in the eighteenth century, shouting wild words in the good-mannered gatherings of the polite, bringing gloomy thoughts to the bright superficial conversations. Edward Young (1683–1765), for instance, with his *Night Thoughts*, a sombre set of meditations on death, graves, yew-trees, the end of life, the end of the world. This set a brief fashion for gloomy poems—Blair's *The Grave* (1743) and Harvey's *Meditations Among the Tombs* (1745–6) and *The Pleasures of Melancholy* (1747) by Thomas Warton. And there was the mad Christopher Smart (1722–71) with his *Song to David*. (It has been suggested that madness was one way out of the repressive rule of eighteenth-century reason. Certainly, Chatterton, Collins, Cowper, as well as Smart, were a little unbalanced.)

Finally, there was William Blake (1757–1827), perhaps one of the greatest of the English poets, certainly one of the most original. Blake is known to most people as the author of the *Songs of Innocence* and such poems as 'Tiger, Tiger, burning bright'. But his achievement is massive and his aim is immense. He wished, using the twin arts of poetry and drawing, to build up a huge mythology of his own, which should portray symbolically the forces always at war with each other in the soul of man. His great poems—*Milton, Jerusalem*—are epics hard to understand until one has found the clues: we have the giant Los, standing for the human imagination, and his opposite, Urizen, who represents the repressive power of law and reason; we have all their progeny and their vast battles —the final impression being not unlike that of the Malayan shadow-play, where gods and goddesses swim into the screen and we hear a strange mystical language from the hidden showmaster. But Blake's powers and gods are solid and huge and sometimes frightening. Blake's philosophy has a simple enough basis: he rejects reason and law and conventional

Blake

Illustration by Blake from Songs of Innocence.

religion, and says that mankind can be fulfilled only through the senses and the imagination. His *Marriage of Heaven and Hell* turns the existing eighteenth-century world upside-down. God, who stands for reason and repression, is set against Satan, who stands for energy and freedom. In Hell (the world of energy and creation) we learn astonishing new truths: 'The road of excess leads to the palace of wisdom'; 'Prisons are built with stones of law, Brothels with bricks of religion'; 'Damn braces. Bless relaxes'. Blake wants every human being to cultivate the imagination to such an extent that it will be capable of perceiving ultimate truth without any help from reason; reason, in fact, is dangerous, so is science; if we all live in a state of unfettered individual freedom, unconcerned with laws, relying on the power of insight and, on a lower level, instinct, we shall achieve that heaven on earth which Blake calls 'Jerusalem' in the Preface to his *Milton*:

> I will not cease from Mental Fight,
> Nor shall my sword sleep in my hand
> Till we have built Jerusalem
> In England's green and pleasant land.

Blake's short poems are always remarkable, always highly individual. At their best, they are forceful indictments of the repressions that he spent his life fighting against—the repressions of law, religion, and science. Some may still believe he was another of the eighteenth-century madmen; to me his madness looks very much like sanity.

> I saw a chapel all of gold
> That none did dare to enter in,
> And many weeping stood without,
> Weeping, mourning, worshipping.
>
> I saw a serpent rise between
> The white pillars of the door,
> And he forced and forced and forced,
> Down the golden hinges tore.
>
> And along the pavement sweet,
> Set with pearls and rubies bright,
> All his slimy length he drew,
> Till upon the altar white
>
> Vomiting his poison out
> On the bread and on the wine.
> So I turned into a sty
> And laid me down among the swine.

16. Prose in the Age of Reason

Despite the interesting body of verse that the eighteenth century produced, the works that have worn best and that still hold the general reader most are in prose. Defoe and Swift and Fielding hardly seem to have dated, while Pope and his followers seem artificial to modern readers, and require to be looked at through the glass of 'historical perspective'.

Beginnings of Newspapers

Daniel Defoe (1660–1731) was a journalist, and that fact itself draws him to our own time. The development of the newspaper and the periodical is an interesting literary sideline of the seventeenth century. The Civil War undoubtedly stimulated a public appetite for up-to-the-minute news (such news then was vital) and the Restoration period, with its interest in men and affairs, its information services in the coffee-houses, was developing that wider interest in news—home and foreign—which is so alive today. Defoe is, in many ways, the father of the modern periodical, purveying opinion more than news, and *The Review*, which he founded in 1704, is the progenitor of a long line of 'well-informed' magazines. Defoe did not see himself primarily as a literary artist: he had things to say to the public, and he said them as clearly as he could, without troubling to polish and revise. There are no stylistic tricks in his writings, no airs and graces, but there is the flavour of colloquial speech, a 'no-nonsense', down-to-earth simplicity. He was—like Swift—capable of irony, however, and his *Shortest Way with the Dissenters* states gravely that those who do not belong to the Church of England should be hanged. (Defoe himself was a Dissenter, of course.) This pamphlet was taken seriously by many, but, when the authorities discovered they had been having their legs pulled, they put Defoe into prison.

Defoe novels

The most interesting of Defoe's 'documentary' works is the *Journal of the Plague Year* (one gets the impression that Defoe was actually present in London during that disastrous time, seriously taking notes, but a glance at his dates will show that this was impossible). But his memory is revered still primarily for his novels, written late in life: *Robinson Crusoe*,

Moll Flanders, *Roxana*, and others. The intention of these works is that the reader should regard them as true, not as fictions, and so Defoe deliberately avoids all art, all fine writing, so that the reader should concentrate only on a series of plausible events, thinking: 'This isn't a storybook, this is autobiography.' Defoe keeps up the straight-faced pretence admirably. In *Moll Flanders* we seem to be reading the real life-story of a 'bad woman', written in the style appropriate to her. In *Robinson Crusoe*, whose appeal to the young can never die, the fascination lies in the bald statement of facts which are quite convincing—even though Defoe never had the experience of being cast away on a desert island and having to fend for himself. The magic of this novel never palls: frequently in England a musical comedy version of it holds the stage during the after-Christmas 'pantomime season'.

Other journalists were Richard Steele (1672–1729) and Joseph Addison (1672–1719). Steele started *The Tatler*, and Addison later joined him, and their writings in this periodical had a moral purpose—they attempted to improve manners, encourage tolerance in religion and politics, condemn fanaticism, and preach a kind of moderation in all things, including the literary art. Addison comes into his own in *The Spectator*, started in 1711, and the most valuable articles of that paper are his. His big achievement is the creation of an imaginary club, its members representing contemporary social types, and one member has become immortal—Sir Roger de Coverley. Sir Roger is the old-type Tory, rather simple-minded, thoroughly good-hearted, never for long away from his country estate, full of prejudices and superstitions which are meant to make us smile, but smile sympathetically. (Addison himself, by the way, was a Whig.) Against Sir Roger is set the Whig merchant, Sir Andrew Freeport, a man of less charm than Sir Roger but of far more intelligence. Addison seems to point to a middle way in politics—there is much good in the old, and one should not scoff at the outmoded ideas of the Tories, but the Whigs stand for progress and with them lies the England of the future. Sir Roger is a fine creation, worthy to rank with any of the eccentrics of eighteenth-century fiction (such as Squire Western in *Tom Jones*). Addison's prose-style is an admirable compromise: it has the grace and polish of the artist, the ease and flow and simplicity of the journalist. If Addison has a fault, it lies in a certain sentimentality: he likes to provoke tears, and his humour has sometimes an over-gentle whimsicality that makes us long for stronger meat.

The greatest prose-writer of the first part—perhaps the whole—of the century is Jonathan Swift (1667–1745). A great humorist and a savage satirist, his meat is sometimes too powerful even for a healthy stomach. He is capable of pure fun—as in some of his poems—and even schoolboy jokes, but there is a core of bitterness in him which revealed itself finally as a mad hatred of mankind. On his own admission, he loved Tom, Dick,

*Other
journalists*

Swift

Illustration from Gulliver's Travels by Rex Whistler.

and Harry, but hated the animal, Man. Yet he strove to do good for his fellow-men, especially the poor of Dublin, where he was Dean of St. Patrick's. The *Drapier's Letters* were a series of attacks on abuses of the currency, and the Government heeded his sharp shafts. The monopoly of minting copper money, which had been given to a man called Wood, was withdrawn, and Swift became a hero. In his *Modest Proposal* he ironically suggested that famine in Ireland could be eased by cannibalism, and that the starving children should be used as food. Some fools took this seriously. His greatest books are *A Tale of a Tub* and *Gulliver's Travels*. The first of these is a satire on the two main non-conformist religions— Catholicism and Presbyterianism. Swift tells the story of three brothers —Jack (Calvin), Martin (Luther), and Peter (St.)—and what they do with their inheritance (the Christian religion). The story is farcical and at times wildly funny, but people of his day could perhaps be forgiven if they found blasphemy in it. It certainly shocked Queen Anne so much that she would not allow Swift to be made a bishop, and this contributed to Swift's inner frustration and bitterness. *Gulliver's Travels* hides much of its satire so cleverly that children still read it as a fairy story. It starts off by making fun of mankind (and especially England and English politics) in a quite gentle way: Gulliver sees in Lilliput a shrunken human race, and its concerns—so important to Lilliput—become shrunken accordingly. But in the second part, in the land of the giants, where tiny Gulliver sees human deformities magnified to a feverous pitch, we have something of this mad horror of the human body which obsesses Swift. (According to Dr. Johnson, Swift washed himself excessively—'with Oriental scrupulosity'—but his terror of dirt and shame at the body's functions never disappeared.) In the fourth part of the book, where the Houyhnhnms—horses with rational souls and the highest moral instincts —are contrasted with the filthy, depraved Yahoos, who are really human beings, Swift's hatred of man reaches its climax. Nothing is more powerful or horrible than the moment when Gulliver reaches home and cannot bear the touch of his wife—her smell is the smell of a Yahoo and makes him want to vomit.

Gulliver

Swift is a very great literary artist, and perhaps only in the present century is his full stature being revealed. He is skilful in verse, as well as in prose, and his influence continues: James Joyce—in his *The Holy Office*—has written Swiftian verse; Aldous Huxley (in *Ape and Essence*) and George Orwell (in *Animal Farm*) have produced satires which are really an act of homage to Swift's genius. Yet *Gulliver's Travels* stands supreme: a fairy story for children, a serious work for men, it has never lost either its allure or its topicality.

The first part of the century is also notable for a number of philosophical and religious works which reflect the new 'rational' spirit. The Deists (powerful in France as well as in England) try to strip Christianity

Religious writing

of its mysteries and to establish an almost Islamic conception of God—a God in whom the Persons of the Christian Trinity shall have no part—and to maintain that this conception is the product of reason, not of faith. On the other hand, there were Christian writers like William Law (1686–1761) and Isaac Watts (1674–1748) who, the first in prose, the second in simple pious verse, tried successfully to stress the importance of pure faith, even of mysticism, in religion. The religious revival which was to be initiated by John Wesley (1703–91) owes a good deal to this spirit, which kept itself alive despite the temptations of 'rationalism'. Joseph Butler (1692–1752) used reason, not to advance the doctrine of Deism, but to affirm the truths of established Christianity. His *Analogy of Religion* is a powerfully argued book. The most important philosopher of the early part of the century is Bishop Berkeley (1685–1753), whose conclusions may be stated briefly: he did not believe that matter had any real existence apart from mind. A tree exists because we see it, and if we are not there to see it, God is always there. Things ultimately exist in the mind of God, not of themselves. He was answered later by David Hume (1711–76), the Scots philosopher, who could not accept the notion of a divine system enclosing everything. He could see little system in the universe: he begins and ends with human nature, which links together a series of impressions, gained by the senses, by means of 'association'. We make systems according to our needs, but there is no system which *really exists* in an absolute sense. There is no ultimate truth, and even God is an idea that man has developed for his own needs. This is a closely argued kind of sceptical philosophy, very different from Berkeley's somewhat mystical acceptance of reality's being the content of the 'Mind of God'.

Development of novel

The novel develops, after the death of Defoe, with Samuel Richardson (1689–1761), a professional printer who took to novel-writing when he was fifty. Richardson liked to help young women with the composition of their love-letters, and was asked by a publisher to write a volume of model letters for use on various occasions. He was inspired to write a novel in the form of a series of letters, a novel which should implant a moral lesson in the minds of its readers (he thought of these readers primarily as women). This novel was *Pamela, or Virtue Rewarded*, which describes the assaults made on the honour of a virtuous housemaid by an unscrupulous young man. Pamela resists, clinging tightly to her code of honour, and her reward is, ultimately, marriage to her would-be seducer, a man who, despite his brutishness, has always secretly attracted her. It is a strange sort of reward, and a strange basis for marriage, according to our modern view, but this moral persists in cheap novelettes and magazines even today—a girl makes herself inaccessible before marriage, and the man who has tried to seduce her, weary of lack of success, at last accepts her terms. Richardson's *Clarissa Harlowe* is about a young lady of wealth and beauty, virtue and innocence, who, in order to avoid a marriage which her parents are trying to arrange, seeks help from Lovelace, a handsome but, again, unscrupulous young man. Lovelace seduces her. Repentant, he asks her to marry him, but she will not: instead, worn out by shame, she dies, leaving Lovelace to his remorse. This is a more remarkable novel than it sounds: close analysis of character, perhaps for the first time in the history of the novel, looks forward to the great French novelists, Flaubert and Stendhal, and Lovelace has a complexity of make-up hardly to be expected in the literature of the age. *Sir Charles Grandison* is Richardson's third novel: its hero, full of the highest virtues, wondering which woman duty should compel him to marry, is anaemic and priggish. (A hero should have something of the devil in him.) This novel is far inferior to the other two.

The greatest novelist of the century is Henry Fielding (1707–54). He started his novel-writing career, like Richardson, almost by accident. Moved to write a parody of *Pamela*, he found his *Joseph Andrews* developing into something far bigger than a mere skit. Joseph, dismissed from service because he will not allow his employer, Lady Booby, to make love to him, takes the road to the village where his sweetheart lives, meets the tremendous Parson Adams—who then becomes virtually the hero of the book—and has many strange adventures on the road, meeting rogues, vagabonds, tricksters of all kinds, but eventually reaching his goal and happiness ever after. With Fielding one is inclined to use the term *picaresque* (from the Spanish *picaro*, meaning 'rogue'), a term originally applicable only to novels in which the leading character is a rogue (such as the popular *Gil Blas* by Le Sage, published between 1715 and 1735). It is a term which lends itself to description of all novels in which the bulk of the action takes place on the road, on a journey, and in which eccentric and low-life characters appear. *Don Quixote* is, in some ways, picaresque; so is Priestley's *The Good Companions*. Fielding's *Jonathan Wild* is truly picaresque, with its boastful, vicious hero who extols the 'greatness' of his every act of villainy (his standards of comparison are, cynically, provided by the so-called virtuous actions of great men) until he meets his end on the gallows or 'tree of glory'. *Tom Jones* is Fielding's masterpiece. It has its picaresque elements—the theme of the journey occupies the greater part of the book—but it would be more accurate to describe it as a mock-epic. It has the bulk and largeness of conception we expect from an epic, and its style sometimes parodies Homer:

Fielding

> Hushed be every ruder breath. May the heathen ruler of the winds confine in iron chains the boisterous limbs of noisy Boreas, and the sharp-pointed nose of bitter-biting Eurus. Do thou, sweet Zephyrus, rising from thy fragrant bed, mount the western sky, and lead on those delicious gales, the charms of which call forth the lovely Flora from her chamber, perfumed with pearly dews . . .

And so on for several hundred words, until eventually we are introduced to the charming, but not quite Homeric, Sophia Western, heroine of the novel and beloved of the quite ordinary but quite likeable hero, Jones himself. The novel introduces a rich variety of characters, contains certain shrewd moral observations, and has an acceptable philosophy— liberal and tolerant, distrustful of too great enthusiasm, recognising the social conventions, but much concerned with reform of the law. (It was Fielding's liberalism which helped along the reform movements of the end of the century.) But we appreciate *Tom Jones* most for its boisterous humour, its good sense, and its vivid characterisation.

Smollett

Tobias Smollett (1721–71) is responsible for *Roderick Random*, *Peregrine Pickle*, and *Humphry Clinker*. The first gives us an insight into the life of the British Navy, which Smollett knew at first hand, having served as a ship's surgeon. The vice and brutality are vividly portrayed, but the satirical tone of the whole book seems to rob it somehow of the force of an indictment—exaggeration is Smollett's technique, not the direct 'reportage' of Defoe. But we are intended to take the novel as entertainment, not as propaganda, and as entertainment it is superb, though strong meat. It is the first of a long line of novels about life at sea, a line which can boast distinguished names like Conrad and Herman Melville. *Peregrine Pickle* is a gentler tale of sailors living on land, and *Humphry Clinker*, which reverts to Richardson's technique of presenting the story in the form of a series of letters, is less a novel than a travel-book—an account of a journey through England and Scotland made by a family from Wales, the letters presenting strongly the distinctive personalities of the writers. What little plot there is centres on a couple of love-affairs and the discovery that Humphry Clinker—servant of the family making the tour—is really the son of Mr. Bramble, the grumpy but golden-hearted head of the family.

Sterne

Laurence Sterne (1713–68) produced a remarkable and eccentric novel in his *Tristram Shandy*, which breaks all the rules, even of language and punctuation, and deliberately excludes all suggestions of a plot, so that— despite the considerable length of the book—nobody gets anywhere, nothing really happens, and the hero does not succeed even in getting himself born until half-way through! The author deliberately hinders all movement: just when we think a story is about to develop, Sterne introduces an incredible digression—a long piece of Latin (with translation on the opposite page), a blank sheet, a page with a marbled design on it, a collection of asterisks—anything to obstruct or mystify. Yet characters emerge: the learned Mr. Shandy, the gentle old soldier Uncle Toby and Trim, his corporal (these last two spend much time reconstructing the Battle of Namur on a bowling-green). There are lewd jokes, patches of sentimentality—often saved, just in time, from becoming mawkish by an ironical stroke—and grotesque Rabelaisian episodes. (Sterne looks back to Rabelais and forward to James Joyce.) Sterne's *Sentimental Journey* is an account of travels through France and Italy, and here tears are shed freely—especially over animals, Sterne being perhaps the first of the English 'poor-dumb-beast' sentimentalists. It was through the copious shedding of tears of pity and sympathy, in writers like Sterne, that the humanitarianism which is now said to be a great characteristic of the English was able to develop. Sentimentality may injure art, but it can improve life.

Oliver Goldsmith, whom we have already met as poet and playwright, contributed to the development of the English novel a country idyll called *The Vicar of Wakefield*. There is sentimentality here, too, in the portrait of the good Dr. Primrose, so good-hearted, so simple-minded, brave in adversity and tolerant and forgiving, but there is characteristic humour also, as well as the lyric gift:

Goldsmith

> When lovely woman stoops to folly,
>   And finds too late that men betray,
> What charm can soothe her melancholy?
>   What art can wash her tears away?

We are trying to trace the course of eighteenth-century prose in fairly strict chronological order. The novels we have just glanced at—from *Pamela* to *Humphry Clinker*—cover thirty years, from 1741 to 1771. Other prose of the time includes attempts at History (Hume produced a *History of Great Britain* and William Robertson a *History of Scotland*, and even Smollett and Goldsmith tried their hands), many interesting collections of letters—including those of Lord Chesterfield to his son, and the vast correspondence of Horace Walpole—and the first book on Economics. This last, *The Wealth of Nations* by Adam Smith (1723–90), lies outside our scope, but we, whose study is literature, can praise it for its brilliance of style, even if we are not concerned with its content. Economics was later to become a 'dismal science', but Smith is not only elegant in the exposition of his revolutionary theory, but even prophetic: his book appeared in 1776, on the very day of the American Declaration of Independence, and it says of the Americans: 'They will be one of the foremost nations of the world.'

The last decades of the eighteenth century were shaken by great political changes. America broke away from England, and, in 1789, the French Revolution took place. English thinkers and politicians were much agitated, taking sides, preaching for and against the new violent movements, and a good deal of the prose of this last period is concerned with such watchwords as Liberty, Anarchy, Justice. William Godwin (1756–1836) wrote a book about Political Justice, preaching a kind of anarchy, extolling the light of pure reason as it comes to the individual soul, denouncing law and marriage and property because these interfere with

Late C18 background

individual freedom. His book had a great influence on Romantic poets like Shelley. Tom Paine (1737–1800) had previously defended the revolt of America, and he now defended, in his *Rights of Man*, the Revolution in France. Edmund Burke (1729–97), despite his Liberalism, attacked this same Revolution, and stated that tradition was more important than rational political theories—society was like a plant or a human body, growing, working out its salvation according to laws of its own, and it was dangerous to interfere with that process.

Gibbon

This period produced the great historian, Edward Gibbon (1737–94), whose *The Decline and Fall of the Roman Empire* reached completion in 1788, a year before the fall of the Bastille. This is a great achievement, written in the most polished prose of the age, and it surveys about thirteen centuries of European history—from the reign of the Emperor Trajan to the fall of Constantinople, covering the rise of Christianity and Islam, the great migrations of the Teutonic peoples, and analysing the forces which turned the old world into the modern world. It is not a compassionate work: it chastises man for his follies much more than it extols his discoveries and virtues, and exhibits more of the author's personality than is perhaps proper in a history; but for literary skill and width of scope it is perhaps still unsurpassed among the larger historical studies.

Fanny Burney

The later days of the eighteenth-century novel produce names like Fanny Burney (1752–1840), whose *Evelina* and *Cecilia* are realistic, humorous, and full of credible characters. But much more typical of the age are those novels of terror which Horace Walpole ushered in, and novels which showed the influence of the Frenchman Jean-Jacques Rousseau.

Rousseau

Rousseau (1712–78) was one of the forerunners of the Romantic movement, and also one of the prophets of the French Revolution. He was by nature a rebel—against existing conceptions of religion, art, education, marriage, government, and in book after book he propounded his own theories on these subjects. Rousseau advocated a return to nature. In the natural state, he held, man is happy and good, and it is only society that, by making life artificial, produces evil. His *Émile*, a treatise on education, advocated that children should be brought up in an atmosphere of truth, and it condemned the elaborate lies that society imposed on the average child—including myths and fairy-stories. The result, in England, was a whole series of instructive books for children (including the incredibly priggish *Sandford and Merton* of Thomas Day) which was only broken by the thoroughly fanciful, and much healthier, children's books of men like Thackeray and Lewis Carroll in the nineteenth century. It was Rousseau's doctrine of the noble 'natural man', and his attack on the corrupting power of civilisation, that produced novels by minor writers like Bage, Holcroft, and the *Caleb Williams* of William Godwin, in which the spirit of revolt is expressed through central characters who have no

religion or morality (like the hero of Bage's *Hermsprong*) or, like Godwin's hero, are a living witness to the corruption of a society in which the
evil flourish and the good are victimised.

There were novels of 'mystery and imagination' by writers like Mrs.   *Gothic novels*
Ann Radcliffe (1764–1822) and Matthew Gregory Lewis (1775–1818),
who followed the example set in 1764 by *The Castle of Otranto*—a 'Gothic'
story by Horace Walpole (1717–97). (This term 'Gothic' is primarily an
architectural one, denoting that kind of European building which
flourished in the Middle Ages and showed the influence of neither the
Greeks nor the Romans. Gothic architecture, with its pointed arches,
began to come back to England in the middle of the eighteenth century—
Walpole himself built a 'little Gothic castle' at Strawberry Hill, near
Twickenham, London. This kind of building suggested mystery, romance, revolt against classical order, wildness, through its associations
with mediaeval ruins—ivy-covered, haunted by owls, washed by moon-
light, shadowy, mysterious, and so on.) *The Castle of Otranto* is a melodramatic curiosity; Mrs. Radcliffe's *The Romance of the Forest*, *The Mysteries of Udolpho*, and *The Italian* are skilfully written, her mysteries always
have a rational explanation at the end, and she never offends conventional
morality. Lewis's *The Monk*—with its devils, horror, torture, perver-
sions, magic, and murder—is very different: its lack of taste does not
compensate for its undoubted power, and its popularity was understand-
ably short-lived. We ought to mention in this context a work produced
a good deal later—*Frankenstein* by Mary Shelley (1797–1851). This was
written during a wet summer in Switzerland, when her husband (the
poet) and Lord Byron were amusing themselves by writing ghost-stories
and she herself was asked to compose one. She could never have guessed
that her story of the scientist who makes an artificial man—by which he
is eventually destroyed—would give a new word to the language, and
become so well known among even the near-illiterate (thanks chiefly to
Hollywood) that its subject would rise from humble fiction to universal
myth.

I have reserved to the end of this chapter mention of the man whose   *Johnson*
personality seems to dominate the whole of the Augustan Age—Dr.
Samuel Johnson (1709–84). Boswell's biography—perhaps the finest
biography ever written—gives so vivid and detailed a portrait of the
'Grand Cham of Literature' and his times, that Johnson the person has,
from the end of the eighteenth century to the present day, tended to overshadow Johnson the writer. There are a thousand people who can quote
one of Johnson's conversational sallies to one who can give a sentence
from *The Rambler* or a line from *London*. When Johnson the writer *is*
quoted, it is usually something to his disparagement that we hear, like
the tautological opening of *The Vanity of Human Wishes*:

> Let observation with extensive view
> Survey mankind from China to Peru,

or some extreme example of his highly Latinised style. Yet Johnson is worth reading. He attempted most of the literary forms of the day— drama, poetry (lyrical and didactic), the novel (his *Rasselas* is in the Oriental tradition, like Beckford's *Vathek*, and has the same sort of theme as Voltaire's *Candide*), and the moral essay, as in *The Rambler* and *The Idler*. He wrote sermons, prayers and meditations, admirable biography (*The Lives of the Poets*), dedications, prologues, speeches, political pamphlets— he leaves few branches of literature, journalism, and 'current affairs' untouched. But his name as a scholar will live chiefly because of his *Dictionary of the English Language* and his critical writings. The *Dictionary* is a great achievement—a work that can still be consulted, and, for the light it throws on Johnson's personality, even read. Johnson the critic is best met in *The Lives of the Poets* (especially in the Life of Cowley, where he has wise things to say about the Metaphysical Poets, and the long essay on Milton) and the preface to his edition of Shakespeare. The following may seem cruel, but there is truth in it:

> A quibble is, to Shakespeare, what luminous vapours are to the traveller; he follows it at all adventures; it is sure to lead him out of his way, and sure to engulf him in the mire. It has some malignant power over his mind, and its fascinations are irresistible. . . . A quibble is the golden apple for which he will always turn aside from his career, or stoop from his elevation. . . . A quibble was to him the fatal Cleopatra for which he lost the world, and was content to lose it.

Johnson was incapable of giving veneration to any writer just because of that writer's reputation. As a critic he was honest, and honesty and independence shine throughout all his writings, as they shine throughout the record of his personal career.

To an understanding of the whole of the eighteenth-century literary world, Boswell's *Life of Johnson* is indispensable. In it we meet all the writers we have been hearing about—Goldsmith, Sheridan, Burke, and the rest—and, more than that, we get the 'feel', the very smell, of the Augustan Age. It is a remarkable record of a remarkable era.

17. The Romantics

It would be convenient (as well as romantic) to believe that the Romantic Movement in Literature began with the storming of the Bastille in Paris and the first spilling of blood in the French Revolution. But, as we have seen, Romanticism was trying to stir all the way through the Age of Reason: the eighteenth century had a number of rebels, individualists, madmen, who—often unsuccessfully, because of the difficulty of language—worked at a literature of instinct, emotion, enthusiasm, tried to return to the old way of the Elizabethans and even the mediaeval poets. It was perhaps because of the influence of the great conservative classicist, Dr. Johnson, that a Romantic literature did not come earlier. Only when the philosophies of men like Rousseau, Locke, and Hume began to be translated into revolutionary action did feeling stir sufficiently to make the new kind of literature seem *natural*. What had been unorthodox became orthodox. Romanticism developed its own rules and standards, and the rebels became the lawful government.

The new orthodoxy

Nevertheless, there were still old conservatives to contend with. Wordsworth had to fight almost incessantly against those who still clung to the standards of the past; Keats was soundly trounced by the critics; Shelley was roundly condemned. But the very fact that, by about 1830, all the literary men of talent can be classified roughly as members of one movement, is a sign that they represent the new orthodoxy. The Romantics are still, in our own age, the orthodox writers: we are brought up at school on Wordsworth and Coleridge, not on Pope and Dryden, and Dylan Thomas fired the public imagination more than T. S. Eliot (Thomas the wild visionary; Eliot the precise classicist). When, however, we consider that the Romantics were really *returning* to the old way of writing (the way of the Elizabethans and even of the ballad-poets), we can then see the classical age in truer perspective. It was Dryden and Pope who broke away from the great English tradition and joined, for a brief age of stability, the classical tradition of France. Now, as revolutionary France became less the home of 'Liberty, Equality, Fraternity' and more

Influence of France and Germany

the home of tyranny, the country that had inspired classicism and fired the Romantic spirit ceased to have any influence on English literature. Poets like Coleridge, Wordsworth, Southey, Scott, Byron, and Shelley learned more from Germany than from the nearer neighbour, and Germany helped to sustain English Romanticism for a long time. And we may note here that even this tendency towards the Germanic is evident, in its small way, in the 'transitional' poets of the Augustan Age: Gray's Pindaric Odes go to Scandinavian mythology as well as Celtic history; 'Gothic' implies Teutonic culture.

Wordsworth's Manifesto

The key year for English Romanticism is not 1789, but 1798. 1789 saw the fall of the Bastille, but 1798 saw the publication of the *Lyrical Ballads* by William Wordsworth (1770–1850) and Samuel Taylor Coleridge (1772–1834). In the Preface to the second and third editions of this book, Wordsworth laid down the principles on which he thought the composition of poetry should be founded. He was insistent that the language of poetry should be the language of ordinary men and women, found at its unspoilt in the speech of rural people. He was against 'poetic diction'. He was also against the rationalist content of the Augustan poets; he wanted a return to imagination, legend, the human heart. He also conceived of poetry—as did all the Romantics—as more than the mere correct versification of philosophical truths: the poet was a prophet, not the transcriber of other men's truths but the initiator of truth itself. To be a poet meant a tremendous responsibility—the poet had the key to the hidden mysteries of the heart, of life itself; the poet was not a mere embellisher of everyday life, but the man who gave life its meaning. In

Poetry as a vocation

the eighteenth century poetry was still something of a spare-time gentlemanly hobby; with the Romantics it became a vocation. Shelley made this claim: 'Poets are the trumpets which sing to battle; poets are the unacknowledged legislators of the world.'

Wordsworth certainly took his vocation seriously. His profession was that of a poet; he had no other trade. In his early days, true, he had been much given to philosophy, hammering out, on the lines of Godwin, a rationalist system of politics and morals he could follow. But in 1798, with the publication of his—and Coleridge's—manifesto, he knew that his way lay not in rationalism, but in intuition, in a kind of mysticism,

Wordsworth's pantheism

and that Nature meant more to him than all the systems. Wordsworth's attitude to Nature is original and remarkable. Nature is the great teacher of morals, and the prime bringer of happiness, but Nature is much more than that: in Nature resides God. Wordsworth is aware, in contact with the woods and mountains and lakes and trees of his own northern county of Cumberland, or of less rugged regions, of—

> A presence that disturbs me with the joy
> Of elevated thoughts; a sense sublime

> Of something far more deeply interfused,
> Whose dwelling is the light of setting suns,
> And the round ocean and the living air,
> And the blue sky, and in the mind of man.
>
> (*Tintern Abbey*: lines 94–9)

Man and nature become fused through participation in the one 'mighty being', so that the most elemental natural objects become 'humanised':

> The birds around me hopped and played,
> Their thoughts I cannot measure:—
> But the least motion which they made,
> It seemed a thrill of pleasure.
>
> The budding twigs spread out their fan,
> To catch the breezy air;
> And I must think, do all I can,
> That there was pleasure there.

Wordsworth is neither Christian, deist, nor rationalist. He is best described as a *Pantheist*, one who identifies the natural universe with God, and thus denies that God is *over* everything or possesses a distinct 'personality'.

   This worship of Nature leads Wordsworth to venerate the simple folk who live 'in the eye of Nature': they are purer, wiser than town-dwellers, and their language is less corrupt. Thus, Wordsworth's theory of poetic language derives from his deeper nature-philosophy, but such a theory lets him down badly at times. Nobody can be more eloquent than Wordsworth, but he can also, in trying to be too simple and 'everyday', produce banalities like this:

> We talked with open heart, and tongue
> Affectionate and true,
> A pair of friends, though I was young,
> And Matthew seventy-two.

Or this opening to a sonnet:

> Spade, with which Wilkinson hath tilled his lands!

And it is true to say that some of the heroes of Wordsworth's narrative-poems—old men like Michael, the Leech-gatherer, the Old Cumberland Beggar—are not in themselves very interesting; Wordsworth sees in them rather symbols of the power of Nature or living guides to natural conduct, and so on. Ultimately, Wordsworth was to regard children—unspoilt as yet by education, uncorrupted by the world—as the real repositories of virtue and even wisdom, and his great Ode—*Intimations of*

Immortality from Recollections of Early Childhood—states this belief most eloquently. The Child is addressed as:

> Thou, whose exterior semblance doth belie
>   Thy soul's immensity;
> Thou best philosopher, who yet dost keep
> Thy heritage, thou eye among the blind,
> That, deaf and silent, read'st the eternal deep,
> Haunted for ever by the eternal mind . . .

Rarely in Wordsworth will you catch any hint or echo of eighteenth-century thought or technique. His language is his own, his natural descriptions are fresh and immediate; he is a poet of the particular scene, not the general abstract image. No other poet has caught so well the colour and scent of flowers, or the zest of spring ('The hare is running races in her mirth'), or the terror of the high lonely mountains. Technically, his range is very wide: the blank verse of *The Prelude* and *The Excursion* (the two long autobiographical poems), though originally owing something to Milton, emerges as recognisably Wordsworth's own; the Italian sonnet-form is exploited in a quite individual way; a variety of stanza-forms and the free Pindaric metre are used with mastery. Wordsworth, when he fails, fails more dismally than any other major poet has ever done; his much more frequent successes are as triumphant as anything in Shakespeare.

Coleridge

The supernatural

Coleridge's contribution to the Romantic movement lay in a return to the magical and mysterious. It was on this question of the introduction of the supernatural into poetry that Coleridge and Wordsworth could never see eye to eye. Wordsworth wanted poetry to stay on the ground and extract thrills from the commonplace; Coleridge wanted it to fly into the regions of the marvellous and choose themes that, though fantastic, should be acceptable through 'willing suspension of disbelief for the moment, which constitutes poetic faith'. Coleridge's three great poems —*The Rime of the Ancient Mariner, Christabel,* and *Kubla Khan*—are coloured with the mysterious and the supernatural. The Ancient Mariner kills an albatross and is forthwith tormented with the most frightening visions and visitations, all of which are presented in the style and metre of the old ballads, but with far greater imagination and astonishing imagery. *Christabel*, with its flexible metre anticipating Gerard Manley Hopkins, but also reminding us of pre-Chaucerian rhythms—sometimes eight syllables to the line, sometimes twelve, but always four steady beats —is full of the mystery of evil. The beautiful Geraldine, whom Christabel meets in the forest, discloses her evil qualities in subtle ways—only Christabel is aware of her malevolent force, and she herself cannot bring even her own father to see it: it is a nightmare situation and a nightmare poem, touched with the glamour of old castles and a mediaeval remoteness. Coleridge turns to the past for mystery and wonder—unlike Wordsworth, who takes the present and the everyday. *Kubla Khan*—like *Christabel*, unfinished—is a poem which goes to the fabulous ancient Orient for its theme, and it contains the quintessence of Coleridge's magic. Composed under the influence of opium—indeed, not so much composed as welling up spontaneously from the unconscious mind of the poet—*Kubla Khan* is a fantastic invocation of a 'sunny pleasure-dome with caves of ice', with sinister images of a 'woman wailing for her demon-lover' and 'ancestral voices prophesying war'. The end of the poem is pure magic:

> Weave a circle round him thrice
> And close your eyes with holy dread,
> For he on honey-dew hath fed,
> And drunk the milk of paradise.

Both Wordsworth and Coleridge lived long enough to regard their early enthusiasm, especially for the French Revolution ('Bliss was it in that dawn to be alive,' says Wordsworth, 'but to be young was very heaven'), as vaguely discreditable. Wordsworth ended his days respectably, writing the *Ecclesiastical Sonnets*, even accepting the Poet Laureateship; Coleridge took to philosophy and criticism (remarkable criticism too, especially that on Wordsworth in the *Biographia Literaria*). The Romantic spirit, it seemed, had to be associated with youth, and indeed it was in the work of men who died when they were still young—Lord Byron (1788–1824), Percy Bysshe Shelley (1792–1822), and John Keats (1795–1821)—that the peculiar *immaturity* of Romanticism found its voice.

Byron's reputation in Europe has always been greater than his reputation in England. He became a legend—the handsome cynic with the club-foot, the man who swam the Hellespont like Leander of old, the great lover, the debauchee and atheist, the hero who eventually lost his life dying for the cause of Greek independence. His poetry is essentially self-centred—he is the hero of *Childe Harold*, of the remarkable anti-religious drama *Cain*, of *The Corsair* and *The Siege of Corinth*. Exiled from England because of the scandal surrounding his private life, in his later days he became the great sneerer at the laws and conventions of his country, and a spirit of satire which allies him to Pope (whom he admired) came out strongly in his masterpiece *Don Juan*. *Don Juan* is perhaps not strictly a Romantic poem at all: there is too much laughter in it, too much of the sharp edge of social criticism:

Byron

Satire

> This is the patent age of new inventions
>   For killing bodies, and for saving souls,
> All propagated with the best intentions;

> Sir Humphry Davy's lantern, by which coals
> Are safely mined for in the mode he mentions,
> Tombuctoo travels, voyages to the Poles,
> Are ways to benefit mankind, as true,
> Perhaps, as shooting them at Waterloo.

But occasionally the Romantic voice comes out in such lyrics as that beginning:

> The isles of Greece, the isles of Greece!
> Where burning Sappho loved and sung,
> Where grew the arts of war and peace,
> Where Delos rose, and Phoebus sprung!
> Eternal summer gilds them yet,
> But all, except their sun, is set.

And yet both the satire and the pouring-forth of feeling seem reconcilable to each other. They are both aspects of a somewhat adolescent mind, a mind impatient of everything, even of the demands of poetic craftsmanship. Byron is not a satirist of the true Augustan order, chiefly because he refuses to take trouble with his poetic technique: Pope, approving some of the humour, would have been appalled at the carelessness of much of the writing. Byron is the young spoilt darling who sulks and sneers if he cannot have his own way. He died heroically, true, after writing one of his finest lyrics—'My days are in the yellow leaf'— but even his fighting for Greece against the Turks was an adolescent attempt at making himself a Homeric hero—it was the ancient epic Greece that was in his imagination, not the real resurgent modern Greece.

Shelley Shelley's adolescence expresses itself in terms of Godwinian revolt against all existing laws, customs, religion. Revolt was in his nature (he was lucky to be able to afford to indulge it: his family was aristocratic, he himself financially independent). At twenty-one he wrote *Queen Mab*, a long philosophical poem with learned notes, in which he professes himself an atheist, a vegetarian, an opponent of existing marriage-laws, a republican, an advocate of universal love. His longer poems all take up the theme of revolt, of suffering humanity in chains: *The Revolt of Islam*, *Prometheus Unbound*, *Hellas* (which hymns the Greek rising against Turkish rule). But he also presents his positive philosophy of the indestructibility of beauty (*The Sensitive Plant*) and of the power of love, as in *Epipsychidion*. He has considerable dramatic power, which makes his *The Cenci* one of the few actable plays of the Romantic period, but it is as the lyrical poet of Nature that Shelley makes the greatest appeal. He has the same sensitivity as Wordsworth, and perhaps a far greater melodic power, revealed at its best in the *Ode to the West Wind*:

> O thou
> Who chariotest to their dark wintry bed
> The winged seeds, where they lie cold and low,
> Each like a corpse within its grave, until
> Thine azure sister of the Spring shall blow
> Her clarion o'er the dreaming earth and fill
> (Driving sweet buds like flocks to feed in air)
> With living hues and odours plain and hill.

Yet one is sometimes repelled by a kind of spinelessness, a kind of 'death-urge', which expresses itself in lines like:

> I fall upon the thorns of life! I bleed!

or:

> I could lie down like a tired child
> And weep away this life of care.

or:

> Oh, lift me from the grass!
> I die, I faint, I fail!

It is a kind of adolescent spirit, self-pitying, over-intense, as immature as a rash of acne or of religious mania. It is from such aspects of Romanticism as this that we gladly rush back to the mature 'good sense' of Dryden, or even of Donne. But that, of course, is not the whole of Shelley. In poems like *Adonais* (an elegy on the death of Keats) we meet a mature mysticism, a serene philosophy of life which denies death and affirms the immortality of the human spirit, and throughout his work we find a technical mastery of traditional verse-forms—Spenserian stanza, couplets, blank verse, *terza rima* (the form Dante used in the *Divine Comedy*)— and an eloquence and music unmatched among English poets of the time.

Perhaps John Keats, had he lived beyond his mere twenty-six years, would have become one of the great poets of all time. So many, aware of his sensuous gift and flood of rich language, believe, thinking also that his *Letters* show the beginnings of a mature and incisive intellect that might, given time, have tempered his lush Romanticism to something like a Shakespearian quality. But the poems of Keats that remain to us are models of the purely *sensuous* aspect of the Romantic movement. His themes are simple enough: beauty in art and nature; the wish to die; happy and unhappy love; the glamour of the classical past. He is a pagan, and the gods of ancient Greece are enough for him. The Miltonic epic he left unfinished—*Hyperion*—was to tell of the downfall of the old gods and the rising of the new gods of strength and beauty. But for the most part

Keats

he is content with the pleasures of the senses—wine, love, and the sights and sounds of nature:

> Thou shalt, at one glance, behold
> The daisy and the marigold;
> White-plumed lilies, and the first
> Hedge-grown primrose that hath burst,
> Shaded hyacinth, alway
> Sapphire queen of the mid-May . . .

> And full-grown lambs loud bleat from hilly bourn;
> Hedge-crickets sing; and now with treble soft
> The redbreast whistles from a garden-croft;
> And gathering swallows twitter in the skies.

But the heart-ache of his poems comes from their awareness that beauty dies. It is there in the *Ode to a Nightingale* and the *Ode on Melancholy* and in the wistful *Ode on a Grecian Urn*, where the figures on the urn are addressed as eternal types of beauty—they are caught forever in certain attitudes, they cannot change or decay, their beauty is truth in the sense that truth is eternal. And the song of the nightingale goes on forever, taunting the world of change that hears it. There is also the heart-ache of love expressed in those last sonnets (Shakespearian in form), and the terrible mystery of love in *La Belle Dame Sans Merci*. But it is the 'simple, sensuous, and passionate' poet that stands out above all, in love with the world of the senses.

Minor Romantic poets

Minor poets of the age are many. Robert Southey (1774–1843) is now chiefly read as the biographer of Lord Nelson, and his long epics are forgotten. He loved the exotic, and his *Thalaba* deals with the Islamic world, as *The Curse of Kehama* goes to India for its theme. Thomas Moore (1779–1852) wrote an Oriental poem, *Lalla Rookh*, but his fame rests on

Exoticism

the lyrical poems which he set to old Irish tunes. Still, the exotic was in the air, and helped to shape Romanticism. As the Elgin Marbles gave Keats a vision of Greece, so China was invoked in the architecture of Brighton (a seaside resort beloved of the Prince Regent). Byron had a harem-scene in *Don Juan* and in 1824 James Morier produced his *Hajji Baba of Ispahan*—the East, near or far, fascinated the Romantics (and this, of course, was being prepared in the Age of Reason, with Voltaire's *Candide* and Beckford's *Vathek*). Thomas Campbell (1777–1844) is best known for his battle poems (*Hohenlinden* and *The Battle of the Baltic*); Thomas Hood (1799–1845) for pathetic humanitarian poems like *The Song of the Shirt* and *The Bridge of Sighs*. One minor poet, John Clare (1793–1864), has come into favour comparatively recently. His end, like that of Keats and Shelley and Byron, was unfortunate. Keats died of tuberculosis, Shelley was drowned, Byron died of fever, Clare went mad. But there is no madness in his delicate studies of country scenes; he had a true lyric gift. Walter Savage Landor (1775–1864) represents a return to the discipline of the classical writers, a Ben Jonson of his age:

> Stand close around, ye Stygian set,
>> With Dirce in one boat convey'd!
> Or Charon, seeing, may forget
>> That he is old and she a shade.

And Thomas Lovell Beddoes (1803–49) goes back to the Elizabethan dramatists, particularly Webster and Tourneur, in his *The Bride's Tragedy* and *Death's Jest Book*. America made a considerable contribution to the Romantic movement, with the prose and verse of Edgar Poe (1809–49). His stories remain as models of the eerie, but his poems are less easy to assess. They had a great influence on the French Romantics, and Poe may well be regarded as the father of a whole nineteenth-century literary movement in France, but English readers sometimes find them crude, noisy, tasteless:

Influence of Poe

> I dwelt alone
> In a world of moan,
> And my soul was a stagnant tide,
> Till the fair and gentle Eulalie became my blushing bride—
> Till the yellow-haired young Eulalie became my smiling bride.

But Poe's voice is at least individual, and his experiments in verse, though often extravagant, look forward to a greater freedom of the poetic line than the English Romantics (with their love of traditional forms) would have approved.

Sir Walter Scott (1771–1832) was both poet and novelist. He first established himself (after an apprenticeship of translating from the German dramatists and poets) as a great writer of narrative verse. Poems which glorified Scotland's scenery and history—*The Lay of the Last Minstrel*, *Marmion*, *The Lady of the Lake*—made him wealthy and famous, but the poetical gift does not seem able to stay with the Romantics for long. Scott seems to have realised, at the age of forty-three, that his poetic genius was exhausted, and he turned then to the writing of novels. Nowadays we feel that he wrote too many novels, and wrote them too carelessly. This was not altogether his fault. His printers and publishers, with whom he was in partnership, went bankrupt, and Scott was faced with the task of paying off a debt of £147,000. This meant turning himself into a kind of writing-machine, churning out book after book, and sacrificing quality to quantity. After five years Scott was able to pay back £130,000, but then his health broke. He died at sixty, leaving behind a vast number of romantic novels which are not as popular as they were, and a few poems which attest to a genuine poetic genius. In verse, with

Scott

the need to compress and to make every word work hard, Scott was able to express memorably certain simple emotions—patriotism, love, the joy of battle. The fault of his novels is their long-windedness.

Scott's historical novels

Scott's themes are historical. They deal with European history—sometimes French, as in *Quentin Durward*, but more often English or Scottish. The novels about Scotland's past include *Waverley*, *Old Mortality*, *Rob Roy*, *The Heart of Midlothian*, *The Bride of Lammermoor*; England in the time of the Tudors and Stuarts is the theme of *The Fortunes of Nigel*, *Kenilworth*, *Peveril of the Peak*, and so on. What interests him most are the great political and religious conflicts of the past—the Puritans and the Jacobites (the followers of the exiled Stuarts) fascinate him especially, and against a big tapestry of historical events he tells his stories of personal hate, of revenge, of love, of the hard lives of the common people and their earthy humour. Scott has a scholar's approach to history: he is accurate and, for the most part, unbiased. His Toryism led him to choose periods when the old values flourished—chivalry, honour, courtly manners, fealty to the king—and this affects his attitude to his invented characters: the women are often too good to be true, the men too honourable or chivalrous. His style is not distinguished, and his dialogue sometimes absurdly stilted. Here is an example from *The Talisman*. (The English are fighting the Saracens; it is the age of King Richard the Lionhearted)—

'My watch hath neither been vigilant, safe nor honourable,' said Sir Kenneth. 'The banner of England has been carried off.'

'And thou alive to tell it?' said Richard in a tone of derisive incredulity. 'Away, it cannot be. There is not even a scratch on thy face. Why dost thou stand thus mute? Speak the truth—it is ill jesting with a king—yet I will forgive thee if thou hast lied.'

'Lied, Sir King!' returned the unfortunate knight, with fierce emphasis, and one glance of fire in his eye, bright and transient as the flash from the cold and stony flint. 'But this also must be endured—I have spoken the truth.'

'By God and by St. George!' said the King—[and so on].

This kind of prose became a standard for writers of historical novels. The 'out on thee, false varlet' and 'speakest thou so, sirrah?' which we now cannot take very seriously, derive from Scott. It is only fair to say that Scott has even now many ardent admirers, especially among people who love Scottish scenery. But his reputation generally is not what it was.

Jane Austen

The reputation of Jane Austen (1775–1817), on the other hand, has never been higher. She has not dated: her novels have a freshness and humour sadly lacking in Scott, a delicacy we can appreciate more than his 'big bow-wow style'. The first important woman novelist, she stands above both the classical and romantic movements; in a sense she bridges the gap between the eighteenth and nineteenth centuries, but she can be assigned to no group—she is unique. In her novels—*Sense and Sensibility*, *Pride and Prejudice*, *Mansfield Park*, *Emma*, *Northanger Abbey*, and *Persuasion*—she attempts no more than to show a small corner of English society as it was in her day—the sedate little world of the moderately well-to-do county families. This world provides her with all her material; the great historical movements rumbling outside mean little to her, and the Napoleonic Wars are hardly mentioned. Jane Austen's primary interest is people, not ideas, and her achievement lies in the meticulously exact presentation of human situations, the delineation of characters who are really living creatures, with faults and virtues mixed as they are in real life. Her plots are straightforward; there is little action. In this, and in her preoccupation with character as opposed to 'types' (the static hero and heroine and villain, beloved of Victorian novelists) she shows herself closer to our own day than any other novelist of the period. She has humour and is the creator of a gallery of richly and subtly comic portraits —Mr. Woodhouse in *Emma*, Mrs. Bennet in *Pride and Prejudice*, Sir Walter Elliot in *Persuasion*, to mention but a few. Her prose flows easily and naturally, and her dialogue is admirably true to life. She is not afraid of 'wasting words' in the interests of naturalistic dialogue, but she can also write very concisely when she wishes. A good example of her style can be found at the end of *Persuasion* (perhaps her best novel):

> Anne was tenderness itself, and she had the full worth of it in Captain Wentworth's affection. His profession was all that could ever make her friends wish that tenderness less; the dread of a future war all that could dim her sunshine. She gloried in being a sailor's wife, but she must pay the tax of quick alarm for belonging to that profession which is, if possible, more distinguished in its domestic virtues than in its national importance.

Other novelists

Other women writers included Maria Edgeworth (1767–1849), who, besides producing instructive novels for children, was, with Lady Morgan, first in the field of the Irish novel—an important branch of English literature, culminating in our own century in the *Ulysses* of James Joyce. It was Maria Edgeworth's work which inspired Scott to write of Scotland as she had written of Ireland. The same interest in 'region' inspired Miss Mitford (1786–1855) to celebrate her own village, its inhabitants, customs, and the surrounding countryside in her *Our Village: Sketches of Rural Life, Character and Scenery*.

Thomas Love Peacock (1785–1866)—known also as a poet—wrote a new kind of novel, anti-romantic, satirical, full of sly digs at Wordsworth and Shelley, at the aspirations of all the new writers of 'feeling'. 'Novel' is perhaps not quite the right term, for *Nightmare Abbey*, *Headlong Hall*, *Crotchet Castle*, and the rest are mostly collections of dialogues with little character-interest and hardly any plot. They have attained a new popularity in our own day, and they certainly influenced the early novels of

Aldous Huxley, particularly *Crome Yellow*—an entertaining work in which little is done but plenty is said.

Literary criticism

The most significant prose of the Romantic writers is not to be found in fiction. Four important writers normally grouped together are Charles Lamb (1775–1834), William Hazlitt (1778–1830), Leigh Hunt (1784–1859), and Thomas De Quincey (1785–1859). These specialised in literary criticism, in attempts to popularise the new poets (Leigh Hunt is associated with Keats, the others with Wordsworth), and in the personal literary form called the Essay. Lamb is noted for his *Essays of Elia*, in which he developed a prose-style owing much to Robert Burton, Sir Thomas Browne, and the Elizabethan poets and dramatists. It is as full of archaisms as Sir Walter Scott, but Lamb never takes himself seriously, and his sometimes over-rich style is shot with irony and self-deprecation. He is the father of that kind of English humour which derives its effects from self-mockery—the author has no ear for music, he slips on an icy street, his clothes need mending, the urchins laugh at him, he has no success with women, he makes a fool of himself in society, and so on. Lamb is a true Romantic in his Wordsworthian search for beauty in the commonplace: to him London is the home of indescribable poetic riches, with its fogs and chimney-sweeps, its cobbles and inns, beggars and book-shops. Lamb as a critic did a great deal to revive interest in the Elizabethan dramatists, and his views on the minor authors of the past are acute and imaginative. With his sister Mary Lamb he provided a children's book which is still much read: *Tales from Shakespeare*, a useful series of stepping-stones to the great plays.

Lamb

Hazlitt

Hazlitt has less of Lamb's fantasy, but his prose is vigorous and his love of the poets suffuses his style. Through him, perhaps more than Lamb, has grown the essayist's habit of interlarding his prose with lavish quotations in verse—making the essay a kind of personal anthology or, at its worst, a vehicle for showing off the author's learning. Hazlitt as a critic is still worth reading: his *Lectures on the English Poets* and *Lectures on the English Comic Writers* are admirable in their direct, forceful analysis of the essential quality of a writer, but his *Spirit of the Age*, which deals with his contemporaries, shows certain prejudices, making him unjust to poets like Wordsworth and Coleridge who, in his view, betrayed in their later work the principles they had proclaimed in their earlier writings.

Leigh Hunt

Leigh Hunt is a less important figure, despite Keats's adulation of him. (His influence on Keats was not always a good one: his verse and drama have a good deal of the sentimental, even the 'mawkish' in them, and his taste was unsure.) His essays can be read with pleasure—especially the one in which he catalogues the images of a hot English summer's day and the other in which he wittily discusses the agony of getting up on a cold morning, and his *Autobiography* gives a useful picture of the age and its literary and political personalities.

De Quincey, like Coleridge, was an opium-taker. Opium, still a familiar indulgence in the East, was to certain Romantics a means of entering a fantastic and poetic world in which history and myth came to life as on a gorgeously dressed and brilliantly lighted stage. De Quincey, with incomparable power, presents in his *The Confessions of an English Opium-Eater*, a whole series of his visions and nightmares. His prose comes near to poetry in its eloquence, suggesting Milton. As a critic he is not very important, but his *Reminiscences of the English Lake Poets* (that is, poets associated with the English Lake District—Wordsworth, Coleridge, Southey) are full of interesting and shrewd assessments of the characters of the great Romantics.

Landor I have mentioned as a poet. His classicism, strong in his verse, is as strong in his *Imaginary Conversations*, in which characters of all ages are, as in a kind of heaven or hell in which they become contemporaries of each other, brought together to express Landor's views on life and art. This is a remarkable book. For the rest, we must not forget the critics against whom the Romantics and their partisans fought so hard—critics of the old school, with classical ideas expressed in sometimes vicious attacks on Keats, Byron and, above all, Wordsworth. The *Edinburgh Review*, the *Quarterly Review*, and *Blackwood's Magazine* are, whether Whig or Tory, the voices of reaction in literature. But these voices were not to prevail: Romanticism won the war.

De Quincey

18. The Victorian Age

In devoting only a single chapter to a period of immense literary activity —on both sides of the Atlantic—I am perhaps being unjust. But I am determined that we shall see the Victorian era as a whole, and the only way we can do this is by taking a bird's-eye view, even if this means that certain great literary figures shrink to mere dots on the ground. Injustice is, anyway, a cry that every historian hears as he approaches the modern period: we are still *involved* in the world that the Victorians built, and we have strong individual opinions about its architects. We do not devote space to a writer in proportion to the number of books he wrote, or in proportion to the reputation he had in his day. Our criterion is fixed by asking the question: Is this man still worth reading? or—Is this man still exerting an influence on modern writers? It would seem that quite a number of Victorian writers, once regarded as great, are no longer read because they no longer have much to say to us. Time may reverse all this, and writers I shall treat summarily here may well, in fifty or a hundred years from now, be seen to have recovered the immense reputations they had. But we cannot speak for the future; we can only speak for the present and, however much we try to be impartial, for ourselves. With regard to the Victorians, there are many and diverse opinions about the worth of some of the literary figures, and one man's opinion is as good as another's. But the opinions held today about the Vicrotians—often most diverse—seem slowly to be coming together and forming a general attitude. The greatness of Gerard Manley Hopkins seems now to be universally acknowledged: unpublished in his own day, neglected by many literary histories with quite recent dates of publication, for a long time nobody knew what to make of him. To many critics he is now the greatest of the Victorian poets. Samuel Butler's *The Way of All Flesh* is placed now by some critics above all other Victorian novels—rightly or wrongly. The poet Clough, on the strength of one long poem, has been taken by some as seriously as Browning. Some of the old giants are becoming dwarfs, some of the dwarfs are becoming giants. Evaluation of

Criteria of criticism

Child labour in the textile factories.

the Victorian era is not yet generally fixed, and that is why it is the most difficult of periods to write about.

It seems to us to be, in some ways, a remoter period than the Elizabethan. That is because the Elizabethans were concerned with problems not unlike those of our own age. The Victorians, on the other hand, seem to be obsessed with questions peculiarly their own. First, there were such *Social and* social and political problems as could not be resolved on a purely party *political* basis. Men like William Cobbett (1762–1835) had already been agitating *problems* for parliamentary reform—more genuine representation for the people, less of the corruption and cynicism that animated politics—and, in the Reform Bill of 1832, a progressive move was made in the direction of 'democratising' parliamentary representation. (More reforms took place in 1867 and in 1884, but more were needed after that to produce the present 'universal franchise', in which everybody—except lunatics and peers—has a vote.) Whigs like Sydney Smith (1771–1845) were pressing —through the *Edinburgh Review* and other periodicals—for other reforms, including Catholic Emancipation (achieved in 1829). Slavery was denounced, and the British colonies were officially rid of it in 1833. Philosophers were concerned with important political questions; Jeremy Bentham (1748-1832) taught the doctrine of 'Utilitarianism'—'it is the greatest happiness of the greatest number that is the measure of right and wrong': Thomas Robert Malthus (1766–1834) saw that the problem of poverty could only be solved by artificially limiting the birth rate (he was derided in his day, and long after, but nowadays his theories are being accorded some respect). A bigger problem for writers than any of these was that presented by the challenge of the new science to the old Chris- *Darwin* tian faith. Darwin's Theory of Evolution hit at the Book of Genesis— man had evolved from lower forms of life; he had not been created complete by God. (*The Origin of Species*, presenting his revolutionary theory, appeared in 1859.) Materialism, which denied the existence of everything except matter—man has no soul, and even thought is secreted by the brain as bile is secreted by the liver—was another challenge to orthodox *Marx* belief. Marx's epoch-making *Das Kapital*, written in London and published in 1867, preached a new conception of society and of the distribution of wealth, and it was based on a 'materialist interpretation of history'. The Victorian age thus had a large number of problems to face. In many ways, it was an age of progress—of railway-building, steamships, reforms of all kinds—but it was also an age of doubt. There was too much poverty, too much injustice, too much ugliness, and too little certainty about faith or morals—thus it became also an age of crusaders and reformers and theorists. It was also, with all its ideals, a curiously *Puritanism* puritanical age: it was easily shocked, and subjects like sex were taboo. (Men like Bowdler, who published in 1818 his *Family Shakespeare*, from which all doubtful lines and words had been cut, anticipated the spirit of the period.) It was an age of conventional morality, of large families with the father as a godlike head, and the mother as a submissive creature like Milton's Eve. The strict morality, the holiness of family-life, owed a good deal to the example of Queen Victoria herself, and her indirect influence over literature, as well as social life, was considerable.

One characteristic of Victorian literature—especially prose—is the high moral purpose allied to a Romantic technique: language is rich and highly ornamental, a reflection of the new 'Gothic' architecture with its —to us—tasteless elaboration of design. Our first two writers—Thomas Carlyle (1795–1881) and John Ruskin (1819–1900)—used a sometimes highly involved prose for moral subjects which seemed to the age very important. Carlyle was much concerned with German philosophy and literature (he followed Coleridge and De Quincey in this). He started by interpreting German 'transcendentalism' (the term used for the doctrine of Kant that, beyond outward appearances, exist certain essences that cause these appearances but are outside the limits of knowledge) and produced an astonishing book in *Sartor Resartus* in which, borrowing from Swift's *Tale of a Tub*, he presents an imaginary German philosopher who sees experience as a suit of clothes, through which he must try to find the nakedness of reality. Later, Carlyle takes to history—his masterpiece is *The French Revolution*, a work he had to write twice, because John Stuart Mill's housemaid made the fire with the original manuscript—and his history is full of ardent moral teaching. He hated materialism and material progress: behind the suit of clothes of prosperity lay the naked truth of poverty. Life was real and earnest, and should be spent in trying to reform the world. The world could not be made a better place through democracy, however: chaos could only be overcome by obeying the born leaders, the 'heroes' of his *Heroes and Hero-Worship*. Carlyle anticipated the German Fascists in this doctrine, and indeed his very style seems permeated with the German spirit: he uses German words and German constructions, exaggerating the Germanic element in English as Milton exaggerated the Latin. It is perhaps easy to understand why he is not popular in an age which has seen too much of Carlylian heroes in action, especially in Germany.

Carlyle

Ruskin's concern was with beauty. His early works helped to set a new taste in art by praising, most eloquently, the works of the modern painters and, in books like *The Seven Lamps of Architecture* and *The Stones of Venice*, that Gothic art which came from religious faith, found at its best in the cathedrals of Europe. To Ruskin there was a close connection between art and faith—the pursuit of the beautiful becomes almost a religious duty—and it is with religious fervour that he attacks the Utilitarian doctrine (initiated, as we have seen, by Bentham, given new expression by John Stuart Mill), which seems to Ruskin to be evil. Utilitarianism meant too much freedom in trade and industry, things working

Ruskin

themselves out without reference to the problem of poverty or concern for the lot of the workers. Utilitarianism allowed squalid homes, towns disfigured by factories; denying the importance of the beautiful or the ethical, it was only concerned with profits. Its doctrine of 'economic man' was false, said Ruskin. He tackled the burning questions of poverty and ignorance in *Unto This Last* and *Sesame and Lilies*, advocating national education, social reform, and—again and again—the need to bring beauty and purpose into the lives and jobs of the workers. His prose-style, whatever its subject, maintains its mellifluous eloquence, sometimes a little too rich for modern tastes.

Arnold

The prose-writings of Matthew Arnold (1822–88), with their clarity of style, are refreshing after Carlyle and Ruskin, and his doctrines are, perhaps, more sympathetic to our own age. Ruskin wanted a return to the Middle Ages, Carlyle adored Germany, but Arnold praised Greece and Rome and wished to see something of the old 'classical harmony' in English art and life. It was the Anglo-Saxon element that Arnold disliked in English literature and 'insularity' in the English way of life. England could learn more from the Greeks or the French than from the Germans or from her own past, and could profitably strive for the qualities of 'form' and intellectuality which are typical of the art and thought of Greece or France. The English character, generally, was too dull and heavy; the English did not think enough. In the *Essays in Criticism*—in which he sees a moral purpose in poetry, which is 'a criticism of life'—he attacks the 'philistinism' of the English, their lack of concern with culture—and in *Culture and Anarchy* he makes a wider onslaught on the faults of English society. Arnold was, by profession, an inspector of schools, and his comparison of the educational systems of the Continent, particularly France, with that of England, was eventually to reform English education. He was also, as we shall see, a very important poet.

Other writers of prose—excepting, of course, the novelists—were concerned with fields of precise knowledge: Darwin and Thomas Huxley, the scientists; John Stuart Mill (1806–73), who wrote on logic, political economy, and political theory; Thomas Babington Macaulay (1800–1859) who, well known for his historical verse, such as the *Lays of Ancient Rome*, produced a brilliant, but unfinished, *History of England* which traces the English story from the reign of James II. His *Essays* (including an admirable one on Milton) show wide learning and a clear—if sometimes over-eloquent—prose-style. But philosophical works were being written also; by, among others, Herbert Spencer (1820–1903), whom Carlyle called 'the most immeasurable ass in Christendom', the founder of a philosophy based on the principle of evolution, and of an ethical system which tries to reconcile evolution and utilitarianism. The field of religious controversy produced Keble and Pusey, and greatest of all, Cardinal Newman (1801–90). The Church of England was splitting into

Philosophy and Religion

a 'Broad Church'—much influenced by rational ideas, becoming almost deistical, rejecting a great deal of the old ritual of traditional Christianity as well as its doctrine—and a 'High Church', which inclined towards Catholicism. The 'High Church' wanted a return to Catholic ceremonial and doctrine, and, in certain *Tracts for the Times* initiated at Oxford, the new tendencies are shown. This trend is usually called the Oxford Movement, but sometimes the Tractarian Movement. John Henry Newman went farther than most, rejecting Protestantism completely and joining the Church of Rome. His *Apologia pro Vita Sua* defends his conversion, giving the reasons for it in 'silver-veined' prose (James Joyce's epithet). Newman's poem, *The Dream of Gerontius*, is best-known to lovers of music, as Sir Edward Elgar set it superbly.

And so to the novel. Bulwer Lytton (1803–73) is now scarcely read, though his *Last Days of Pompeii* has been filmed, and his *Rienzi* inspired an opera by Richard Wagner. *The Coming Race* anticipates modern 'science fiction', with its race of underground supermen living on a nourishing substance called *Vril*. Benjamin Disraeli (1804–81) will long be remembered as a great Prime Minister, but his novels—including *Coningsby* and *Sybil*—can be read still for their wit and for the picture they give of Victorian political life. They enshrine many of the Conservative ideas—the new concept of democracy, Disraeli's vision of a great British Empire—which were to be translated into actuality. These novelists, however, are mere fanfares to Charles Dickens (1812–70), perhaps the greatest—if not the most perfect—of Victorian story-tellers.

Victorian novel

Dickens

Everybody is aware of the faults of Dickens—his inability to construct a convincing plot, his clumsy and sometimes ungrammatical prose, his sentimentality, his lack of real characters in the Shakespearian sense—but he is read still, while more finished artists are neglected. The secret of his popularity lies in an immense vitality, comparable to Shakespeare's, which swirls round his creations and creates a special Dickensian world which, if it does not resemble the real world, at least has its own logic and laws and its own special atmosphere. Dickens is a master of the grotesque (he is, as T. S. Eliot points out, in the direct line of Marlowe and Ben Jonson) and his characters are really 'humours'—exaggerations of one human quality to the point of caricature. Mr. Micawber is personified optimism, Uriah Heep mere creeping hypocrisy, Mr. Squeers a monster of ignorance and tyranny—they are grotesques, not human beings at all. In a sense, Dickens's world is mad—most of his characters have single obsessions which appear in practically everything they say or do, and many of them can be identified by catch-phrases like 'Barkis is willin'' or tricks of speech such as Mr. Jingle's clipped 'telegraphese' and Sam Weller's confusion of 'v' and 'w'. (The heroes and heroines are, in comparison with the full-blooded comic monsters, anaemic, conventional, and dull.) The world created by Dickens is mainly a kind of

Phiz illustration from Nicholas Nickleby.

nightmare London of chop-houses, prisons, lawyers' offices, and taverns, dark, foggy, and cold, but very much alive. Dickens's novels are all animated by a sense of injustice and personal wrong; he is concerned with the problems of crime and poverty, but he does not seem to believe that matters can be improved by legislation or reform movements—everything depends on the individual, particularly the wealthy philanthropist

(Pickwick or the Cheeryble brothers). If he has a doctrine, it is one of love.

Dickens is unlearned, his style grotesque, inelegant. But he has a lively ear for the rhythms of the speech of the uneducated, and he is not afraid of either vulgarity or sentimentality. It is his complete lack of restraint which makes for such an atmosphere of bursting vitality and for a warmheartedness that can run to an embarrassing tearfulness, as in the description of Little Nell's death in *The Old Curiosity Shop*. His novels fall roughly into groups. Starting with *Pickwick Papers*, a picaresque masterpiece in which plot does not matter, but everything depends on humorous types and on grotesque incidents (and, incidentally, on a large appetite for convivial fun, as in the picnic and Christmas scenes), Dickens moved towards historical novels—*Barnaby Rudge* and *A Tale of Two Cities*. He also concentrated on the social conditions of his own day, as in *Oliver Twist* and *Hard Times* (an attack on the Utilitarians), and presented, in *A Christmas Carol*, his view of man's duty to man—Scrooge, the miser, miraculously becomes a philanthropist; Christmas symbolises the only way in which the world can be improved—by the exercise of charity. *David Copperfield* is autobiographical in its essence, and, in its long parade of grotesques, it can be associated with *Nicholas Nickleby*. Perhaps the finest of the novels is *Great Expectations*, a long but tightly-knit work, moving, with something like penetration of character, and full of admirably conceived scenes. It is in this book that Dickens reveals, at its finest, his understanding of the mind of the child, his sympathy with its fantasies and its inability to understand the grown-up world. In some ways, Dickens remained a child: it is the weird wonderland of ogres and fairies that one finds perpetually recurring in his books.

This is a convenient place to mention briefly two Victorian writers who frankly, without any disguise, explored the world of fantasy for the benefit of children but were perhaps themselves more at home in that world than in Victorian Utilitarian England. These writers are very widely read—Lewis Carroll, pseudonym of Charles Dodgson (1832–98), and Edward Lear (1812–88). Carroll's *Alice's Adventures in Wonderland* and *Through the Looking-Glass* have a mad Dickensian flavour with a curious undercurrent of logic (Dodgson was a mathematician); Lear's nonsense rhymes are also mad, but far less mad than some of the works of the sane writers. Carroll and Lear are among the literary riches of the Victorian era; they may well be read when Carlyle and Ruskin are forgotten.

Carroll

Lear

It is customary to group with Dickens a novelist who does not resemble him in the slightest—William Makepeace Thackeray (1811–63). Dickens wrote of low life and was a warm-blooded romantic; Thackeray wrote of the upper classes and was anti-romantic. Thackeray started his career as a satirist, and wrote many humorous articles for the comic weekly *Punch*, also a couple of curious works—*The Book of Snobs* and the

Thackeray

Yellowplush Papers—which made fun of the pretensions of the upper-classes and their worshippers in the middle-classes—and then wrote a novel in the manner of Fielding—*The Luck of Barry Lyndon*, which, like Fielding's *Jonathan Wild*, makes a rogue complacently recount his wicked exploits as if they were thoroughly moral and lawful. *Vanity Fair* is still his most-read work: it tells of the careers of two girls with sharply contrasted characters—Becky Sharp, unscrupulous and clever; Amelia Sedley, pretty, moral but unintelligent—and draws clever—wickedly clever—portraits of officers and gentlemen of the time of Waterloo. His historical novels, such as *Esmond* and *The Virginians*, are very different in technique from those of Scott. The first tells, in autobiographical form, of a man who lives through the age of Queen Anne and of the Georges who follow, and it shows a remarkable knowledge of the literature and life of the eighteenth century. In many ways, Thackeray is closer to the Age of Reason than to his own times. But his book for children—*The Rose and the Ring*—is one of the best-loved of all Victorian fantasies, and a certain tenderness that Thackeray hides in such works as *Vanity Fair* appears in *The Newcomes*, with its portrait of the gentle childlike old Colonel. His deathbed scene should be contrasted with Little Nell's: 'He, whose heart was as that of a little child, had answered to his name, and stood in the presence of the Master.' Capable of tenderness, but never of sentimentality, Thackeray is in many ways the superior of Dickens, but he lacks that strange, mad glamour that Dickens shares with Shakespeare.

Brontës

Meanwhile, in the isolation of a Yorkshire vicarage, three sisters, none of them destined to live long, were writing novels and poems. Charlotte Brontë (1816–55), who admired Thackeray, dedicated her most un-Thackerayan novel, *Jane Eyre*, to him. Here, in this story of the governess who falls in love with her master, himself married to a madwoman, we have a passion not to be found in either Thackeray or Dickens, a genuine love-story of great realism, full of sharp observation and not without wit. This story, with its frank love-scenes, was something of a bombshell. Charlotte Brontë's *The Professor*, later re-written—with some quite radical changes—as *Villette*, tells of her own experiences as a teacher in Brussels, and *Shirley* is concerned with industrial Yorkshire. *Jane Eyre*, one of the really significant Victorian novels, remains her masterpiece. Emily Brontë (1818–48) had, if anything, a more remarkable talent than her sister. Her poems are vital and original, and her novel *Wuthering Heights* is the very heart and soul of the romantic spirit, with its story of wild passion set against the Yorkshire moors. Anne Brontë (1820–49), with her *Agnes Grey* and *The Tenant of Wildfell Hall*, is perhaps best remembered now because of her sisters: her talent is smaller than theirs.

Other novelists

Other novelists included Mrs. Gaskell (1810–65), Charles Kingsley (1819–75), Charles Reade (1814–84), and Wilkie Collins (1825–89). The first three are much concerned with social reform. Mrs. Gaskell, most read for *Cranford,* a study of life in a small provincial town, also wrote *Mary Barton* and *Ruth,* full of pity for the down-trodden dwellers in factory towns, the working-class exploited by profit-seeking capitalists. Kingsley preaches a kind of Christian Communism in *Alton Locke* and *Yeast,* but turns to the Elizabethan past in *Westward Ho!* and to the world of the Vikings in *Hereward the Wake. The Water Babies,* a story of a little chimney sweep who runs away from his master and, falling into a river, learns of the under-water world, is a charming fantasy still read. Reade attacked such social abuses as the state of the prisons and the lunatic asylums in *It is Never Too Late to Mend* and *Hard Cash,* but his story of the late Middle Ages, *The Cloister and the Hearth,* keeps his name alive. Wilkie Collins is, at present, enjoying a revival of interest with his *Woman in White* and *The Moonstone.* He is the first great British writer of mystery-stories, and to a gift of maintaining suspense, terror, and a credible plot he adds a clear prose-style which is quite individual.

Anthony Trollope (1815–88) invented a county called Barset and a town called Barchester, and, in novel after novel (*The Warden, Barchester Towers, Dr. Thorne, Framley Parsonage, The Small House at Allington,* and *The Last Chronicle of Barset*) he paints life in a provincial cathedral town atmosphere, with humour and without passion. His work is a little too lacking in warmth for some people, but he has still many devotees. Trollope, who worked in the General Post Office and was busy there, was only able to write by forcing on himself a mechanical routine—so many pages per day, no rest between finishing one book and starting another. This perhaps explains a lack of inspiration in his novels; but, in good, plain, undistinguished prose, he builds up his own world, and this world has a remote charm.

George Eliot (1819–90), whose real name was Mary Ann Evans, is also a writer with admirers, but she has not commanded the same general love as Dickens. There are signs, however, of a new interest in her work, and penetrating critical studies about her have been published (notably Joan Bennett's book). Her life is interesting: she lived, unmarried, with George Henry Lewes from about 1854 to 1878 (the year of his death) and had less than a year of legal marriage (with Walter Cross) before she died. Her strong personality and fine mind are evident from her books— *Scenes of Clerical Life, Adam Bede, The Mill on the Floss, Romola, Middlemarch, Daniel Deronda,* and others. She was interested in German philosophy (some of which she translated) but, despite a strong religious upbringing, could not retain a belief in Christianity. Despite this, she shows sympathy in her novels for the faith of others and she is always concerned with moral problems. She deals mostly with country people (the Tullivers in *The Mill on the Floss* are especially memorable), has a gift for reproducing their speech and a taste for their humour. George Eliot is important because she is prepared (unlike Dickens) to analyse human

George Eliot

conduct, to show the moral consequences of even trivial actions—this makes her very modern—and to show how the minds of even humble people can be made noble through suffering. In a word, it is human dignity she is concerned with, even though she knows how to puncture pretensions with a sharp needle of satire.

Meredith

George Meredith (1828–1909) is perhaps equally important. His verbal gift is shown in his poetry, and it sometimes tends to obscure the content of his novels. He liked verbal smartness, remote references to subjects and books not generally known, and in his last works is sometimes hard to understand. His main novels are *The Ordeal of Richard Feverel*, *The Egoist*, and *Diana of the Crossways*, though he wrote many others, not all of them popular in his day. The reason why he did not make a great appeal to the Victorian mind—but is much more sympathetic to our own—lies in his approach to his characters. He was aware of conflict in man and woman, the conflict between what society demands and the fundamental brute desire for assertion which lies in even the most civilised. This conflict is expressed in terms which are often subtly comic, but Meredith can unleash poetry in depicting human passion. His attitude to women is a world away from the conventional Victorian view: women must assert their own individuality against brutal man, must become more intelligent and willing to understand the forces of human life. *The Egoist* is the best novel with which first to approach Meredith.

Butler

Last of the novelists, and in many ways the man who has most to say to our own age, is Samuel Butler (1835–1902). He wrote *Erewhon* and *Erewhon Revisited* (*Erewhon*, being 'Nowhere' anagrammatised, suggests *Utopia*), which, with characters with names like Nosnibor, are obviously pictures of England, highly satirical, full of attacks on English institutions and English stupidity. The 'Musical Banks', where one can draw money which will only be of use in the next world, are obviously Christian churches, and the 'Book of the Machines' warns that machines may well develop to a point where they can destroy human beings and take over their function. Butler has no mercy on Victorian England, and his masterpiece, *The Way of All Flesh*, is a sustained onslaught on everything the Victorians held dear. It is the story of Ernest Pontifex, his upbringing by tyrannical parents who think themselves models of rectitude; his entry into the Church of England as a curate and his discovery that its brand of formal Christianity is a sham, and his eventual emergence as a man of wealth, tolerance and easy humour. He learns to take little seriously except a belief that evolution works not only in the world of nature but also in the world of mind, and that gradually something like common sense will drive out the old superstitions, whether religious or social. Butler attacks not only the Church but also the family, the institution of marriage, and the false gods of Victorian education. He has had a considerable influence on some modern writers, having suggested to

Bernard Shaw the theory of 'creative evolution' and to others a special brand of ironical humour, and such techniques of novel-writing as enable the author to probe deep into the mind of his characters, uncovering layers which the average Victorian writer hardly knew existed. *The Way of All Flesh* is a very amusing novel, full of masterly character sketches— Dr. Skinner, Mrs. Jupp, Ernest's parents, and, for that matter, the narrator, who is partly Samuel Butler himself. (In order to avoid confusion with the seventeenth-century satirist, you can speak of Hudibras Butler and Erewhon Butler.)

Prose-writings of general interest include the studies of gypsies by George Borrow (1803–81)—*Lavengro* and *The Romany Rye*—and his travel-book *The Bible in Spain*. Borrow is full of the open air and 'the wind on the heath'. A. W. Kinglake (1809–91) wrote about the Muslim world in *Eöthen*, as did Richard Burton (1821–90) who, in disguise, made the pilgrimage to Mecca and wrote about it. He is best known for his translation of the *Arabian Nights*.

We turn now to the poetry of the age. Alfred Tennyson (1809–92), who later was made Lord Tennyson for his contribution to literature, sums up many of the preoccupations of the period in work which is thoroughly Romantic. Romantic, however, with a difference, for Tennyson brings to his sensuous verse a care, a deliberate contrivance of effect, which suggests Pope more than Keats. His music is distinctive, but its flow is by no means 'artless'—nothing is left to chance. The first works are 'irresponsible', delighting in the world of the senses, but the sense of Victorian responsibility is not long in coming, and moral problems begin to intrude. *The Palace of Art* teaches that beauty must be shared (a Ruskinian notion), almost suggesting the substitution of art galleries and public libraries for the aristocratic gloating over personal treasures. Tennyson shows a gift here which is almost macabre—the sudden intrusion of terrible portents—ghosts and corpses—into a world of calm beauty and, frequently, his carefully tended Victorian gardens (as in *Mariana*) become full of the stench of decay. Keats could take a purely aesthetic pleasure in Homeric legend, but Tennyson's *Ulysses* (in a fine, austere blank-verse monologue) stands for the need to strive, to search 'and not to yield'. In *The Two Voices* we hear the conflict of a mind whose orthodox Christianity is troubled by the new materialism; but orthodox belief wins, and Tennyson sees in the Victorian family, on its way to worship, with the church-bells ringing, a symbol of stability and hope. *In Memoriam*, inspired by grief at the death of a friend, Hallam, sets out in greater detail the Victorian dilemma; in his despondency, the poet becomes morbidly aware of how the new science has made man shrink to insignificance in the universe, but, again, Christianity wins—intuition is better than scientific knowledge, Tennyson *knows* that religion has the answer to life's riddles. Again, the final symbol of security is the marriage

Tennyson

of two people pure in heart. Tennyson is most Victorian in his attitude to the sexes: the men and women of his *Idylls of the King*—a return to Arthurian legend—are nothing like Malory's; their morality is Victorian, they may sin, but the code of Victorian respectability always wins. In *Maud* and *Locksley Hall* there may be bitterness towards woman, towards the mealy-mouthed girl who rejects passion for a safe marriage, but generally Tennyson does not grapple with problems of sex; illicit love is nearly always taboo, Christian marriage is unshakable. It is rarely, indeed, that we see the flesh of a woman: even *Oenone*, with its Greek goddesses, seems to be describing the conventional Venus of a Victorian painter. The goddesses appear naked, but their nakedness is as moral as that of an allegorical statue. Finally, Tennyson is an optimist. Some of his visions, as in *Locksley Hall*, are of a happy, liberal future and even 'The Parliament of Man, the Federation of the World'. As a technician, he is unsurpassed, and the skill with which he manages the simple stanza of the long *In Memoriam*—immense variety, no monotony—is superb.

Browning   Robert Browning (1812–89) approaches, in his language and imagery, the poetry of our own time. Both are, to some extent, anti-romantic: there are railway-trains, cigars, grand pianos, 'scrofulous French novels' and trousers; language is often colloquial and even slangy. There is also humour (rarely found in the Romantics) and a kind of self-mockery in the grotesque rhymes that Browning sometimes uses (*The Pied Piper*, his children's poem, shows how far he can go: the ending, with its 'from mice'/'promise' rhyme, is an extreme example). He also suggests the modern poets in his obscurity (as he also suggests Donne), but Browning's obscurity does not derive from complexity of thought; it comes from an impatience with language and a deliberate desire to dazzle the reader—Browning's vocabulary is large and his fondness for little-known words proverbial. His early *Sordello* is so difficult that, of one of the lines, Browning himself said, 'When I wrote that only God and Robert Browning knew what it meant; now God only knows.'

Browning, after first paying homage to Shelley in *Pauline*, thought of himself as a dramatist ('Robert Browning, you writer of plays'). But his stage-plays were not successful, and he found his best dramatic outlet in the form he cultivated most—the dramatic monologue. In *Men and Women* and *Dramatis Personae* he put into the mouths of various historical characters (often obscure painters and musicians of Italy and Germany) certain philosophical themes which, together, make up Browning's answer to the Victorian dilemma. He is aware of division in the human soul and of despondency at failure to achieve happiness: his answer is always 'Act!' He believes that our mere attempts to order our lives—however unsuccessful—find their reward in heaven; whatever we start and leave uncompleted, God himself will complete. His *Abt Vogler* puts it succinctly: 'On earth the broken arcs, in heaven the perfect round.'

His poems about love are vigorous and virile: he believes again in acting rather than vacillating when love is crossed. *The Statue and the Bust* tells of two lovers who, unable to be together because of circumstantial difficulties, die apart; now a statue and a bust, perpetually gazing at each other, mock their timidity. Browning's own courtship of Elizabeth Barrett, and his elopement with her, translated his doctrine into action. Browning's optimism—'God's in his heaven—All's right with the world!'—no longer makes much appeal to an age which finds it hard to be optimistic. We appreciate Browning best as the dramatic realist—his *Ring and the Book*, a long murder-story in verse, has a psychological penetration which is after our own hearts, his technique is always vigorous and fresh, but his message has perhaps lost some of its appeal.

Elizabeth Barrett Browning (1806–61) was, in her day, thought to be superior as a poet to her husband. Her *Aurora Leigh*, a blank-verse novel, was hailed as the greatest thing since Shakespeare, but, though it is readable, we cannot now find many marks of greatness in it. Her lyrics— especially the *Sonnets from the Portuguese*—are pretty, displaying a woman's passion which seems feeble in comparison with Emily Brontë's and technically little more than competent.

Elizabeth Browning

Arthur Hugh Clough (1819–61) is one of those puzzling figures who, at times seeming very much part of his age, can suddenly leap into the present with a modern technique and a modern attitude to life. His *Amours de Voyage*, published in 1849, sounds, in places, as though it were written yesterday:

Clough

> I do not like being moved: for the will is excited; and action
> Is a most dangerous thing; I tremble for something factitious,
> Some malpractice of heart and illegitimate process;
> We are so prone to these things, with our terrible notions of duty.

The division in Clough's soul is a modern division and also an Elizabethan one; the fear of action is Hamlet's sickness and our own. In Matthew Arnold (1822–88), who produced in *Thyrsis* a moving elegy on the death of Clough, we have also something of the modern spirit—a pessimism (as in *Dover Beach*) which cannot be healed either by going back to Christianity or assuming a vigorous but over-simple philosophy like Browning's. In *The Scholar Gipsy* we have a lament over 'this strange disease of modern life' and a yearning to return to an age when faith was sure—but return is impossible. Arnold's technique is classical, restrained, lacking the excessive decoration of some of Tennyson, but he is prepared to experiment and use that 'free verse' which we like to regard as a purely twentieth-century innovation.

Dante Gabriel Rossetti (1828–82), his sister Christina Rossetti (1830–1894), and William Morris (1834–96) belong to the 'Pre-Raphaelite' group. The title is derived from the painter Raphael, who is the first of

Rossettis

'Acanthus' Pattern Wall Paper by William Morris.

the Renaissance painters, with their love of richness and colour, their
devotion to man rather than God. Ruskin had taught a return to the old
simplicity of the Middle Ages, in which art expressed faith, and both
Rossetti and Morris, in their paintings, had striven for an unexciting,

calm simplicity which also found its way into their poems. The faith of the Middle Ages was not so important to these poets as what they believed to be the essential mediaeval qualities of art. They wanted a certain remote strangeness in their work, they sought mediaeval subjects, they avoided the philosophy and controversy of poets like Tennyson and Browning. But Christina Rossetti, in her frightening *Goblin Market*, got something of the moral tone of Tennyson allied to a magic of her own. Her brother's work has echoes of the mediaeval Italian sonnet-writers (in *The House of Life*) and, in *The Blessed Damozel*, he attempts the simplicity of the ballads but produces something quite un-ballad-like. This poem suggests one of Rossetti's own paintings, a certain artificial straining after simplicity, a religious atmosphere which does not seem to spring from religious faith. The achievement of Morris lies not perhaps in the field of poetry but in that more utilitarian one of spreading, like Ruskin, the artistic light in everyday life. Wall-paper, book-binding, printing, painting—Morris 'beautified' all these, but his poems are thin, sweet, pleasant but insubstantial, and his writings were, in their own day, perhaps greatly over-praised.

Algernon Charles Swinburne (1837–1909) is a poet who also deserts thought and hymns beauty. He is much influenced by contemporary French poets, particularly Baudelaire (whose astonishing volume *Fleurs du Mal*—'Flowers of Evil'—came out, like *Aurora Leigh*, in 1857: Mrs. Browning, in retrospect, suffers somewhat from this coincidence). Swinburne takes as his theme some aspect of the old Romantic spirit of revolt —down with morality and religion!—but his main aim seems merely to shock. Shock he did; the *Poems and Ballads* with their sensuality and noise had an almost Byronic impact on the public. Nowadays it is hard to see what the fuss was about. Swinburne has a fine musical gift and can overwhelm the ear with his alliteration and his 'mighty line', but beneath the jewelled words is a great emptiness. He was a thoughtful critic, however, and his work on behalf of the Elizabethan dramatists and William Blake helped to restore interest in writers who were, for the Victorians, somewhat strong meat.

Swinburne

George Meredith shone both as poet and novelist. His *Modern Love* has the same insight into human relationships as is shown in the novels, and his compact verse haunts the ear. He is a fine nature-poet, too, and the magic of such a poem as *The Woods of Westermain*—'Enter these enchanted woods, you who dare'—is the pure stuff of Romanticism. There is a subtlety and obscurity about some of his *Odes* which seems distinctly 'modern', and they proclaim a finer mind than Browning's.

Edward Fitzgerald (1809–83) produced a series of quatrains which are still widely read, though they had to be rescued from obscurity in their own day by Rossetti. These verses are very free translations of the *Rubáiyát* of the Persian poet, Omar Khayyam. To anyone who knows the

Fitzgerald

original, Fitzgerald must seem to miss much of the wit and 'meta-physical' quality of the Muslim tent-maker, but much of his pessimism is retained—life is vanity, therefore drink wine; of life after death we know nothing, therefore make the most of this life. But Fitzgerald brought to a complacent Victorian England at least a little of the fatalistic spirit of the East, and he illustrates one aspect of the impact of science on faith—the complete loss of faith, and a kind of hedonistic scepticism.

Hopkins

Finally, we must glance briefly at Gerard Manley Hopkins (1844–89), a Jesuit priest, follower of Newman, who, after ordination, burned his early poems, but, at the request of his superior, began writing again in his thirties, and produced work that, had it been published in his lifetime, would never have made much appeal. His poems were published in 1918, and he became almost immediately a powerful influence. We see him as a 'modern', but his work belongs to the very heart of the Victorian era. He is a deeply religious poet, perpetually aware of God's power and beauty as manifested in nature, but also convinced of his own unworthiness and, in his final sonnets, even of his damnation. His technique is so revolutionary that it makes Tennyson and Browning look stale and out-moded: the very surface of his verse, with its tight compression, seems hard as steel, and his compound epithets are more daring than anything in Tennyson or Carlyle—'fresh-firecoal chestnut-falls', 'Miracle-in-Mary-of-flame', 'down-dugged ground-hugged grey', 'the O-seal-that-so feature', 'wilful-wavier meal-drift'. He uses language in a highly individual way, but he is always logical, choosing a dialect-word where a Standard English one cannot give his meaning, playing tricks with grammar for the sake of a more forceful emphasis. The new rhythmical system that had 'haunted his ear' during his long poetic silence, rushed into life in the elegy *The Wreck of the Deutschland*, and 'sprung rhythm' at last became a principle in English verse. Traditional English verse acknowledged two factors: a fixed number of stresses, a more or less fixed number of syllables to the line. Thus blank verse had to have, traditionally, five stresses and ten, or eleven, syllables:

It may be that the gulfs will wash us down.—*Tennyson*.

Sprung rhythm reverted almost to the principles of Old English verse: a fixed pattern of stresses, but any number of syllables, the idea being that English stresses are so strong that they can hold the line together, without any need for a syllabic pattern as well. Here is an example from Hopkins's *Duns Scotus's Oxford*:

Towery city and branchy between towers;

Cuckoo-echoing, bell-swarmèd, lark-charmèd, rook-racked,

river-rounded . . .

The Road to the Great Exhibition, London 1851.

This is the opening of a sonnet which, in rhyme-scheme, is almost un-usually regular (Hopkins wrote many sonnets, and never played tricks with the rhyme-scheme, unlike Wordsworth). But the first line has ten syllables, the second line has seventeen syllables. Yet both lines take about the same time to recite, for both lines have the same pattern of five stresses. The principle is roughly that of music, where a bar of four beats can have any number of notes, so long as the fundamental rhythm is not destroyed. Sprung rhythm has meant a good deal to modern poets. Other poetical habits of Hopkins have also been borrowed—the frequent alliteration, internal rhyme, use of compound words—but few poets have been able to borrow his intensity, his clear-sightedness, his sense of con-flict, not only within but in the world without:

> Where, selfwrung, selfstrung, sheath- and shelterless, thoughts against
>
> thoughts in groans grind.

19. Fresh Life in the Drama

Dramatic decline

We have been neglecting the drama, chiefly because the drama, from the death of Sheridan on, neglected itself. The only licensed theatres in London, between the Restoration and the Theatre Regulating Act of 1843, were Drury Lane, Covent Garden, and (from 1766) the Haymarket; the first two of these were very large—large, because they had to accommodate vast numbers which, obviously, could not be dispersed into other theatres. The result of this largeness was a crude kind of drama—only the most grotesque facial distortions of the actors could be seen (and even then, said one critic, a telescope was needed) and only the loudest speeches could be heard. This inevitably meant a drama lacking in subtlety and intimacy and (less of a problem than genuine plays) spectacles, burlesques, pantomimes, simple but lavishly-staged entertainments of all kinds. There were, admittedly, a number of unlicensed theatres in London, but these were only allowed by law to present musical shows. Some of them, however, managed to put on 'straight plays' with many musical interludes or almost continuous musical accompaniments, thus getting round the law, and these plays were called melodramas (literally, music-dramas or plays with music). The features of melodrama are still well-known from revivals (usually meant to be laughed at) of plays like *Sweeney Todd* and *Maria Marten* (authors unknown: we are back now to the mediaeval tradition of anonymity). Villainy is black, virtue too good to be true. Violence, sadism, attempted seduction, posturing, low humour, murder, sensationalism, conventional moralising—all are to be found in the melodramas of the early nineteenth century, and the term 'melodramatic' has ever since been a disparaging one. But when the Regulating Act was passed in 1843, breaking the monopoly of the three theatres holding the Royal Patent (or licence), drama was able to return to the smaller theatres and had a chance to regain its old qualities of subtlety and intimacy: the trouble was that there were so few dramatists able to meet the challenge.

Melodrama

In the early part of the century, practically all the poets—from Keats to Browning—tried their hands at five-act blank-verse plays, but these were foredoomed to failure because they were conceived in the study, not the theatre. It was as though the authors said: 'Shakespeare was a great poet: I am a great poet. Shakespeare was a great dramatist: therefore I can be a great dramatist.' The false logic of this was proved by short runs and scanty box-office returns. The belief also that the future of drama lay in its past—in imitations of Shakespeare, rather than in original and modern experiments—held back a dramatic revival. The superstition about the intrinsic value of blank verse and mythical or historical themes seemed to hold until the present century: Stephen Phillips (1864–1913), with his *Ulysses* and *Paolo and Francesca,* was for a time much admired, but his glamour was only a glamour of association with the glorious Elizabethan era. Perhaps today Christopher Fry (1907–   ) is the same sort of phenomenon, but it is too early to say.

Beginnings of revival   Drama owed more to its producers and actors (men like Henry Irving) than to its authors. But one sees the beginnings of a new dramatic outlook in the work of Thomas William Robertson (1829–71), especially in *Caste* (1867). *Caste* is not a great play, but at least it has a credible story and characters, and its construction points to a genuine knowledge of the theatre. Its subject may now seem out-of-date—a girl of the lower classes should not marry into the upper classes, but there are exceptions, and here is one—but at least it presents a thought-out subject which is worked out logically. The play has pathos, comedy, 'situations', it is not too long and it does not bore. This is a great deal to be thankful for. Henry Arthur Jones (1851–1929) learned a lot from France, especially Sardou, and began to specialise in the 'well-made' play which Sardou is noted for (he can be noted for little else). Jones introduced contemporary problems, contemporary speech, and wished to startle Victorian audiences into regarding the drama as a serious entertainment. His plays number altogether about sixty, and some of them—*The Liars, The Silver King, Saints and Sinners,* for example—are occasionally revived. Arthur Wing Pinero (1855–1934) went even farther than Jones, presenting in *The Second Mrs. Tanqueray* a 'dissolute-woman' theme which still has power to shock sensitive audiences. Other plays of his, especially *Trelawny of the 'Wells'* (the old *Caste* subject, with the actress meeting opposition from the family of the aristocrat she wants to marry), *Mid-Channel* (the problems of a married couple who have reached a critical point in their relationship), and *The Weaker Sex,* show a mastery of form and knowledge of the stage which even very 'modern' playwrights like Noel Coward (1899–1973) have thought it worth while to copy.

Wilde   But English drama in its renascent stage needed other elements than a mere attempt at 'realism'—it needed fantasy and wit. Oscar Wilde (1854–1900) gave it wit in his admirable artificial comedy *The Importance of Being Earnest,* one of the most amusing plays ever written, a comedy of man-
Gilbert and Sullivan ners worthy to rank with Sheridan. W. S. Gilbert (1836–1911) produced

with Arthur Sullivan the famous series of comic operas—*H.M.S. Pinafore, Patience, The Mikado,* and the rest—which combined satire with smart lyrics and ravishing music. These operas are inimitable, a phenomenon that only comes once in theatrical history: their originality of theme and treatment is attested by the fact that they can be described only as 'Gilbertian'. Gilbert's skill as a stage-producer, and especially his concern with clarity of speech, helped also to improve standards of acting in the theatre generally.

But the really great dramatic genius of the age was to come, not from England, but from Norway. Henrik Ibsen's work cannot be considered here, but we must note the tremendous impact it made on the English theatre. Ibsen (1828–1906) delved deep into the social and domestic problems of his age (problems common to both Scandinavia and England), and his presentation of a failed marriage in *A Doll's House,* and the sins of the fathers being visited on their children in *Ghosts*, caused a sensation when William Archer translated these plays into English for production in London. George Bernard Shaw (1856–1950) defended Ibsen against the attacks of the critics, and stated that this was the way the new drama should go—it should not be afraid to shock, it should concentrate on ideas, it should rely on its own inner life rather than on external 'accidents' like spectacle and comic turns. Shaw put his own notions of drama into practice, and from *Widowers' Houses* (1892) onward he dominated the European theatre. *Influence of Ibsen*

Shaw

Shaw had many things to say, all of them important, but he should not be regarded as a mere preacher who used the stage as a platform. Being an Irishman like Wilde and Sheridan, he had a native gift of eloquence and wit, and—much helped by his interest in music—a sharp ear for the tones and rhythms of contemporary speech. For the 'well-made' play he had little use: he constructed his dramas on rules of his own, some of them most irregular, but he knew that, whatever tricks he played, his ability to hold the audience's attention through sheer *words* would carry him through. Thus, *Getting Married* is written in one huge act, lasting over two hours; *Back to Methuselah* lasts for five nights; *Man and Superman* shifts the main characters to a mythological plane right in the middle of the story, and keeps them there for a long time arguing philosophically. Shaw deliberately uses anachronism, making Cain in the Garden of Eden quote Tennyson, and Cleopatra speak in the words of Shelley; early Christians sing a hymn by Sir Arthur Sullivan, and Queen Elizabeth I use a line of Lady Macbeth's long before Shakespeare wrote it. Strict realism is not necessary to Shaw's purpose: speech can be, at one moment, colloquial, and, at another, biblical; history can be distorted and probability ignored—it does not matter in the least.

Shaw was a disciple of Samuel Butler, but of other philosophers as well. His doctrine of the Superman comes from Germany—Friedrich *Shaw's iconoclasm*

Nietzsche (1844–1900)—and his theory of Creative Evolution owes something to Henri Bergson (1859–1941). But he had his own views on practically everything. Generally, the aim in his early plays is to make audiences (and readers) examine their consciences and overhaul their conventional beliefs. Thus, he attacks those people who derive their rents from slums in *Widowers' Houses,* faces the question of prostitution in *Mrs. Warren's Profession,* subjects the medical profession to critical scrutiny in *The Doctor's Dilemma,* and deflates the glory of war in *Arms and the Man.* He turns the conventional assumptions of English society upside-down, so that woman becomes the stronger sex and man the weaker, man the dreamer, woman the realist, woman the pursuer, man the pursued. This is an important idea in Shaw, and is the basis of *Man and Superman.* Shaw conceives of a great creative will in the universe, which is endeavouring to produce higher and higher forms of life (Creative Evolution). As woman has the greater part to play in the making of new life, it follows that, perhaps quite unconsciously, she will look for a man in whom the germs of human superiority lie, pursue him, mate him, and help forward the evolution of the Superman. The power of *will* is also the theme of *Back to Methuselah* which, in five separate plays, whose action starts with Adam and Eve and ends in the remotest possible future, presents the thesis that only by living longer can man become wiser; longevity is a matter of will: as Adam and Eve willed individual death but immortality for the race, so we can will individual immortality.

Shaw was fascinated by ideas of all kinds, and he used his outstanding dramatic skill to publicise all sorts of notions—from the importance of the science of phonetics (*Pygmalion*) to the 'Protestantism' of Joan of Arc (*St. Joan*). He attacked everything (being a born rebel) but, strangely, he never lays a finger on the Christian religion—the Church, yes, but belief, no. Shaw was a great rationalist, very like the Frenchman Voltaire, *His mysticism* but there was a deep core of mysticism in him. At times he sounds like an Old Testament prophet, and his finest speeches (as of Lilith at the end of *Back to Methuselah*) are in the great tradition of English biblical prose. Finally, his work will endure for its dramatic coherence, its wit, its common sense, and a literary gift which prevented him from ever writing a dull line.

Shaw's influence   The Shavian influence is to be found mainly in the work of the Scotsman James Bridie (Dr. Osborne Henry Mavor) (1888–1951). Certain Shavian tricks occur in play after play—*The Black Eye, Tobias and the Angel, A Sleeping Clergyman*—where impatience with the orthodox Pinero-esque forms make him experiment with dialogue, staging, and plot in Shaw's manner. He has the same concern with morals as Shaw, and the same desire to uncover the truth that lies beneath conventions and superstitions. (Even T. S. Eliot cannot resist giving to his four knights in *Murder in the Cathedral* long Shavian speeches, and this after pages and pages of dramatic poetry which go back, in form, to *Everyman*.)

Dramatists who owed more to Ibsen in their tense grappling with social problems were Harley Granville-Barker (1877–1946), John Galsworthy (1867–1933), and St. John Ervine (1883–   ), though, because some of their social problems no longer exist, they have dated somewhat. They liked to throw a challenge to the audience, to make them think deeply about injustice and inequality and perhaps puzzle out an answer to certain problems for themselves. Galsworthy, for example, wonders, in *Strife*, whether workers' strikes really achieve anything, and, in *The Silver Box*, whether the law for the poor is really the same as the law for the rich, and, in *Escape*, whether perhaps the answer to many of our problems lies not in external reforms but in fundamental human 'decency'. *Social problems in drama*

In Ireland there were certain important dramatists who found a platform in the Abbey Theatre, Dublin, which was founded in 1904. In effect, there were two movements—a realistic one which followed Ibsen and a poetic one which sought inspiration in Irish myth and legend. But, the Irish mind being what it is, and the Irish approach to English being naturally poetical, all the new Irish drama has a vitality and colour that Galsworthy and the rest could never approach. William Butler Yeats (1865–1939) is the first great name. In *Cathleen ni Houlihan, The Countess Cathleen, The Land of Heart's Desire,* and others he used blank verse— individual in tone, but sometimes too dreamy and lyrical to be effective on the stage—and drew on old stories and traditions—even superstitions—of the Irish people. All the plays he wrote eventually found their way to the Abbey Theatre, where they tended to excite anger and opposition from conservative Irish audiences. Perhaps a greater dramatist was John Millington Synge (1871–1909), whose *Playboy of the Western World, Riders to the Sea, The Tinker's Wedding,* and others, dealt with the Irish peasantry and used a wonderfully rich and poetical style which was itself based on Irish peasant speech. The plays are completely realistic, and, because Irish audiences thought that Synge was defaming the Irish character when he was merely telling the truth about human character, they met with a stormy reception. Synge's genius is now universally acknowledged. Sean O'Casey (1884–1964) is responsible for plays about the Dublin slums which touch the rock-bottom of reality. *Juno and the Paycock* is a masterpiece, tragic but shot with uproarious comedy, and *The Shadow of a Gunman* and *The Plough and the Stars* are brilliantly realistic. Non-realistic effects—symbolism, song, poetry, soliloquy—are to be found in later plays like *Within the Gates* and *Red Roses for Me,* as though O'Casey has stirring within him the poetic urge which no Irishman (not even Shaw) can completely subdue. *Irish Drama* *Yeats* *O'Casey*

There is not a great deal to be proud of in the work of *English* dramatists in the modern period. Fantasy came with a Scotsman—James Matthew Barrie (1860–1937)—to give the English theatre a touch of *English dramatists*

Hardy.

T. S. Eliot.

W. B. Yeats.

Conrad.

'faery'. Barrie is not in favour at present (except with children, who love *Peter Pan*), chiefly because of a strong sentimentality which disfigures such plays as *Mary Rose, Alice-Sit-By-The-Fire,* and *A Kiss for Cinderella.* But the construction of his plays is sound, he is capable of quite robust humour, and he has interesting ideas, as is shown in *Dear Brutus* and *The Admirable Crichton.* Dramatists of English blood (Shakespeare's blood) tended to follow the tradition of the 'well-made' play established by Pinero. William Somerset Maugham (1874–1965) wrote three-act *drames* (the French term for plays which are neither comedy nor tragedy) on social themes—marriage, adultery, the conflict between children and parents. His last play, *Sheppey,* is among his most original, with its ironical but touching examination of the place of human charity in a non-religious age. Noel Coward (1899–1973), the complete 'man of the theatre', shows skill rather than depth, but he interprets adequately (sometimes sentimentally) the disillusioned world of the 1920s. Terence Rattigan (1912–   ) continued the tradition of social comedy, but in *The Browning Version* seems to have gone deeper with his analysis of a stoical schoolmaster's soul.

John Boynton Priestley (1894–   ), known principally as the author of such novels as *The Good Companions* and *Angel Pavement,* has written social dramas which appear profounder than they really are, but has experimented in *Time and the Conways, Dangerous Corner,* and *I Have Been Here Before.* Priestley was much struck with J. W. Dunne's book *An Experiment With Time,* which seemed to show that time was like any other dimension and, as one can walk backwards and forwards in space, so one should be able to go backwards and forwards in time. (H. G. Wells, of course, had presented this idea as pure fantasy in *The Time Machine.*) Priestley deliberately reverses the order of events in his plays, or presents the notion of two parallel courses of action, both of which exist but only one of which need be chosen. In *Johnson Over Jordan* he went to the Tibetan Book of the Dead for his theme: a business-man, just dead, is shown in an intermediate world beyond the grave, reliving his past in symbolic form, shedding the flaws which he cannot take on the final journey. Priestley has dramatic skill, but he is hampered by the inability to write telling dialogue, and in his soul there is no poetry.

On the Continent, and in America, more fruitful experiments have been tried. Expressionism, which used any and every possible theatrical device to *express* a single idea, produced remarkable results in the work of Ernst Toller, a German Communist, and in plays like *R.U.R.* (which gave to the world the word *Robot*), by the Czech Liberal Karel Čapek. Behind these experiments was the achievement of the great demented Swede, August Strindberg, whose *Miss Julie, The Spook Sonata* and *The Father* are terrifying experiences. America's most notable Expressionist play was *The Adding Machine,* by Elmer Rice (1892–1967), a satire on

Foreign drama

American materialism, which, in telling of the life, crime, death, and re-incarnation of the timid little clerk, Mr. Zero, used such devices as a re-volving stage, a mass of sound effects, special lighting, soliloquy, internal monologue, and other 'non-realistic' tricks. Rice was an important play-wright: his grasp of the stage and his Expressionist passion for ideas and humanitarian sympathies can be seen in *Street Scene* and *Judgment Day*. Eugene O'Neill (1888–1953), perhaps America's finest dramatist, shows the same audacity in the use of fresh devices—masks, fantasy, asides, soliloquies—in his *The Emperor Jones, The Great God Brown, Strange Inter-lude,* and other plays. His masterpiece, *Mourning Becomes Electra*, is a re-telling in more modern terms of a Greek tragic theme, and it approaches Shaw's indifference to length in requiring three nights for its performance. America continues to produce notable work in 'legitimate drama', with such writers as Tennessee Williams, Arthur Miller and Edward Albee, and it is leading in the field of the musical play.

Use of verse in drama

England's contributions to drama was, in the 1930s, most noteworthy in the few attempts to return to the use of verse, made by W. H. Auden (1907–1973) and Christopher Isherwood (1904–   ) in collaboration, and by Thomas Stearns Eliot (1888–1965) on his own. Auden and Isherwood used the stage for left-wing propaganda in *The Dance of Death* and *The Dog Beneath the Skin,* plays which employed verse of a racy, colloquial kind, songs in popular idiom, and various Expressionist devices. No twentieth-century poetic dramatist could, it seemed, dispense with the use of a chorus (on the Greek model) in the first days of verse-drama, and it is the choral comments of *The Dog Beneath the Skin* that have survived better than the play. *The Ascent of F6* is a remarkable achievement, with all its crudities and frightful Wordsworthian blank-verse. It is a vital examina-tion of the problem of power, presented in terms of an attack on the highest mountain in the world (higher than Everest) and the conflict that goes on in the mind of the leader of the exepedition—'What is my real motive for bringing these men to a highly probable death? Is it a dis-interested desire to conquer a mountain, or a hunger for the fame and power which will follow success?' The mountain-climbing episodes are commented on by Mr. and Mrs. A., typical 'ordinary people', and by a radio-studio, situated in stage-boxes, left and right of the proscenium. Popular songs, the inevitable chorus, Expressionist nightmare—all find their place in this disturbing but diverting play.

Eliot

T. S. Eliot's *Murder in the Cathedral* tells the story of the last days of Archbishop Thomas à Becket, his temptations, and his final martyrdom. Its central theme is expressed in the lines:

> The last temptation is the greatest treason:
> To do the right deed for the wrong reason . . .

The conflict in Thomas's mind is skilfully dramatised—through words more than action—and the agony of his inability to know whether he is right or wrong in seeking martyrdom, is the theme of the first act. After a moving prose sermon, violent action animates the play: Thomas is murdered, the assassins try to justify their act, and, through the words of the chorus, we are given the means of 'cathartising' our emotions, seeing all this conflict and violence as contained in the Will of God. It is a deeply touching play, rising to moments of poetical magnificence. Eliot's later plays, *The Family Reunion, The Cocktail Party,* and *The Confidential Clerk,* are less obviously 'poetical': they are written in a verse so close to prose that the average auditor cannot tell the difference. This, however, is intentional; the rhythm of verse, working on the unconscious mind, prepares it for sudden outburst of genuine poetry which, in a prose play, would be out of place and embarrassing. *The Family Reunion,* with its theme of guilt for the misdeed of one man spread throughout that man's family, finally expiated in the man's son, is a moving play, though there is not enough action. *The Cocktail Party* is more interesting for its philosophy than its verse (poetry, long-expected, only comes in the last act in a quotation from Shelley!). *The Confidential Clerk* is probably a competent play, but we expect from Eliot something more than competence. One fragment of an early play—*Sweeney Agonistes*—has been collected with Eliot's poems. This, with its jazz rhythms, songs, symbols, is the most frightening picture of Hell that modern literature has produced. It should be performed more often.

The British theatre experienced a remarkable renascence in the 1950s. It flamed into new life with the *Look Back in Anger* of John Osborne (1929–), which, while dramaturgically traditional enough, expressed with highly original power the disaffection of a sector of the British population which had previously had no real voice—the 'angry young men' of the provinces, bitter at the stranglehold on British life of a public-school and 'Oxbridge' Establishment, resentful of hypocrisy in both church and state, filled with a hopeless nostalgia for a virile romantic England—Edwardian or eighteenth-century—which had perhaps never really existed. Osborne showed himself capable of tackling a wide range of subjects—the German Reformation, for instance, in *Luther,* which succeeds in making the Augustinian monk a convincingly modern figure —a kind of angry young man of the sixteenth century. *Inadmissible Evidence*, despite its inordinate length and its shapelessness (it is more of a monologue than a true play) opened up areas of middle-class sensibility, particularly the sexual zone, which had previously been ignored in the theatre. Arnold Wesker (1932–) wrote plays about a newly articulate rural or artisan class, such as *Roots* and *Chicken Soup with Barley*, and, in *Chips with Everything*, uncovered the ignorance and complacency which, in his view, were holding back the working class. Wesker's politics, needless to say, are left wing, and he has been strenuous in his attempts to establish a new British left-wing theatre. The work of John Whiting (1917–63), John Arden (1930–), and Robert Bolt (1925–)—

Modern British drama

while it has no class axe to grind—has been notable for a new tough eloquence. Bolt showed, in his Sir Thomas More play, *A Man for All Seasons,* that *Luther* was no mere flash in the pan, and that a new approach to historical drama was possible. This was confirmed by Peter Schaeffer, in his remarkable play about the Aztecs and the Conquistadores, *The Royal Hunt of the Sun.* To help further the revivification of the British stage, new influences from abroad were being admitted.

Foreign influence   The concept of 'absurdity', which derives properly from the writings of the late Albert Camus, showed man less as a Renaissance wonder in control of the universe than as a lonely creature confronted by a vast indifferent emptiness, in which his acts are of no significance but have to be performed to confirm his human identity. Existential man, desperately asserting himself, stoically hopeless and yet curiously heroic, had been the hero of Camus's work as well as Jean-Paul Sarte's, but he was followed, in the plays and novels of the Irishman Samuel Beckett (1906–), who writes in French, by totally deprived creatures—like the tramps in *Waiting for Godot*—filling in empty time on an eternal Saturday which follows Good Friday but never becomes Easter Sunday. God has failed man by not existing; man has little to do except hang on to a few scraps of life, finding a minimal identity in the mere fact of being able to communicate. But communication is no more than time-filling words that lead to no action. In the plays of Ionesco (1912–), there is the same pathetic absurdity of language as a mere time-filling device, and his *Bald Prima Donna* draws its dialogue from an English language primer. Both Beckett and Ionesco have exerted an influence on Harold Pinter (1930–), who nevertheless has his own voice. His plays, particularly *The Caretaker* and *The Birthday Party* have a sinister-comic quality: an end of some violence, deriving from no discernible motivation on the part of the characters, comes after long stretches of dialogue in which nothing is really said. Pinter's exploitation of everyday speech is remarkable. He recognises that language is primarily phatic—a device of human contact, not (as was the traditional view) a vehicle for ideas.

Influence of Television   The theatre in Britain, as in America, serves a small section of the community only, and it can hardly survive commercially without help from the state or private foundations. Nevertheless, at least in Britain, there is a new vast audience which at least is able to distinguish between the nature of stage drama and that of film, chiefly because television plays—however much they use film technique—are an offshoot of the stage and provide a living for artists who regard themselves primarily as stage-actors. Both Pinter and Osborne have written for television, and stage-works like Osborne's *A Matter of Scandal and Concern* and Pinter's *The Lover* had their first showings on the small screen. It is likely, however, that television will kill the theatre. It can satisfy, at a lesser cost and in greater comfort, the appetite for drama that it arouses.

20. *The Coming of the Modern Age*

Queen Victoria's reign ended in 1901, but the Victorian age ended about twenty years earlier. That peculiar spirit called 'Victorianism'—a mixture of optimism, doubt, and guilt—began to disappear with men like Swinburne the rebel, Fitzgerald the pessimist, Butler the satirist, and others. The literature produced from about 1880 to 1914 is characterised either by an attempt to find substitutes for a religion which seems dead, or by a kind of spiritual emptiness—a sense of the hopelessness of trying to believe in anything.

Death of Religion

There were many possible substitutes for religion. One was Art, and Walter Pater (1839–94) was its prophet. 'Art for art's sake' (very different from Ruskin's highly moral doctrines) was the theme of books like *Marius the Epicurean* and *Studies in the History of the Renaissance*. It was one's duty, said Pater (in the most exquisite prose), to cultivate pleasure, to drink deep from the fountains of natural and created beauty. In other words, he advocated *hedonism* as a way of life. Pater does not preach, however. He is mainly concerned with shaping his wonderful prose, concentrating (following his own doctrine) on his art, and letting the philosophy filter gently through.

Art

Hedonism was the thesis of some of Oscar Wilde's witty essays, as also of his novel *The Picture of Dorian Gray*. Wilde (1856–1900) seems, in the latter book, however, to be concerned with showing the dangers of asking for too much from life. The beautiful Dorian Gray—Faustus-like—wishes that he should remain eternally young and handsome, while his picture, painted in the finest flush of his beauty, should grow old in his stead. The wish is granted: Dorian remains ever-young, but his portrait shows signs of ever-increasing age and, moreover, the scars of the crimes attendant on asking for too much (a murder, the ruining of many women, unnameable debauchery). Dorian, repentant, tries to destroy his portrait, symbolically quelling his sins, but—magically—it is he himself who dies, monstrous with age and ugliness, and his portrait that reverts to its former perfection of youthful beauty. The sense of guilt—as much mediaeval as Victorian—intrudes into Wilde's bright godless world un-expectedly, and this book prepares us for those later works of his—written under the shadow and shame of his prison-sentence—which lack the old wit and contain a sombre seriousness—*The Ballad of Reading Gaol* and *De Profundis*.

Imperialism

Another substitute for religion was Imperialism (with undertones of Freemasonry), and Rudyard Kipling (1865–1936) was the great singer of Empire. Born in India, Kipling knew the British Empire from the inside, not merely, like so many stay-at-home newspaper-readers, as a series of red splashes on the map of the world. This concern with Empire expres-ses itself in many forms—the sympathy with the soldiers who fought the frontier wars, kept peace in the Empire, did glorious work for a mere pittance and the reward of civilian contempt; the stress on the white man's responsibility to his brothers who, despite difference of colour and creed, acknowledged the same Queen; the *value* of an Empire as the creator of a new, rich civilisation. Kipling's reputation as a poet has always been precarious among the 'intellectuals': they have looked askance at his mixture of soldier's slang and biblical idiom, his jaunty rhythms and 'open-air' subjects. Recently Kipling was rehabilitated by T. S. Eliot, in his long essay prefacing his selection of Kipling's verse, and George Orwell has said, in an essay on Eliot's essay, valuable things which put Kipling firmly in his place: he is not a great poet, but he sums up for all time a certain phase in English history; he has the gift of stating the obvious—not, as with Pope, for the men of reason and learning, but for the man in the street—with pithy memorableness. He is a poet who knows the East, and certain lines of his (as in *The Road to Mandalay*) evoke the sun and the palm-trees, and the oriental nostalgia of many a repatri-ated Englishman, with real power. As a prose-writer, Kipling is known for one novel (*Kim*) and a host of excellent short stories, also for a school-boy's classic, *Stalky and Co*. He has, in both verse and prose, a vigour and an occasional vulgarity that are refreshing after men like William Morris, Swinburne, and Rossetti.

Pessimism

The other side of the coin is shown in the poems of writers like John Davidson (1857–1909), Ernest Dowson (1867–1900) and A. E. Housman (1859–1936), who expressed a consistent mood of pessimism. In Hous-man's *A Shropshire Lad* we have exquisite classical verse—regular forms, great compression—devoted to the futility of life, the certainty of death, the certainty of nothing after death. There is a certain Stoicism: the lads of his poems maintain a 'stiff upper lip' despite disappointment in love and their sense of an untrustworthy world about them. Some of the poems express the beauty of nature in a clipped, restrained way which still suggests a full-blooded Romanticism. But other poets of the same period sought a new meaning for life in the Catholic faith—Francis Thompson (1859–1907), who, following Coventry Patmore (1823–96), expressed the everyday from a 'God's eye' point of view (as in the brief *In No Strange Land*) but turned to a rich, highly-coloured style in *The Hound of Heaven*—a mixture of the Romantic and the Metaphysical; and Alice Meynell (1850–1922), who wrote highly individual Christian lyrics.

Pessimism reigned in the novel. Thomas Hardy (1840–1928) produced a whole series of books dedicated to the life of his native Dorset, full of the sense of man's bond with nature and with the past—a past revealed in the age-old trees, heaths, fields, and in the prehistoric remains of the Celts, the ruined camps of the Romans. In his novels, man never seems to be free: the weight of time and place presses heavily on him, and, above everything, there are mysterious forces which control his life. Man is a puppet whose strings are worked by fates which are either hostile or indifferent to him. There is no message of hope in *Tess of the D'Urbervilles* (when Tess is finally hanged we hear: '. . . And so the President of the Immortals had finished his sport with Tess') nor in *The Mayor of Casterbridge* or *Jude the Obscure*. The reception of this last work, with its gloomy 'Curst be the day in which I was born' and its occasional brutal frankness, was so hostile that Hardy turned from the novel to verse. Today it seems that his stature as a poet is considerable, and that both as poet and novelist he will be remembered. His verse expresses the irony of life—man's thwarted schemes, the need for resignation in the face of a hostile fate—but also he expresses lighter moods, writes charming nature-poems, even love-lyrics. Hardy's skill at depicting nature, his eye for close detail, is eminently apparent in the novels, and it comes to full flower in the poems. His verse occasionally suffers from a 'clotted' quality—consonants cluster together in Anglo-Saxon violence ('hill-hid tides throb, throe on throe')—but this is an aspect of his masculine force. An ability to produce a verse-composition of epic length was shown in *The Dynasts*, a vast un-actable drama meant to be presented on the stage of the reader's own imagination, dealing with the Napoleonic Wars as seen from the viewpoint not only of men but of the Immortal Fates, who watch, direct, and comment.

George Gissing (1857–1903), whose importance has slowly been revealed in our own age, presents grim pictures of futility with a classical restraint. *The Unclassed* shows the effect of poverty upon human character; *Demos* seems to show that, no matter how much the depressed classes may agitate, they cannot build a juster world; *New Grub Street* tells something of Gissing's own story—the writer of merit struggling to make a living by churning out trashy novels at starvation-rates, contrasted with the glib, successful book-reviewer who is successful because he has no literary conscience. Gissing's concern with showing the 'other side' of life (*The Nether World* is a ruthless study of slum-life) owes something to Dickens, though Gissing does not possess Dickens's fantasy, robustness,

Novels—
Hardy

Gissing

or humour; but his critical study of Dickens is one of the most penetrating books ever written about that master.

A return to optimism is shown in the verse and prose of Robert Louis
Stevenson (1850–94), but it is a rather superficial one, for Stevenson is a
rather superficial writer. He is at his best in adventure stories which show
the influence of his fellow-countryman, Walter Scott—*Kidnapped, The
Master of Ballantrae*—and boys' books like *Treasure Island*, a juvenile
masterpiece. *Dr. Jekyll and Mr. Hyde* deals with the duality of good and
evil within the same man, but it is perhaps little more than a well-written
thriller. The poems, especially those for children, are charming, and the
essays, which have little to say, say that little very well. His short stories
are good, and we may note here that the short story was becoming an
accepted form—writers had to learn how to express themselves succinctly, using great compression in plot, characterisation, and dialogue—
heralding the approach of an age less leisurely than the Victorian, with
no time for three-volume novels, and demanding its stories in quick
mouthfuls.

Liberalism   A new faith, more compelling than Pater's hedonism or Kipling's
Imperialism, was still needed, and Bernard Shaw and H. G. Wells (1866–
1946) found one in what may be called Liberalism—the belief that man's
future lies on earth, not in heaven, and that, with scientific and social
progress, an earthly paradise may eventually be built. Wells is one of the
great figures of modern literature. He owed a lot to Dickens in such
novels as *Kipps* and *The History of Mr. Polly*—works which borrow
Dickens's prose-style, his humour, and his love of eccentrics, and which
deal affectionately with working people—but he found themes of his own
in the scientific novels. *The Time Machine, The First Men in the Moon, The
War of the Worlds, The Invisible Man, When the Sleeper Awakes*, and *The
Food of the Gods* all seem concerned not merely with telling a strange and
entertaining story but with showing that, to science, everything is theo-
retically possible. The glorification of scientific discovery leads Wells to
think that time and space can easily be conquered, and so we can travel
to the moon, or Martians can attack us; we can travel forward to the
future, and back again to the present. The old Newtonian world, with its
fixed dimensions, begins to melt and dissolve in the imaginative stories
of Wells: flesh can be made as transparent as glass, human size can be
increased indefinitely, a man can sleep for a couple of centuries and wake
up in the strange Wellsian future; a man can work miracles; a newspaper
from the future can be delivered by mistake; a man can lose weight without bulk and drift like a balloon.

Wells sometimes described himself as a 'Utopiographer'. He was
always planning worlds in which science had achieved its last victories
over religion and superstition, in which reason reigned, in which everybody was healthy, clean, happy, and enlightened. The Wellsian future

has been, for many years, one of the furnishings of our minds—sky-scrapers, the heavens full of aircraft, men and women dressed something like ancient Greeks, rational conversation over a rational meal of vitamin-pills. To build Utopia, Wells wanted—like Shaw—to destroy all the vestiges of the past which cluttered the modern world—class-distinction, relics of feudalism, directionless education, unenlightened and self-seeking politicians, economic inequality. In other words, both Shaw and Wells wanted a kind of Socialism. Rejecting the doctrine of sin, they believed that man's mistakes and crimes came from stupidity, or from an unfavourable environment, and they set to work to blueprint the devices which would put everything right.

Wells, in book after book, tackles the major social problems. In *Ann Veronica* we have the theme of woman's new equal status with men; in *Joan and Peter* education is examined; in *The Soul of a Bishop* we hear of the new religion of the rational age; in *The New Machiavelli* we have Wells's philosophy of politics. But these works remain novels, charac-terised by a Dickensian richness of character and not lacking in love-interest. *Tono-Bungay* is about commerce, *Mr. Blettsworthy on Rampole Island* a satire on our 'savage' social conventions, *The Dream* a story of the muddle of twentieth-century life as seen from the viewpoint of a thousand years ahead. Wells was a prolific writer and, when he kept to a story, always an interesting one. His preaching is now a little out of date, and his very hope for the future, rudely shattered by the Second World War, turned to a kind of wild despair: mankind would have to be super-seded by some new species, *Homo Sapiens* had had his day; 'You fools,' he said in the preface to a reprint made just before his death, 'you damned fools.' Optimistic Liberalism died with him.

John Galsworthy (1867–1933) is best known for his *Forsyte Saga*, a series of six novels which trace the story of a typically English upper-class family from Victorian days to the nineteen-twenties—presenting their reactions to great events which, in effect, spell the doom of all they stand for, including World War I, the growth of Socialism, the General Strike of 1926. Galsworthy had shown himself, in his early *The Island Pharisees*, to be critical of the old standards—the philistinism, decadence, dullness, atrophy of feeling which characterised the so-called 'ruling class'. *The Forsyte Saga*, in trying to view this dying class dispassionately —with occasional irony—nevertheless seems to develop a sympathy for the hero of *The Man of Property*, Soames Forsyte, the epitome of the money-seeking class which Galsworthy is supposed to detest. Gals-worthy, in fact, is himself drawn into the family of Forsytes, becomes in-volved with its fortunes, and what starts off as a work of social criticism ends in acceptance of the very principles it attacks. This work is still widely read, though it is not greatly esteemed by the modern critics. It came into its own as a television serial in the 1960s.

Galsworthy

Walpole

Hugh Walpole (1884–1941) also wrote a saga—*The Herries Chronicle*—which owes something to Scott in its love of 'period' and adventure. Walpole is not a distinguished writer: perhaps his early *Mr. Perrin and Mr. Traill*—a story of rivalry between two schoolmasters—is his best work. Walpole's reputation was great with the middle-classes, he made much money, but critics united in condemning a lack of depth and a too great facility: Walpole had too much 'flow' and too little capacity to criticise his own writing. Arnold Bennett (1867–1931) similarly can be

Bennett

condemned for a lack of distinction and imagination in style. A realist on the French pattern (he owed much to Balzac and Zola) he was at his best in the works which dealt with the pottery district of Staffordshire, where he was born—*Anna of the Five Towns*, *The Old Wives' Tale*, *Clayhanger*, and others. *The Old Wives' Tale* is considered to be his greatest work, though some find it difficult to read.

Conrad

Joseph Conrad (1857–1924) brought a new quality into the novel. Conrad was a Pole (his real name was Teodor Josef Konrad Korzeniowski), born in the Ukraine, in love with the sea from an early age. This led him eventually to a British merchant ship, a Master's certificate, and a mastery of the English language. Conrad produced his first novel at the age of forty, but then made up for lost time by turning out a book every year. He normally writes of the sea, of the Eastern islands, of the English character as seen against a background of the exotic or faced with difficulties. His handling of English is distinctive, a little foreign in its lack of restraint and its high colour, but admirably suited to the description of storms, labouring ships with skippers shouting through high winds, the hot calm of a pilgrim-ship in the Red Sea. Conrad's finest book is perhaps *Lord Jim*, where moral conflict is admirably presented in the character of the young Englishman who loses his honour through leaping overboard when his ship seems to be in danger, but expiates his sin by dying heroically at the end. A good brief introduction to Conrad is the short *Youth*, with its action, swift character-studies, and its vision of the mystical, magical East at the close of the voyage. Other novels are *Typhoon*, *The Nigger of the Narcissus*, *Nostromo*, and *The Secret Agent*.

Ford

Associated with Conrad is Ford Madox Ford (1873–1939), who collaborated with him in the writing of *Romance* and *The Inheritors*. Ford is neglected, though there are signs that he is at last being recognised by a few as one of the great novelists of the period. His four novels on Christopher Tietjens ('the last Tory') are a study of England during World War I, as well as a penetrating satire on the new forces against which Tietjens, with his outmoded standards of honour and honesty, must contend. They are called *Some Do Not*, *No More Parades*, *A Man Could Stand Up*, and *Last Post* and, as a collective entity, carry the title *Parade's End*. Stylistically, Ford is the superior of bigger names of the period, and his analytical skill is shown at its best in *The Good Soldier*, a tragic novel which is one of the really important pieces of literature of the twentieth century.

Ford takes as his mythology a decaying set of Tory values, enshrined in an admirable but occasionally absurd human figure. G. K. Chesterton (1874–1936) and Hilaire Belloc (1870–1953) choose a brand of Catholic Christianity almost of their own invention. Chesterton especially is the singer of a joyful, beer-drinking, colour-loving spirituality which, in his view, is mediaeval, closer to Chaucer than to Cardinal Newman. Chesterton's vigour is infectious, and his love of paradox and fun sometimes a little tiresome (he begins a book with: 'The human race, to which so many of my readers belong . . .'). He wanted to shock his audience into a realisation of how dull their lives were without faith. His novels are excellent, especially *The Man Who Was Thursday* and *The Flying Inn*, and his poems rousing if a little unsubtle. As a critic he is best left alone, but as a general, rather fantastic, essayist he is amusing and sometimes genuinely thoughtful. His *Father Brown* detective-stories are in the great tradition started by Sir Arthur Conan Doyle (1859–1930), whose tales of Sherlock Holmes are likely to be immortal. Belloc seems a less forceful figure than Chesterton: his works on faith and history are scholarly, but it is through his verse, especially his light verse, that he has become generally known. Belloc was French, and his long poem *In Praise of Wine* has more of the Mediterranean in it than the North Sea; it shows a mastery of the traditional style of verse-writing, a style almost dead in his own day.

Chesterton

Verse generally did not flourish in the England of the early modern period. Besides those poets already mentioned, there were a number of versifiers who wrote pleasantly of love and country matters, among them a man who perhaps gained more admiration than he altogether deserved —Robert Bridges (1844–1930), friend and editor of Hopkins, whose long poetic life was crowned with *The Testament of Beauty*, a philosophical poem (possibly of no great depth), in 1929. Poets who breathed a new and rather uninspired Romanticism, like Rupert Brooke, had no chance to develop, for the First World War swallowed many of them. Edward Thomas, Walter de la Mare, Edmund Blunden, and John Masefield have shown a sturdier Romanticism, and one young Romantic, Wilfred Owen (1893–1918), lived long enough to be influenced by his war experiences in the direction of a new and terrible poetry, sometimes, in its dignity and haunting music, resembling even Dante. Satire came out of that War, as in the poems of Siegfried Sassoon and Robert Graves, and a new movement we shall discuss later, but, generally speaking, the poet who had most virtues and most facets was the Irishman, William Butler Yeats (1865–1939), and he may be said to dominate the greater part of the early modern period.

Lack of poetry

Yeats

Yeats's early work is full of Irish melancholy, breathing the spirit of the 'Celtic Twilight'. Exquisite music, evocation of Irish myth and Irish landscape, and a quality of eerie mystery are to be found in the earlier volumes, but in later life the inspiration and form of his work changed radically. Yeats forged his own philosophy, made a personal mythology (based on the image of ancient Byzantium, a symbol of the undying in art), and wrote a rough, terse verse, avoiding true rhyme, capable of expressing abstruse ideas or of speaking all-too-intelligible home-truths about life, religion, and love. His influence, even on very young poets, is considerable, and, though he has recently been under attack for the alleged reactionary quality of his thought, his toughly bound syntax and rhetorical power remain among the most incredible achievements of the English language.

21. *To the Present Day*

The twentieth century has been much concerned with finding something to believe in—it has that in common with the last twenty years of the Victorian era. But whereas the first of our moderns were satisfied with their hedonism or liberalism or mediaevalism, the later age has demanded something deeper—it has wanted the sense of a *continuous tradition*, the sense of being involved in a civilisation. This is difficult to make clear, but if we consider that most of the writers we discussed in the last chapter were trying to *manufacture* something to believe in, and that most of the more modern writers want to belong to something already there, but perhaps hidden, then we can understand the main difference. An artist has to have subject matter—a civilisation, a religion, a myth, and the emotions of people who belong to these things, but it should not have to be the artist's job to create his subject matter—it should be ready, waiting. Shaw and Wells, Chesterton and Belloc are sometimes weakened by having to tell the reader what they are writing about before they start writing about it. An artist who can look back to a few hundred years of continuous belief and tradition based on belief, and take it for granted, is in a far happier position.

Even Ford Madox Ford, in his Tietjens novels, is using a kind of Don Quixote as hero—the last of his race, and hence somewhat absurd. Conrad takes, in effect, the easy way out by choosing the sea (an eternal myth, but only available to those who have made it their life). The religion of Francis Thompson is a personal creed, mystical, outside the general tradition. Galsworthy's world is a dying one. Liberalism, with its great shout of progress, was to turn sour on people who experienced the First World War and found that science meant gas and guns. Where were new writers to look?

Americans sick of two aspects of American life—Puritanism and materialism—found a myth in the continuity of European culture, especially as revealed in the Latin countries. Henry James (1843–1916) proclaims

Americans in Europe

James

Collage of modern authors.

1. Elizabeth Bowen.   2. Stan Barstow.   3. Virginia Woolf.   4. Colin MacInnes.
5. Brigid Brophy.   6. John Osborne.   7. Alan Sillitoe.   8. D. H. Lawrence.   9. Iris
Murdoch.   10. Muriel Spark.   11. John Braine.   12. John Wain.   13. E. M. Forster.
14. Keith Waterhouse.   15. Rebecca West.   16. Kingsley Amis.   17. Edna O'Brien.

in his dates a kinship with writers already discussed, but the spirit of his books anticipates T. S. Eliot, who produced his first book of poems a year after James's death. James was an American, born in New York, educated at Harvard, a member of a great American family that had produced in Henry James senior a remarkable writer on philosophy, and in William James (the brother of Henry James junior) one of the most important original philosophers of the age. Henry James felt that his spiritual home was Europe, despite the tremendous 'Liberal' advances that America was making. His most significant novels—beginning with *The American* and ending with *The Ambassadors* and *The Golden Bowl*— deal with the theme of the impact of Europe on visiting Americans: the Americans feel themselves uncivilised, young, inexperienced, and Europe seems so old, wise, and beautiful. Europe absorbs America—it has continuity of tradition, and the tradition itself is old and valuable; the Americans of *The Ambassadors* are bewitched by a civilisation almost against their will.

Ezra Pound (1885–1972) and Thomas Stearns Eliot (1888–1965), both *Pound, Eliot* Americans, made their homes in Europe, like their senior compatriot. Both have seemed concerned with trying to conserve what is best in European culture before European civilisation is finally destroyed. Pound followed Browning and various Italian and French poets of the Middle Ages, translated Chinese and Anglo-Saxon, looking for something to build on. He came to fruition of his talent in *Hugh Selwyn Mauberley*, an autobiographical poem which sums up his position as a poet who detests the civilisation of Materialism, and is trying to build up a culture based on the past. Eliot, after satirising the puritanical world of New England and condemning its philistinism, produced in 1922 an epoch-making poem of some 400 lines, *The Waste Land*, which set out in *The Waste Land* a new poetical technique a picture of a materialistic age dying of lack of belief in anything: the solution to the problem of living in such an arid Waste Land of a civilisation seemed to be to accept it as a kind of fiery purgation (he quotes Dante: *Poi s'ascose nel foco che gli affina*—'Then he hid in the fire which refines them') and to gather together such scraps of civilisation and faith as have not yet been destroyed ('These fragments I have shored against my ruins'). *The Waste Land* makes tough demands on the reader: it quotes frequently from the literatures of Europe and India (in the original), uses a rapidly shifting point-of-view (sometimes it is the poet speaking, sometimes a woman in a pub, sometimes a prostitute, sometimes the Greek mythical figure Tiresias, who is half-man and half-woman and thus contains in himself all the other characters), and uses verse which owes something to practically every English poet of the past, though Eliot's voice is always heard clearly enough. Eliot's distinctive verse-form is a kind of free verse derived from the blank verse of the late Elizabethan playwrights: it is supple and capable of much variety, also highly dramatic. *The Waste Land* is a closely organised poem, and not a word is wasted: it repays the trouble spent on it and is, in fact, a sort of door into European literature—a concise summary of a civilisation which is contrasted sharply with the present age.

Pound spent much of the last part of his life on a very long poem, the *Cantos*. In it he ranges over the civilisations of the past—Eastern as well as Western—and fragments of Chinese appear, as well as Greek, Latin, and the modern European tongues. The general theme is—Usury as the cause of a civilisation's decline. But the *Cantos* can be read as a shimmering history of civilisation, in which time and place are not important and all ages are seen as one. Eliot's finest work after *The Waste Land* was the *Four Quartets*—four poems organised on the analogy of musical pieces, in which the old concern for European civilisation has been changed into a very Christian preoccupation with 'the intersection of time with the timeless'—the way in which eternity can redeem the mistakes of history. The technique is remarkable, though we notice clearly one characteristic of modern poetry which is frequently condemned—the tendency for verse to sound like prose. In our age the dividing-line between prose and poetry is very thin indeed.

Ulysses

In 1922 there appeared an important work in prose which (inevitably) sometimes sounds like verse. This was *Ulysses*, by the Irishman James Joyce (1882–1941), a novel of enormous length dealing with the events of a single day in the life of a single town—the author's native Dublin. Joyce had previously published some charming but not outstanding verse, a volume of short stories called *Dubliners*, and a striking autobiographical novel—*Portrait of the Artist as a Young Man*. The hero of this novel—Stephen Dedalus—appears again in *Ulysses*, this time subordinated in a secondary role: the hero is a Hungarian Jew, long-settled in Dublin, called Leopold Bloom. The novel has no real plot. Like the Greek hero whose name provides the title, Bloom wanders from place to place, but has very un-heroic adventures, and finally meets Stephen, who then takes on the role of a sort of spiritual son. After this the book ends. But the eight hundred pages are not filled with padding; never was a novel written in conciser prose. We are allowed to enter the minds of the chief characters, are presented with their thoughts and feelings in a continuous stream (the technique is called 'interior monologue'). The book is mostly a never-ending stream of Bloom's half-articulate impressions of the day, but Joyce prevents the book from being nothing but that, by imposing on it a very rigid form. Each chapter corresponds to an episode in Homer's *Odyssey* and has a distinct style of its own; for instance, in the Maternity Hospital scene the prose imitates all the English literary styles from *Beowulf* to Carlyle and beyond, symbolising the growth of the foetus in the womb in its steady movement through time. The skill of the book is amazing, and when we pick up a novel by Arnold Bennett or Hugh

Walpole after reading *Ulysses* we find it hard to be impressed by ways of writing which seem dull, unaware, half-asleep. *Ulysses* is the most carefully-written novel of the twentieth century.

In *Finnegans Wake* Joyce tried to present the whole of human history as a dream in the mind of a Dublin inn-keeper called H. C. Earwicker, and here the style—on which Joyce, going blind, expended immense labour—is appropriate to dream, the language shifting and changing, words becoming glued together, suggesting the merging of images in a dream, and enabling Joyce to present history and myth as a single image, with all the characters of history becoming a few eternal types, finally identified by Earwicker with himself, his wife, and three children. This great and difficult work probably marks the limit of experiment in language—it would be hard for any writer to go farther than Joyce. In both *Ulysses* and *Finnegans Wake* Joyce shows himself to have found a positive creed: man must believe in the *City* (symbolised by Dublin), the human society which must change, being human, but which will always change in a circular fashion. Time goes round, the river flows into the sea, but the source of the river is perpetually refreshed by rain from the sea: nothing can be destroyed, life is always renewed, even if the 'etym' 'abnihilises' us. The end of *Ulysses* is a triumphant 'Yes'; the end of *Finnegans Wake* is the beginning of a sentence whose continuation starts the book.

Finnegans Wake

One reaction against the Liberalism of Wells and Shaw was to be found in the novels and poems of the Englishman David Herbert Lawrence (1885–1930), who in effect rejected civilisation and, like Blake, wanted men to go back to the 'natural world' of instinct. Lawrence's novels—*Sons and Lovers, The Plumed Serpent, Aaron's Rod,* and *Lady Chatterley's Lover*, to mention a few—are much concerned with the relationship between man and woman, and he seems to regard this relationship as the great source of vitality and integration (*Lady Chatterley's Lover* was banned until 1960 because it too frankly glorified physical love). Lawrence will have nothing of science: instinct is more important; even religions are too rational, and, if man wants a faith, he must worship the 'dark gods' of primitive peoples. Nobody has ever presented human passion, man's relationship to nature, the sense of the presence of life in all things, like Lawrence. His poems, which express with intimate knowledge the 'essences' of natural phenomena and of the human instincts, are also capable of bitter satire on the 'dehumanisation' of man in the twentieth century.

Lawrence

Often associated with Lawrence is Aldous Huxley (1894–1963), whose early novels—especially *Antic Hay, Those Barren Leaves,* and *Point Counter Point*—showed a world without aim or direction (artists, rich people, the Waste Land of post-war London) and offered no solution to the puzzle of a seemingly meaningless existence. *Point Counter Point* especially

Huxley

seemed to show that man is a creature too mixed, too divided by 'passion and reason' to find much happiness. This book tried certain experiments —several stories going on at the same time, on the analogy of musical counterpoint; the employment of vast scientific knowledge in ironic descriptions of human actions—as though to say, 'Science has no solution either'. *Brave New World* brilliantly satirised Wellsian Utopias, showing that, if man became completely happy and society completely efficient, he would cease to be human and it would become intolerable. Huxley found a faith in brotherly love and (at a time when war perpetually threatened) in non-violence, in *Eyeless in Gaza*, a novel which plays tricks with the time-sequence with, it seems to me, great success. In later works he has turned to satire—*After Many a Summer*, *Ape and Essence*—and shown little faith in man's capacity to become a more selfless or more rational creature. Huxley's works on mysticism (*Grey Eminence*, *The Devils of Loudun*) are learned and interesting, and his essays show him keenly absorbed in the problems of science, art, and civilisation.

Waugh

Evelyn Waugh (1903–66) proved himself one of the best modern humorists in his early *Decline and Fall* and *Vile Bodies*, which, among other things, depicted the empty search for amusement which animated 'bright young people' of the leisured classes after the First World War. Waugh became a Catholic, but—except for a brilliant study of the English martyr, Edmund Campion—hardly let his religion affect the tenor of his novels before the coming of the Second World War. *A Handful of Dust*—perhaps his best work—was a story of the break-up of a marriage, and the consequent destruction of a stability symbolised by one of the old landed estates; it is significant that the hero leaves England, after his wife leaves him, to seek a lost city in the wilds of Brazil. Only in the delirium of fever does he find it, and then it appears as his own abandoned estate. *Brideshead Revisited*, published at the end of the Second World War, is the story of an old aristocratic Catholic family and the way in which its faith, though seemingly decaying, comes back in times of crisis. The book, sometimes resembling Henry James (but a more poetical James) in its highly-organised sentences, is a reaffirmation of the value of traditional English Catholicism. In *Men at Arms* and *Officers and Gentlemen*, Waugh chronicles the first years in the army of a rather pathetic Tietjens character, seemingly trying, though unsuccessfully, to find stability in the army myth. These books, admirably reporting the first years of the War, are often uproariously funny. *The Loved One* is a satire on American myth (particularly American burial-customs) told heartlessly but brilliantly.

Greene

Graham Greene (1904–   ), another Catholic convert, has been obsessed with the problem of good and evil, and his books are a curious compound of theology and stark modern realism. Greene sees the spiritual struggle of man against a background of 'seedy' town life

(*Brighton Rock*) or in the Mexican jungle (*The Power and the Glory*) or in wartime West Africa (*The Heart of the Matter*). In this last work, and also in the moving *The End of the Affair*, Greene shows a concern with the paradox of the man or woman who, technically a sinner, is really a saint. Some of his works have conflicted with Catholic orthodoxy (especially in Ireland). *The Quiet American*, dealing with the Indo-China War, turns to a moral theme—how far are good intentions enough? Greene's lighter novels—'Entertainments', as he calls them—are distinguished by fine construction and admirably terse prose.

It is hard to say how far E. M. Forster (1879–1970) fits into any pattern. His influence on the construction of the novel has been great, but he has no real 'message', except about the value of individual life, the need not to take too seriously out-moded moral shibboleths (*A Room With a View*, which affirms passion rather than control). *Howard's End* and *Where Angels Fear to Tread* are distinguished by very taut construction and the creation of suspense through incident—Forster does not think a plot very important. *A Passage to India*—perhaps his finest novel—deals with the East and West duality: can the two really meet? After a long analysis of the differences, expressed in terms of a vividly realised India, against which the puppets of English rulers parade, Forster comes to the conclusion that they cannot—at least, not yet. Forster's book, *Aspects of the Novel*, is admirable criticism and entertaining reading.

Forster

Virginia Woolf (1882–1941) is another novelist hard to classify. She dispenses with plot and even characterisation, preferring to analyse in the closest possible detail a mood or thought as presented at a given moment in time. Like Joyce, she uses an interior monologue device to depict 'the stream of consciousness' of her characters. Her prose is careful, exquisitely light, approaching poetry in its power to evoke mood and sensation. Her view of the novel was a comprehensive one; she did not wish to limit herself to the mere story-telling of men like Arnold Bennett and Hugh Walpole, but wanted to see the novel absorb as many literary devices as possible, even, occasionally, to break away from prose and use verse instead. To many readers her novels do not appear to be works of fiction at all: they seem too static, too lacking in action and human interest—a kind of literary form which is neither true poetry nor true prose, neither completely dramatic nor completely lyrical. Perhaps her best works are *Mrs. Dalloway*, *To the Lighthouse*, and *The Waves*. *Orlando* is a curious work—it presents a picture of English history from the Renaissance to modern times, as seen through the eyes of a character who is, presumably, immortal and, moreover, changes from hero to heroine exactly half-way through the book! Here Virginia Woolf's great literary gifts are to be seen at their most dazzling. Her two books of literary criticism—*The Common Reader*, 1 and 2—show a penetrating intellect and great good taste.

Woolf

We may note here—in parenthesis—that the twentieth century has been the great age for women novelists,[1] though perhaps none has approached the genius of Jane Austen. Virginia Woolf is certainly the most important, but Ivy Compton-Burnett has her devotees, who see in her a great and remarkable genius firmly rooted in tradition. All her novels deal with family relationships, all her settings are upper middle-class homes in the late Victorian period, and character is revealed through endless, rather stylised, dialogue. Like Virginia Woolf, she has no interest in plot, and is content to let her revelations of human character unfold slowly, deliberately eschewing tricks which will 'charm' the reader and make him want to read on. Ivy Compton-Burnett is an acquired taste, but perhaps her contribution to the modern novel will eventually be seen as an important one.

Franz Kafka, a Czech who wrote in German, had a good deal of influence in England, with his *The Castle* and *The Trial*. These novels, using the technique of allegory, seem to show that man is subject to powers greater than himself and carries a burden of guilt for a crime which is never specified but which must be punished. It is, in a sense, Christian allegory, though Kafka never provides a key to his strange stories. The hero of *The Trial* is arraigned for a crime which his judges will not name and which he is certain he has never committed. Gradually, in the long tortuous process of the trial, the hero comes to develop a sense of guilt (Original Sin) and his final execution (two polite men stick a knife in his heart) seems somehow just. Rex Warner (1905–   ) followed Kafka's technique in *The Wild Goose Chase* and *The Aerodrome*. The Kafka-esque style gives to these novels a peculiar quality of mystery and foreboding, and the choice raised in *The Aerodrome*—between the efficient, rational air-station and the depraved but all-too-human village nearby—has profound political (if not religious) significance. William Sansom used the same Kafka-esque technique (with its telling, flat, rather wordy prose) in the volume of short stories called *Fireman Flower*. In his novels, *The Body* (a fine study of middle-aged jealousy), *The Face of Innocence*, and *A Bed of Roses*, his aim seems to have been rather to poeticise the ordinary details of everyday life, in a prose which sometimes becomes lyrical and, in its rhythm and alliteration, approaches verse.

Other novelists—senior novelists—have been content to push on with their plain story-telling, without any desire apparently for a faith to express, or for a technique more original than that of the nineteenth century. William Somerset Maugham (1874–1965) has told good stories, showing himself not unconcerned with the paradoxes in human behaviour, but fundamentally he is the mere observer who refuses to be too deeply involved in humanity. His attitude to morals is a simple Utilitarian one, except that he seems grateful when people behave out-

[1] See Chapter 22.

rageously, because they thus supply him with a new theme for a story. His alleged masterpiece, *Of Human Bondage,* is distinguished by frequently clumsy prose and a length which hardly seems justified by the subject. Maugham's wittiest and warmest book—one of the best of the age—is *Cakes and Ale,* the story of an eminent novelist whose background is not all that his admirers would like. *The Razor's Edge* dallies with the question of faith, but superficially. Maugham is perhaps best as a writer of short stories—especially about British expatriates in the Far East.

Some novelists found their subject matter in modern political ideologies, and one of the most important of these was George Orwell (1904–50), whose early works expressed pungently a profound dissatisfaction with the economic inequalities, the hypocrisies, the social anachronisms of English life in the nineteen-thirties, but whose last and finest novels attack the Socialist panaceas which, earlier, seemed so attractive. Orwell was a born radical, champion of the small man who is 'pushed around' by bosses of all denominations, and something of Swift's 'savage indignation' as well as his humanitarianism is to be found in *Animal Farm* and *Nineteen Eighty-Four.* The former is a parable of the reaction which supervenes on all high-minded revolutions: the animals take over the farm on which they have been exploited for the selfish ends of the farmer, but gradually the pigs—ostensibly in the name of democracy—create a dictatorship over the other animals far worse than anything known in the days of human management. The final farm-slogan— 'All animals are equal, but some are more equal than other'—has become one of the bitter catch-phrases of our cynical age. *Nineteen Eighty-Four* is a sick man's prophecy of the future (Orwell was dying of tuberculosis when he wrote it) and with its nightmare picture of a totalitarian world it has helped to create a new series of myths. The eternal dictator, Big Brother, the concept of 'double-think', the notion of the mutability of the past—these have become common furniture of our minds.

Political influence on Orwell

Politics provided an inspiration for poets too. Three who expressed a left-wing faith in their early days were W. H. Auden (1907–   ), Cecil Day Lewis (1904–72), and Stephen Spender (1909–   ). The first two found the sprung rhythm and alliteration of Gerard Manley Hopkins congenial for their near-propagandist purpose, while Spender's technique was more reminiscent of Georgian poets like Rupert Brooke. Auden especially was telling and vigorous, but the faith that nourished his early work did not survive the Second World War. When, at the outbreak of that War, he went to America with the novelist Christopher Isherwood, to become, like him, an American citizen, a more attractive creed seemed to be Anglican Christianity, and Auden has produced fine work—*New Year Letter, For the Time Being, The Age of Anxiety*—rooted in traditional belief and traditional technique. (Auden's main contribution to the tech-

Poets

nique of modern verse has been the introduction of scientific and slang terms into its vocabulary, and, by taking in religious, philosophical, political, and psychological themes of a specifically modern kind, he has enormously increased its range.) Day Lewis, much of whose early work reads like a series of parodies of Hopkins, and whose subject matter used to be uncompromisingly 'revolutionary', became a traditional poet owing much to Hardy, deliberately limiting his range to a few themes. Louis MacNeice (1907–63)—a poet once associated with Auden, Spender, and Day Lewis—was, in fact, a member of no school: he never had an axe to grind, and, with a classical background, an Irish temperament, and a very supple technique, he has produced some of the finest love-poetry of the age.

Thomas

A poet who emerged just before the War was Dylan Thomas (1914–1953), a Welshman with Welsh fire and eloquence and a technique that borrowed freely from Hopkins, Joyce, and the Bible. His best poems affirm the unity of life (man with nature, growth with decay, life with death) and, in the exultant tones of Traherne, glorify the innocence of childhood. His images are a curious mixture of the erotic and the biblical (though, even in this, he shows the underlying fertility themes of religion), and the originality of his very concise language, with its Romantic overtones, injected new vigour into an art threatening to become (under Eliot's influence) a little too passionless and intellectual. Dylan Thomas's early death deprived literature of an important poet, a fine prose-writer, and a promising dramatist.

Modern poets

English poetry has reacted against the 'bardic' romanticism of Thomas but has not, since his death, produced any name approaching his in stature. Nevertheless, excellent work is being done by those poets who belong, or belonged, to the 'Group' founded by Philip Hobsbaum in 1955—Edward Lucie-Smith, Peter Redgrove, Martin Bell. Peter Porter, an Australian settled in London, is now established as a poet of considerable distinction, and the same must be said of Philip Larkin, who, working as a librarian in Hull, brings to his work those admirable 'provincial' settings which remind us that poets need not go to London to find either a voice or a reputation. Other poets are W. S. Graham, Kathleen Raine, David Gascoyne, Roy Fuller, Anthony Thwaite, Ted Hughes, and D. J. Enright, though none has yet achieved the glamour of the neo-classic Eliot or the neo-romantic Dylan Thomas. One important senior poet, William Empson, seems content now to assert his influence through literary criticism: his *Seven Types of Ambiguity* has—ever since its first appearance in 1930—encouraged other poets to regard words as complex chords, ringing with overtones, and not just as plain slabs of unequivocal meaning. And, finally, the Scottish poet Hugh Macdiarmid, a self-taught practitioner in Lallans, or Scots, as well as Standard English, continues to produce his highly idiosyncratic explorations of sensibility and language, influencing few, influenced by none.

The novel remains, in England as in America, the literary form in
which talent seeks most to express itself, and it is proper to conclude this
book with a survey of the British novel since (the date is arbitrary but
convenient) the death of Orwell in 1950. The American novel is a subject to be studied on its own as, indeed, is the whole field of American
literature from the early nineteenth century on. But ties of sentiment, as
well as factors of history, demand that the fiction of the British Commonwealth be glanced at along with that of the mother country.

22. The British Novel Since 1950

It is convenient, for the student as well as his teacher, to bundle today's novelists into rough categories of subject matter or form or even (though this may be unfair, since all artists are a kind of hermaphrodite) sex, rather than to set them on a chronological treadmill. And it is appropriate, since we are beginning our survey of the British novel in the year of the death of George Orwell, to start with one very significant category of subject matter—that visionary kind which either hopes for much from the future or fears that the future will be even worse than the present. The novel which presents an optimistic vision of the future is called *utopian*, and its greatest practitioner was H. G. Wells. The most frightening forecast is, of course, to be found in Orwell's *Nineteen Eighty-four*, and this novel may be termed *dystopian*. Aldous Huxley (1894–1963) was the pioneer, with his *Brave New World*, of the dystopian novel in English, but, the year before his death, he published a book called *Island* in which a feasible modern utopia is presented, though it is disrupted by human ambition and malice. A fine dystopian novel by L. P. Hartley (1895–1972) is called *Facial Justice*, in which the levelling process already at work in the contemporary socialist state reaches its bizarre limit in a state philosophy which forbids citizens to be either beautiful or ugly— only mediocre. Hartley's earlier novels—*The Shrimp and the Anemone, Eustace and Hilda, The Go-Between*—are in the Jamesian tradition, but their powerful moral content is highly personal. *The Brickfield* (1964) and *The Betrayal* (1966) are vigorous and original. Hartley still needs a larger audience than the mainly British one he commands, but there are signs that he is at last being taken seriously in America and even Europe.

The Utopian Novel

The War Novel

The war novel is a distinct category of contemporary fiction, and perhaps the best evocations of World War II are to be found in America— with Norman Mailer's *The Naked and the Dead*, Joseph Heller's *Catch-22*, and Kurt Vonnegut's *Slaughterhouse Five*, but Evelyn Waugh's *Sword of Honour* was revealed as not only his finest work but as the sole major British contribution to the category. The trilogy which began with *Men at Arms* and *Officers and Gentlemen* was completed in 1961 with *Unconditional Surrender*, and the three novels, much revised, were eventually issued as a single volume called *Sword of Honour*. Waugh died suddenly in 1966, and his œuvre is at last being seen, on both sides of the Atlantic, as more than a mere collection of witty and elegant entertainments. He has chronicled the decline and fall of an era with matchless skill and a previously undescried profundity.

Waugh was a Catholic novelist, concerned, as he says in a prefatory note to *Brideshead Revisited*, with eschatological matters (or with death, judgement, hell and heaven), and one of the ways in which he compares with Graham Greene—whom otherwise he resembles little—is in this assumption of a set of divine standards by which even the actions of characters in fictional entertainments must be measured. Greene himself has continued to explore the human conscience, mainly in exotic settings. His major achievements since 1950 have been *A Burnt-Out Case* and *The Comedians*, but he has shown himself capable of a new humour and lightness of touch in the delightful *Travels With My Aunt* (1970), as well as having made admirable contributions to the art of the short story. William Golding (1911–   ), without taking a specifically Catholic viewpoint, has been preoccupied with the great absolutes of good and evil in *Lord of the Flies* (1954), which is about the functioning of original sin among boys wrecked on an island, *The Inheritors* (1955), which seems to teach that *homo sapiens* first defined himself in prehistory through his capacity to perform evil, *Pincher Martin* (1956), with its nightmare image of the soul of a wrecked sailor confronting a God who exposes its wretched emptiness, and *Free Fall* (1959), which deals with man's capacity to choose either good or evil: his fall from grace cannot be blamed on any deterministic process but only on his open-eyed election of damnation.

Good and Evil

The work of Pamela Hansford Johnson (1912–   ) has been regarded ever since her first novel (*This Bed Thy Centre*, 1935) as distinguished social commentary or comedy, but she began to disclose a concern with the deeper moral problems in novels like *An Error of Judgment* (1962), at the same time practising a taut and astringent soul-surgery in *The Unspeakable Skipton* (1958) and *Night and Silence! Who is Here?* (1963). In this field of moral concern, the novels of P. H. Newby (1918–   ) must be mentioned, especially such probings of the human spirit as are to be found in *The Barbary Light* (1962) and *One of the Founders* (1965). He too has a comic gift, best seen in his studies of east–west confrontation—*The Picnic at Sakkara* (1955) and *A Guest and His Going* (1959). But two names stand out among those that came to special prominence in the post-war period as delvers into the tortured depth of the human spirit—Malcolm Lowry (1909–57), whose masterly *Under the Volcano* (first published, to little acclaim, in 1947) began to be perceived as a study in self-damnation

Social Comment

of almost Faustian proportions, and the Australian Patrick White (1912–   ), whose *The Tree of Man* (1955), *Voss* (1957), and *Riders in the Chariot* (1961) rise above mere Australian 'regionalism' and probably will earn, sooner or later, the kind of praise accorded to such great dead Russians as Dostoevsky and Turgeniev.

The modern British novel owes much to the Irish, and the same may be said of the contemporary French novel, one of whose glories is Samuel Beckett (1906–   ), a Dubliner and friend of James Joyce who elected to write in French and, in works like *Molloy* and *Malone Dies*, explores a margin of fiction long neglected—the world of the totally deprived, the rejected of God and man who yet keep alive the spark of human identity. Another Irishman, Joyce Cary (1888–1957), is, since his death, finding a place in the great pantheon of original creators, and his works—whether they deal with Africa, as in *Mister Johnson* and *Aissa Saved*, or the world of the young, as in *Charley is my Darling* and *A House of Children*, or, in the great sequence which contains *Herself Surprised*, *To Be a Pilgrim* and *The Horse's Mouth*, with a whole swathe of British social history—are seen to come close to William Blake in their affirmation of the holiness of the human imagination. A third Irishman, Flann O'Brien (1910–66), published a masterpiece—acclaimed as such by Joyce—in 1939, but this still awaits the general recognition that is its due. The book is *At Swim-Two-Birds* and, with lesser novels like *The Hard Life* and *The Dalkey Archive*, it is unique in its experimental power, its lightly carried learning, its fusing of fantasy and Irish realism.

Roman fleuve   The period since 1950 has seen the flowering of the *roman fleuve* in England—the long novel-sequence which makes obeisance to Marcel Proust's *A la Recherche du Temps Perdu* and presents, in a series of books which may be read as separate entities but gradually reveal themselves as a single unified conception, human society in a state of change. Anthony Powell (1905–   ) has been working on *The Music of Time* since 1951, when *A Question of Upbringing* appeared, and the whole emergent sequence, with its portrait of that area of British life where the bohemian and aristocratic conjoin, promises to be a great novel hardly inferior to Proust's in respect of the variety of its characters, its wit, and its recreation of a whole society. C. P. Snow (1905–   ), husband of Pamela Hansford-Johnson, has at last completed his long sequence *Strangers and Brothers*, with its pictures of an England painfully trying to adjust itself to social change, war, the new horrors of science, new concepts of moral responsibility. Seen from the viewpoint of a public man of obscure origins, this England is different from Powell's, but the two sequences together form a remarkable and enlightening synoptic picture of the history of our own times. To these two river-novels must be added the long autobiographical *Chronicles of Ancient Sunlight* by Henry Williamson (1895–   ), strangely neglected but, in its old-fashioned way, compelling and moving.

Certain novelists, unwilling to commit themselves, and their whole lives, to the endless labour of a *roman fleuve*, have compromised by producing tetralogies and trilogies, whose unity derives from place more than time. I might mention my own *Malayan Trilogy* here (entitled *The Long Day Wanes* in America), which attempts to depict the end of colonial rule in the Far East. Olivia Manning has, with her *Balkan Trilogy*, rendered for all time the very essence of life in Rumania and Greece, as it appeared to a pair of British expatriates, during the imminent Nazi invasions. Lawrence Durrell (1912–   ) completed in 1960 a poetically bizarre study of passion and guilt and intrigue in Alexandria. This is a tetralogy built on the 'relativist principle', in which the events are viewed from different angles, and the whole work is called, appropriately, the *Alexandria Quartet*. Doris Lessing (1919–   ) has, in her pentateuch *Children of Violence*, written an autobiographical sequence which presents the main preoccupations of a left-wing feminist who has seen intolerance in many areas—in the political system of South Africa, in the man-dominated ethos of Britain, in the whole sick post-war world. Her work is sometimes wearisomely didactic, neglecting form for theme and entertainment for instruction, but it is an achievement that it is unwise to ignore.

The writer of the really long novel labours under disadvantages that were unknown in, say, Dickens's time, when serialisation permitted a long slow work to emerge piecemeal in public. One sometimes feels that Angus Wilson (1913–   ) would be happier if he could fulfil his Dickensian propensities in serial form. As it is, he produces rare novels of less than Dickensian length, though the canvas is large enough and the portrait gallery sufficiently massive. Works like *Hemlock and After* (1952) and *Anglo-Saxon Attitudes* (1956) show a remarkable wit, reveal a sardonic eye, make statements of permanent value about life in modern England, while *The Middle Age of Mrs. Eliot* (1958) and *Late Call* (1964) show an ability to delve into the female mind that is worthy of George Eliot. And Wilson has made fictional statements about the homosexual sensibility quite unavailable to his Victorian masters, who were hampered by ignorance as well as an imposed reticence.

Since her death, Ivy Compton-Burnett has been subjected to the serious critical assessment which was lacking in her lifetime, when her novels, all of whose titles were similarly structured—*The Present and the Past*, *A Heritage and its History*, *The Mighty and their Fall* and so on, seemed to be eccentric sports, entertaining but perhaps fundamentally frivolous under the pose of Victorian gravity. The recent essay by Mary McCarthy seems to demonstrate that Ivy Compton-Burnett was prophetic, despite the old-fashioned surface of her settings and style; she dealt in those social *structures* which have become so important to French anthropologists rather than in traditional fictional properties like character, morality, nemesis. Among other British women novelists, undistinguished

Women novelists

by such quirky originality but nevertheless important, is Elizabeth Bowen (1899–1972), who added fresh lustre to a reputation gained as early as 1927 (*The Hotel*) and consolidated with *The Death of the Heart* (1938) and *The Heat of the Day* (1949), by producing *A World of Love* in 1955 and *The Little Girls* in 1964. Her near-contemporaries, Storm Jameson (1894–   ), Rosamond Lehmann (1903–   ) and Rebecca West (1892–   ) continue to write with the energy and scrupulous delicacy which relates the entire generation of women novelists to Henry James. Storm Jameson has produced at least a dozen novels since 1950. Rosamond Lehmann, whose masterpieces are *Dusty Answer* (1927) and *The Ballad and the Source* (1944), has been comparatively silent since her remarkable *The Echoing Grove* in 1953. Rebecca West's *The Birds Fall Down* (1966) shows a firm grasp of the dilemmas of our time, particularly that treasonable impulse which was the subject of a long philosophical study by Miss West.

Younger women novelists include Iris Murdoch (1919–   ) who, in such early works as *Under the Net*, *The Sandcastle* and *The Bell*, disclosed a capacity for blending naturalism and symbolism and touching on complex, almost inarticulable, psychological states. *A Severed Head* (1961), which has not been well understood though it has been dramatised and even filmed, seemed to flirt with structuralism, combining the characters in sexual patterns of a purely cerebral nature. Later books like *An Unofficial Rose*, *The Unicorn*, *The Italian Girl*, are exercises in a new kind of Gothic—poetic, erotic, even violent—while *The Red and the Green* (1965) was a not very successful attempt to make a historical romance out of the Irish rebellion of 1916. A perhaps more interesting novelist is Muriel Spark, a Catholic convert who views human life almost from the lofty heights of the Church Triumphant—brilliantly detached, savagely comic. She has created new myths in *Memento Mori* (1959) and *The Prime of Miss Jean Brodie* (1961) and shown herself capable of the traditional large-canvas novel in *The Mandelbaum Gate* (1964). Edna O'Brien (1932–   ), with her strong erotic content, has brought to the British novel a very frank, even devastating, exposure of women's sexual needs (as in *The Country Girls* and *August is a Wicked Month*), and the same may be said of Brigid Brophy (1929–   ), a novelist of great intelligence whose purpose, like that of Doris Lessing, is to deflate the lordly pretensions of man. Other fine novelists of this younger generation are Elizabeth Jane Howard (*The Beautiful Visit*, *The Sea Change*) and Penelope Mortimer (*Daddy's Gone A-Hunting*, *The Pumpkin Eater*).

Historical novel

The historical novel, to which may be added the novel of ancient myth, is a form frequently associated with women, perhaps because of the reputations earned by popular novelists like Margaret Mitchell (*Gone With the Wind*) and Kathleen Winsor (*Forever Amber*), but perhaps also because women—more aware of identity than change in the passing of time—are better qualified than men to see through historical 'accidents' (dress and speech and manners) and hit the human essence underneath. Certainly, in the serious field of historical and mythical conjuration, women have done better than men in the present period. Helen Waddell's *Peter Abelard* and Bryher's evocations of life in early Britain, Mary Renault's *The Last of the Wine, The King Must Die, The Bull from the Sea*, even Georgette Heyer's light romances of Georgian English life, attest that the bringing of the past to life can be very much woman's work. But certain men must not be neglected—Robert Graves (1895–), with his *I, Claudius* and *Claudius the God* and a whole series of fictional biographical studies, from *King Jesus* to *Wife to Mr. Milton*; Alfred Duggan (1903–66), the 'professional' historical novelist, who would write on any period, so long as it was in the past; Peter Green, evoker of ancient Greece and Rome; Henry Treece, specialist in myth.

Arthur Koestler (1905–), who wrote in Hungarian and German before he wrote in English, is responsible for a different kind of historical fiction. *The Gladiators* tells the story of Spartacus and the slaves' revolt which the Roman historians say so little about, but it asks the question: in a new state founded on hatred of oppression, how far is its ruler himself permitted to use oppression to keep law and order? In other words, Koestler is using the past to illuminate modern political problems. His masterpiece, *Darkness at Noon*, deals with the Soviet purges and as such joins those books which are near-historical, illustrative of a recent past which goes on influencing the present. But to *use* the past—as also in Koestler's *Thieves in the Night*, a tale of the Palestinian Jews and their state-building problems—as a device for speaking of the present is not perhaps the way of the real historical novel.

All novels become, in time, historical. They express their own period, and that period passes, leaving the novel behind as a gloss in its margin. The nineteen-fifties, a period of middle-class rebellion in Britain, produced John Osborne's *Look Back in Anger* but also John Wain's *Hurry On Down*, Keith Waterhouse's *Billy Liar*, Stan Barstow's *A Kind of Loving* and Kingsley Amis's *Lucky Jim*. These novelists are still at work, but their subject matter has inevitably changed. Amis (1922–) is an important comic writer who, having attacked bourgeois hypocrisy and dented the armour of the British Establishment in *That Uncertain Feeling*, *I Like It Here* and *Take a Girl Like You*, has settled to a kind of brilliant professionalism, in which such popular forms as the spy-novel and even the ghost-story are ennobled in his hands and become devices for expressing 'new Tory' convictions. Amis began as a Socialist but is now a pillar of middle-class values, like his contemporary John Braine (1922–), whose *Room at the Top* and *Life at the Top* articulated the bitter dissatisfaction of the provincial working classes at their exclusion from the great feast of privilege. Alan Sillitoe (1928–) was even bitterer

Anti-Establishment Novels

and bolder in *Saturday Night and Sunday Morning*, a novel which presents class warfare as the natural state of British life.

The first of the British rebels appeared in *Scenes from Provincial Life* (1950) by William Cooper (1910–), but they have sprung up in many quarters since, or have stimulated the novelist's concern with a kind of human being who wants to be accepted on his own terms, or those of his class, and not merely to be absorbed into the Establishment. Colin Mac-Innes (1914–) has, in *City of Spades* and *Absolute Beginners*, given a voice to both the West Indian immigrants of Britain and the working-class young. John Wain (1925–), with *Hurry On Down, Living in the Present*, and *The Contenders*, presents working-class values as something to be embraced actively, even by those born in privilege, since they represent a greater solidity and offer a richer happiness than the stewed-out conventions of upper-class culture. The provinces become, in the novels of Stanley Middleton (1919–)—particularly *Harris's Requiem*—and Keith Waterhouse (1929–), author of *Billy Liar* and *Jubb*, a region to be taken quite as seriously as the metropolis.

Commonwealth Novelists

More than the mere provinces of the mother-island have entered the novel since the Second World War. The whole of the British Commonwealth has found a voice, often in works produced by writers to whom English is not a first language but an auxiliary imposed by colonial rule. In Africa, Chinua Achebe (1930–) has chronicled with great wit and some bitterness the agonies of the coming of independence, particularly in *No Longer At Ease* and *A Man of the People*. On the same continent, Cyprian Ekwense (1921–) has—particularly in *Jagua Nana*—shown the new corruptions available to a simple tribal people confronting the material values borrowed from the West. South Africa has produced a magnificent literature of protest. To Doris Lessing's achievement may be added those of Nadine Gordimer (1923–), Alan Paton (1903–), whose *Cry the Beloved Country* has a world readership, and Dan Jacobson (1929–).

India's novelists include R. K. Narayan (1907–), gentle, humorous, and perceptive in *The English Teacher* and *The Maneater of Malgudi*, Raja Rao (1909–) whose *The Serpent and the Rope* may well be the outstanding triumph of modern Indian literature in English, and the scholarly, witty Balachandra Rajan (1920–), with his *The Dark Dancer* and *Too Long in the West*. The work of the Sikh, Khushwant Singh (1915–), especially his powerful *I Shall Not Hear the Nightingale*, has already gained a large reputation in America, though it needs to be better known in England.

The important West Indian names are V. S. Naipaul (1932–), whose *A House for Mr. Biswas* and *The Mimic Men* are already well-known in Europe, George Lamming (*In the Castle of My Skin, The Pleasures of Exile*), John Hearne (1926–), who is best approached through *Land of the Living*, and the late Edgar Austin Mittelholzer (1909–66), whose violent suicide put an end to a life of high production and little recognition. English-born novelists who have made exotic or imperial territories their subject matter include D. J. Enright (*Academic Year*), Francis King (*The Custom House*), Susan Yorke (*Capitan China*) and Katherine Sim (*Malacca Boy*).

Finally, it remains to mention certain important novelists who cannot easily be classified. There is Christine Brooke-Rose, who has brought the spirit of experimentalism to be found in the French *anti-roman* into the English novel; her husband, Jerzy Peterkiewicz, whose first language, like Conrad's, is Polish, but whose novels in English are a fresh contribution to modes of using the language; Philip Toynbee, another experimentalist, who has written some of his fiction in verse; and the great original Henry Green, who practises a very individual symbolism in works like *Loving, Nothing, Back*.

The British novel is flourishing, though its readership is not. The story of English literature, viewed aesthetically, is one thing; the story of English writers is quite another. The price of contributing to the greatest literature the world has ever seen is often struggle and penury: art is still too often its own reward. It is salutary sometimes to think of the early deaths of Keats, Shelley, Byron, Chatterton, Dylan Thomas, of the Grub Street struggles of Dr. Johnson, the despair of Gissing and Francis Thompson. That so many writers have been prepared to accept a kind of martyrdom is the best tribute that flesh can pay to the living spirit of man as expressed in his literature. One cannot doubt that the martyrdom will continue to be gladly embraced. To some of us, the wresting of beauty out of language is the only thing in the world that matters.

English Verse Forms

The smallest unit of verse is the *metrical foot*. This consists of a strong, or accented, syllable and one or more weak, or unaccented, syllables. Traditional prosody isolated four main types of foot:

  ⌣— ⌣ — ⌣ —
  The iambic (weak syllable followed by strong): away; come here; to-night.

  — ⌣ — ⌣ — ⌣
  The trochaic (strong syllable followed by weak): father; sister; Monday.

  ⌣ ⌣— ⌣ ⌣ —
  The anapaestic (two weak followed by one strong): go away; not at all.

  — ⌣ ⌣ — ⌣ ⌣
  The dactylic (one strong followed by two weak): merrily; murderous.

Gerard Manley Hopkins, however, showed that it was possible to have

  — ⌣ ⌣ ⌣
metrical feet with three, four, or more weak syllables (river-rounded;
  — ⌣ ⌣⌣⌣
cuckoo-echoing) or with no weak syllables at all (from *The Wreck of the*
  ⌣ — — ⌣ ⌣ —

Single lines *Deutschland:* World's | strand, | sway of the | sea). A regular line of verse is expected to choose one type of metrical foot and repeat it, thus producing the simplest kind of verse-pattern. Classical prosody counts the number of feet in a line and gives the total in Greek: iambic monometer (one iambic foot); trochaic dimeter (two trochaic feet); anapaestic trimeter (three anapaestic feet); dactylic tetrameter (four dactylic feet); iambic pentameter (five iambic feet); trochaic hexameter (six trochaic feet); iambic heptameter (seven iambic feet); trochaic octameter (eight trochaic feet). Here are some examples:

  ⌣ — ⌣ — ⌣ — ⌣ — ⌣ —
  The day | is hot, | the Mont|agues | abroad | (iambic pentameter).
  — ⌣ — ⌣ — ⌣ — ⌣
  Minne|haha, | laughing | water | (trochaic tetrameter).

˘ ˘ – ˘ ˘ – ˘ ˘ –

We are they | who come fast|er than fate | (anapaestic trimeter).

– ˘ ˘ – ˘ ˘

Sisterly, | brotherly | (dactylic dimeter).

The use of Greek nomenclature for English verse-units is not really convenient, as the English language (unlike the classical and Romance tongues) is a heavily stressed one and prefers to generate its rhythms—like music—out of the regular recurrence of a strong beat, paying little heed to the number of weak syllables that come between the repetitions. 'Scanning' a line on the Greek pattern produces many anomalies, and it is better, with the greater part of English verse, to speak of 'so many beats to the line'. By this means we are able to describe, in the same terms, both traditional verse and 'sprung rhythm' (see below). The following piece of classical scanning is manifestly absurd:

˘ – ˘ – ˘ – ˘ – ˘ – ˘

To-morr|ow and | to-mor|row and | to-mor|(row).

This is not iambic pentameter at all. Two of the stresses are only heard in the imagination:

˘ – ˘ – ˘ ˘ – ˘ – ˘ ˘ – ˘

To-morrow( )and to-morrow( )and to-morrow.

Some kinds of English verse admit of no greater organisation than the single line—dramatic and narrative blank verse, for example. The bigger unit known as the 'verse paragraph' depends on sense, on meaning, and not on the technical resources of verse alone. The minimal verse-unit greater than the single line is the *couplet*:

Couplets

Had we but world enough and time,	(a)
This coyness, lady, were no crime.	(a)
We would sit down and think which way	(b)
To walk, and pass our long love's day.	(b)

Here rhyme is used to bind two successive lines into a single unit (letters indicate the rhyme-scheme). These are, of course, 'four-beat couplets'. Five-beat couplets are known as *heroic couplets*:

A little learning is a dangerous thing:	(a)
Drink deep, or taste not the Pierian spring.	(a)
There shallow draughts intoxicate the brain,	(b)
And drinking largely sobers us again.	(b)

A couplet is a verse-unit, but not quite a *stanza*. A stanza, as its setting-forth on the printed page clearly shows, is 'framed in silence'—in other words, its sense is complete enough for it to be followed by a lengthy

Stanza

Quatrain

pause: a couplet, though it may make a pithy and memorable statement, always seems to require qualification or amplification from another couplet, and so couplets tend to 'go on for ever'. The commonest stanza-form is the *quatrain*, and here are some examples of typical rhyme-schemes:

> Tiger! tiger! burning bright
> In the forests of the night,
> What immortal hand or eye
> Could frame thy fearful symmetry?
> > (William Blake).

(Four-beat line, rhyme-scheme aabb)

> The curfew tolls the knell of parting day,
> The lowing herd wind slowly o'er the lea,
> The ploughman homeward plods his weary way,
> And leaves the world to darkness and to me.
> > (Thomas Gray).

(Five-beat line, rhyme-scheme abab. This is known as the *Heroic Stanza*.)

> Then he pulled out his bright, brown sword,
> And dried it on his sleeve,
> And he smote off that vile lad's head
> And asked for no man's leave.
> > (The ballad 'Glasgerion'.)

(Four beats alternating with three beats, rhyme-scheme abcb. This is the *Ballad Stanza*.)

> I held it truth, with him who sings
> To one clear harp in divers tones,
> That men may rise on stepping-stones
> Of their dead selves to higher things.
> > (Tennyson.)

(Four-beat line, rhyme-scheme abba. Often called, because Tennyson employed it consistently in the long poem of that name, the *In Memoriam Stanza*.)

> Awake, for morning in the bowl of night
> Has flung the stone that puts the stars to flight,
> And, lo, the hunter of the East has caught
> The Sultan's turret in a noose of light.
> > (Fitzgerald.)

(Five-beat line, rhyme-scheme aaba. A Persian form, adopted by Edward Fitzgerald for his translation of Omar Khayyam's *Rubaiyat*, and often called the *Omar Khayyam Stanza*.)

Many variants of the quatrain are possible. Andrew Marvell, in his *Horatian Ode on Cromwell's Return from Ireland*, rendered Horace's ode-stanza as follows:

> He nothing common did or mean
> Upon that memorable scene,
>   But with his keener eye
>   The axe's edge did try.

(First two lines have four beats, last two lines have three beats, rhyme-scheme aabb.) Collins, in his *Ode to Evening*, attempted a similar rendering of Horace's stanza without using rhyme:

> Now air is hush'd, save where the weak-ey'd bat
> With short shrill shriek flits by on leathern wing,
> Or where the beetle winds
> His small but sullen horn . . .

(First two lines have five beats, last two lines have three beats, no rhyme.)

Three-line stanzas are less common than quatrains, chiefly perhaps because of the need for an aaa rhyme-scheme, which obviously presents more technical difficulties than any dual rhyme-scheme like aabb or abab. The Earl of Rochester's poem *Upon Nothing* is a triumphant example of the use of a three-line stanza: *3 line stanza*

> Nothing! thou elder brother ev'n to Shade,
> Thou hadst a being ere the world was made,
> And (well fixt) art alone of ending not afraid.

(First two lines have five beats, last line has six beats—a six-beat line is sometimes called an *Alexandrine*; rhyme-scheme aaa.)

A form not properly stanzaic, but based on a three-line unit, is the *Terza Rima* used by Dante in his *Divine Comedy*. Here lines interlock as follows: aba bcb cdc ded efe . . . The sequence may run for over a hundred lines, and it is brought to a close with an extra line in the following way: yzy z. Shelley uses terza rima in his *Ode to the West Wind*, but the sequence is compressed to a stanza of fourteen lines with a final couplet. *3 line unit*

If I were a dead leaf thou mightest bear;	(a)
If I were a swift cloud to fly with thee;	(b)
A wave to pant beneath thy power, and share	(a)
The impulse of thy strength, only less free	(b)
Than thou, O uncontrollable! If even	(c)
I were as in my boyhood, and could be	(b)

The comrade of thy wanderings over Heaven,   (c)
As then, when to outstrip thy skiey speed   (d)
Scarce seemed a vision; I would ne'er have striven (c)

As thus with thee in prayer in my sore need.   (d)
Oh, lift me as a wave, a leaf, a cloud!   (e)
I fall upon the thorns of life! I bleed!   (d)

A heavy weight of hours has chained and bowed   (e)
One too like thee: tameless, and swift, and proud. (e)

Sapphic form

A stanza-form that seems to suggest both the quatrain and the three-line stanza is the *Sapphic* (named after the Grecian poetess Sappho):

Sit like a fool then, crassly emptying
Glass after wineglass in some foul tavern,
Watching the night and its candles gutter,
Snoring at sunrise.

A. B.

(First three lines have four beats, last line has two beats; no rhyme.)

Complex stanzas

I shall now list three 'standard' complex stanza-forms.

Rime Royal

It was no dream; for I lay broad awaking:
But all is turned now through my gentleness
Into a bitter fashion of forsaking,
And I have leave to go of her goodness,
And she also to use new-fangledness.
But since that I unkindly so am served:
'How like you this,' what hath she now deserved?

(Sir Thomas Wyatt.)

(Seven five-beat lines, rhyme-scheme ababbcc.)

Spenserian Stanza

St. Agnes' Eve—ah, bitter chill it was!
The owl, for all his feathers, was a-cold;
The hare limp'd trembling through the frozen grass,
And silent was the flock in woolly fold:
Numb were the the Beadsman's fingers while he told
His rosary, and while his frosted breath,
Like pious incense from a censer old,
Seemed taking flight for heaven without a death,
Past the sweet Virgin's picture, while his prayer he saith.

(John Keats.)

(Eight five-beat lines followed by one six-beat line or Alexandrine; rhyme-scheme ababbcbcc.)

Byronic Stanza

> O Hesperus! thou bringest all good things—
> Home to the weary, to the hungry cheer,
> To the young bird the parent's brooding wings,
> The welcome stall to the o'erlaboured steer:
> Whate'er of peace about our hearthstone clings,
> Whate'er our household gods protect of dear,
> Are gathered round us by thy look of rest;
> Thou bring'st the child, too, to the mother's breast.
>
> (from *Don Juan*: Lord Byron.)

(Eight lines, all with five beats; rhyme-scheme abababcc.)

An infinite number of other complex stanza-forms is, of course, possible, and many poets invent their own, use them, perhaps once, in a particular poem, and then discard them.

The other 'standard' verse-forms are not stanzaic, because they are not units but entities: the whole point of a stanza is that it appears more than once in a poem, whereas the following make complete poems in themselves:

The Sonnet

Examples are to be found in this book of the two main sonnet-forms used in English—the Shakespearian and the Petrarchan. We can summarise them as follows: Shakespearian: fourteen lines, each containing five beats, divided into three quatrains and a final couplet; rhyme-scheme abab cdcd efef gg. Petrarchan: fourteen lines, each containing five beats, divided into an octave (eight lines) and a sestet (six lines). The octave rhymes abba abba, the sestet cde cde or cdc dcd or any other combination of two or three rhymes. Strictly, a final couplet should be avoided. The point of change-over from octave to sestet is known as the *volta*, though the statement made in the octave is often not completed until the middle of the first line of the sestet: the volta is then said to be delayed.

Variations on these two sonnet-forms have been attempted. Milton and Hopkins have written sonnets with *codas* or 'tails', in other words, extra lines added as afterthoughts to the strict fourteen. Hopkins has written two 'curtal-sonnets'—ten lines with a coda of one foot, rhyming abcabc dbcdbd—one of which is the well-known *Pied Beauty*. Hopkins is perhaps also the first English poet to write sonnets with six-beat lines or Alexandrines (on the French model) and his sonnet *Spelt From Sybil's Leaves* has eight-beat lines with a marked *caesura* between each four. (A caesura is a pause, real or imaginary, cutting a long line into two halves. It is only found when the total number of beats in the line is a multiple of two.)

The sonnet-form is, in origin, Italian. Those that follow now were first used by mediaeval French poets.

The Ballade

A poem of three eight-line stanzas and a half-stanza called the *Envoy* or *Envoi*. The number of stresses to the line is immaterial, but the rhyme-scheme is strict: ababbcbc ababbcbc ababbcbc *Envoy* bcbc. The envoy is a message to some great person, living or dead, real or fictitious, frequently unnamed, and its characteristic beginning is 'Prince!' The three stanzas and the envoy all carry the same final line as a refrain.

A Ballade of Studying English Literature.

Extol the virtue of the verse,
    The myriad wonders of the prose;
And then with reverent breath rehearse
    The marvels that the plays disclose.
    Show me the endless serried rows
Where sleep the masters, great and small.
    Yet I a minor problem pose:
    How can I ever read them all?

Glittering the gold and rich the purse:
    The Muses blessed us when they chose
This island as the bounteous nurse
    Of poesy that, the world well knows,
    Is the world's writing's reddest rose,
Its brightest-woven coronal.
    But still the problem swells and grows:
How can I ever read them all?

Surely this richness is a curse?
    For my ascetic instinct flows
Not to the better, but the worse—
    The meanest that the Muse bestows.
    Count me not one of learning's foes
That I for sham and shoddy fall;
    The great repel with countless blows:
How can I ever read them all?

ENVOY

Prince! Twitch not a disgusted nose,
    Nor bite me with a fang of gall.

'All or nothing.' Thus it goes—
And how can I ever read them all?

A. B.

Once used, by men like Villon in France and Chaucer in England, for themes of high seriousness, the ballade-form is now most in favour with writers of light and facetious verse. (A very amusing ballade by J. C. Squire has for refrain: 'I'm not so think as you drunk I am.')

The Rondel

Again, a form which insists on economy in rhyming and makes use of a refrain. The refrain is, properly, the opening phrase of the poem, which is heard again at the end of the second and third stanzas. The following improvisation is based on a phrase from Browning—'In England now'.

In England now the wind blows high
And clouds brush rudely at the sky;
The blood runs thinly through my frame,
I half-caress the hearthstone's flame,
Oppressed by autumn's desolate cry.

Then homesick for the south am I,
For where the lucky swallows fly,
But each warm land is just a name
In England now.

The luckless workers I espy
With chins dipped low and collars high,
Walk into winter, do not blame
The shifting globe. A gust of shame
Represses my unmanly sigh
In England now.

A. B.

The Triolet

A light, brief but difficult form, using two rhymes and a refrain. The scheme is: a (refrain—first half) b (refrain—second half) a a (refrain—first half) ab a (refrain—first half) b (refrain—second half).

What can I say of any worth
In lines as crabbed and crimped as these?
I scan the sky and then the earth:
What can I say of any worth?
The poem comes, at last, to birth
Only to meet its obsequies!

What *can* I say of any worth
In lines as crabbed and crimped as these?

A. B.

The Villanelle

Like the triolet, this has a two-line refrain which only appears as such at the very end of the poem. The scheme is:

a (refrain 1) b a (refrain 2)
a   b a (refrain 1)
a   b a (refrain 2)
a   b a (refrain 1) a (refrain 2)

This writing of a villanelle
  Takes lots of paper, ink and time.
It's difficult to do it well.

Each verse is like a prison-cell;
  Tricky as dancing on a dime,
This writing of a villanelle.

More blood and tears than tongue can tell
  Must go to juggling with the rhyme.
It's difficult to do it well.

To poets whom the gods impel
  To tame in words the vast sublime,
This writing of a villanelle,

This tinkling of a tiny bell,
  Must seem a waste of time, a crime!
It's difficult to do it well,

However; it's a hill that's hell
  (Though sound your wind and limb) to climb,
This writing of a villanelle.
It's difficult to do it well.

A. B.

This form has, in our own day, carried serious and moving themes. One of the finest modern examples is Dylan Thomas's, addressed to his dying father, based on the lines: 'Do not go gentle into that good night./ Rage, rage against the dying of the light.'

Last of these strict verse-forms I must mention the *Sestina*, Italian in origin, which, though no rhyme is used, is certainly the most difficult of all. There are six stanzas of six lines each and a half-stanza to conclude. Melody is provided through the repetition of certain key-words, first heard at the ends of the first six lines, then appearing in the five following stanzas, at the ends of the lines, but not in the order in which they first appeared. Here is an example of an opening stanza:

> On that still night, in that autumnal weather,
> When all the air was silver-drenched in starlight,
> We stood entranced, crowning that grassy hill-top,
> With, all below us, leagues of murmuring ocean,
> And, though so high, we knew no fear of falling;
> More than embracing arms would keep us steady.

The key-words are 'weather', 'starlight', 'hill-top', 'ocean', 'falling', and 'steady'. Each key-word must have a chance to come at the end of a first line and at the end of a last line. 'Steady' ends the first stanza, so the first line of the second stanza might run:

> Come highest winds, love keeps the vessel steady . . .

In the concluding half-stanza the key-words appear at the end of half-lines:

> Changed our hearts' weather, for the glass is falling,
> Now no more starlight, rain will patter steady,
> Misted the hill-top, menacing the ocean.

Finally, we must consider briefly some aspects of the technique of modern poetry.

Free Verse (or *Vers Libre*)

This is verse which obeys no rules as to number of stresses in a line or (where rhyme is used) to regular rhyme-pattern. It is the antithesis of the forms we have just been discussing. There first appears a hint of free verse in the blank verse of Shakespeare's last plays and in the plays of other Jacobean dramatists, where frequently a line cannot be 'scanned' into five beats: the rhythms are as close as possible to those of natural speech, almost, but not quite, suggesting prose. In the Augustan Age, the *Pindaric Ode* (ostensibly following the example of the Greek poet Pindar) gave great freedom, anticipating modern free verse. (Examine the two great musical odes of Dryden, for example.) Wordsworth's *Intimations of Immortality* Ode exhibits a similar freedom. But the first hints of modern practice are to be found in certain Victorian poets— Matthew Arnold, Coventry Patmore and the American Walt Whitman. (Most of the work of this latter poet suggests prose—'cadenced prose'— rather than verse.) T. S. Eliot's free verse derives from two sources: the break-up of the blank-verse line with the Jacobean dramatists and the break-up of the regular Alexandrine in France (with poets like Jules

Laforgue). Because of the lack of restriction, bad free verse is all too easy to write:

> I look up
> From my empty tea-cup,
> At the picture on the wall, a phalanx of grey
> Victorian faces, they ticking away
> In their own time, I
> In mine. And there is no way
> Of bridging the gap. They
> See me as dead, perhaps as I
> See them.

Experiments in Rhyme

W. B. Yeats, Wilfred Owen, W. H. Auden, and others, found the 'full chime' of rhyme too unsubtle, so they deliberately introduced 'imperfect rhyme' or 'slant rhyme'. Thus Owen rhymes 'groined' with 'groaned'; 'tigress' with 'progress'; 'escaped' with 'scooped'. Yeats rhymes 'wall' with 'soul'; 'one' with 'man'; 'dull' with 'school' and 'full'.

Sprung Rhythm

The letter which Hopkins wrote to Robert Bridges, explaining Sprung Rhythm, and printed as the Introduction to his *Poems*, is the best account of it we have. But some general idea of its nature may be gained from study of the following lines. First, an orthodox four-beat line, which could be scanned easily in the classical way as 'iambic tetrameter':

> The morn, the noon, the eve, the night.

The four stresses (on 'morn', 'noon', 'eve', and 'night') come at regular intervals, as in a bar of music. Thus the essential 'beat' of the line remains if we eliminate the unstressed syllables:

> \   \   \   \
> Morn, noon, eve, night

and if we increase the number of unstressed syllables to an extent unknown to classical practice:

> \   \   \   \
> Morn, noon, in the evening, during the night.

The characteristic flavour of Sprung Rhythm is compounded of musical rhythms and speech-rhythms: two or more strong beats coming together for weighty or harsh effects, a scurrying cluster of unstressed syllables seeming to express excitement, speed, even a stuttering neurosis.

Chronological Table

Ruler	Political, Social, Religious Events	Literary Events
	477 The first invasions by Angles and Saxons from North Germany. By the time these Germanic peoples had settled in Britain, the Danes began their raids. 787 Danish invasion of England, followed by almost continual raids. As England was divided into five kingdoms, each under its own ruler, it was difficult to combat them. This was the position when Alfred became King of Wessex, one of the five kingdoms, in 871.	*Beowulf* and other poems were brought over to England by the new settlers. 670 Caedmon flourished. 735 Venerable Bede died.
Alfred the Great, reigned 871–899.	878 Alfred defeats the Danes at Ethandune (now Edington). Their rule is confined to the Eastern part of England.	891 (*circa*) beginnings of the Anglo-Saxon Chronicle. In Alfred's reign much literature is translated into the Wessex dialect of English.
Edward the Elder, 899–924.		
Athelstan, 924–39.	937 The Battle of Brunanburh.	
The six 'boy kings' (all under 20 on accession): Edmund, Edred, Edwy, Edgar, Edward, Ethelred, 939–1016.	991 The Battle of Maldon. 1013 Sweyn of Denmark subdues the English. Ethelred flees to Normandy and the Dane Canute becomes King of England in 1016.	
Canute, 1016–35.		1023 Archbishop Wulfstan dies.
Harold I, 1035–40.		
Hardicanute, 1040–42.		
Edward the Confessor, 1042–66.		

Ruler	Political, Social, Religious Events	Literary Events
Harold II, 1066.	1066 The English are defeated by the Normans at Hastings. William of Normandy becomes King.	

NORMANS

Ruler	Political, Social, Religious Events	Literary Events
William the Conqueror, 1066–87.	Now begins the 'Feudal System' of land tenure, under which the 'serfs' (the lowest class) are more or less slaves. During the two centuries following, however, this class gradually disappears. 1086 Completion of Domesday Book.	
William II, 1087–1100.	1095 The First Crusade.	
Henry I, 1100–35.	1119 The Order of Knights Templar established.	
Stephen, 1135–41; 1141–54.		1140 (*circa*) Geoffrey of Monmouth's *History of the Britons*.
Matilda, 1141 (Mar.–Dec.).		

PLANTAGENETS

Ruler	Political, Social, Religious Events	Literary Events
Henry II, 1154–89.	1146 Second Crusade. 1154 Nicholas Brakespeare—an Englishman—becomes Pope. 1170 Assassination of Thomas à Becket, Archbishop of Canterbury. 1181 Carthusian monasteries established in England. 1189 Third Crusade.	1154 Geoffrey of Monmouth dies.
Richard I, 1189–99.	The Crusades continue.	
John (Lackland), 1199–1216.	1202 Fourth Crusade. 1204 Crusaders conquer Constantinople. 1209 Franciscan Order established. 1215 Magna Carta signed by King John.	1200 (*circa*) Layamon's *Brut*, The *Ormulum*, The *Ancrene Riwle*.
Henry III, 1216–72.	1218 Fifth Crusade. 1228 Sixth Crusade. 1229 Jerusalem ceded to the Christians. 1248 Seventh Crusade. 1265 First British Commons meet. (St. Thomas Aquinas and Roger Bacon flourished.)	
Edward I, 1272–1307.	1282 Edward I conquers Wales. 1295 First regular English Parliament. 1296 Edward I subdues Scotland.	1300 (*circa*) Robert Mannyng's *Handlyng Sinne*.
Edward II, 1307–27.	1311 Papal decree that Corpus Christi shall be celebrated with all due ceremony.	1311 (*circa*) beginning of Guild plays in England. 1324 Wycliff born.
Edward III, 1327–77. [*cont. over*]	1333 Edward III defeats the Scots. 1339 Edward invades France.	Much literary activity: 1340 (*circa*) Richard Rolle's *Pricke of Conscience*.

Ruler	Political, Social, Religious Events	Literary Events
Edward III, 1327–77.—*cont.*	1346 Battle of Crecy: French defeated. 1348 The 'Black Death' comes to England. 1351 'Statute of Labourers' passed. 1356 Battle of Poitiers: French defeated.	Mid-century: *Pearl*; *the Owl and the Nightingale*; *Sir Gawayn and the Green Knight*. 'Sir John Mande-ville's' *Travels*. 1340? Chaucer born. 1362 Langland's *Piers Plowman*.
Richard II, 1377–99.	1381 Peasants' Revolt under Wat Tyler. 1385 Scots invade England. 1399 Richard deposed by Bolingbroke.	1384 Wycliff dies. 1390 Gower's *Confessio Amantis*. 1394 King James I of Scotland born.
Henry IV (Boling-broke), 1399–1413.	1400 Revolt in Wales. 1402 Scots defeated.	1400 Chaucer and Langland die.
Henry V, 1413–22.	1415 Henry defeats the French at Agincourt. 1420 Henry becomes Regent of France.	1422 William Caxton born.
Henry VI, 1422–61.	1422 Henry VI King of France. 1431 Joan of Arc burnt at the stake. 1440 Printing invented. 1450 Insurrection in England under Jack Cade. 1455 Wars of the Roses begin.	1437 King James I of Scotland dies.
Edward IV, 1461–1483.	1476 Caxton sets up his printing-press at Westminster.	1471 Sir Thomas Malory dies.
Edward V, 1483 (two months only). Richard III, 1483–85.	1485 Richard III killed at Battle of Bosworth. Henry Tudor becomes king. End of Wars of the Roses.	1485 Malory's *Morte D'Arthur* printed.
TUDORS		
Henry VII, 1485–1509.	By 1485 the Feudal System in England had died out. A new era has already begun. 1492 Columbus discovers the West Indies. 1497 The Cabots discover Newfoundland. Vasca da Gama rounds Cape of Good Hope. 1498 Columbus touches American mainland. Vasco da Gama discovers sea-route to India. 1500 Discovery of Brazil.	1491 Caxton dies. 1508 (*circa*) Robert Henryson (born *c.* 1429) dies. 1508 (*circa*) William Dunbar's *Lament for the Makers*.
Henry VIII, 1509–47. [*cont. over*]	1513 Battle of Flodden: Scots defeated. 1517 Luther's theses at Wittenberg. 1521 Luther excommunicated. 1534 Act of Supremacy: Papal power in England abolished. 1536 Wales united to England. 1538 Pope Paul III excommunicates Henry VIII. 1539 General dissolution of monasteries in England. *Note:* Coverdale's translation of the Bible was made, printed and generally used during this reign (from about 1537).	1516 More's *Utopia*. 1522 (*circa*) Gavin Douglas dies (born *c.* 1475). 1526 Tyndale's New Testament. 1529 John Skelton dies (born 1460?). 1530 (*circa*) Dunbar dies (born *c.* 1460). 1535 Sir Thomas More executed (born 1478). 1542 Sir Thomas Wyatt dies (born 1503).

Ruler	Political, Social, Religious Events	Literary Events
Henry VIII, 1509–47.—*cont.*		1547 Earl of Surrey executed (born 1517).
Edward VI, 1547–53.	1549 Act of Uniformity (intended to make the nation conform to the religious changes introduced by Henry VIII). First form of the Book of Common Prayer.	1552 Edmund Spenser born. 1553 François Rabelais dies.
Mary, 1553—8.	1554 Mary marries Philip of Spain. 1555–6 Ridley, Latimer and Cranmer burnt at the stake for refusing to conform to the Church of Rome (Mary was attempting to re-establish Catholicism in England). 1558 Calais taken by the French. Mary Queen of Scots marries heir-apparent to the French throne.	1557 Tottel's *Miscellany*—an anthology containing poems by Surrey, Wyatt and others.
Elizabeth I, 1558–1603.	1560 Reformation established in Scotland. 1564 Death of Calvin. 1577–80 Drake's first voyage round the world. 1587 Mary Queen of Scots beheaded for alleged treason. 1588 Defeat of the Spanish Armada. (*Notes:* Religion in England represented a middle way between Marian Catholicism and Lutheran Protestantism, with the reigning monarch as head of the Church. Drama and music flourished, but so did bear-baiting and cock-fighting. Many social changes, especially in the Poor Laws, and attempts to suppress vagrancy were made.)	1562 *Gorboduc* presented. 1563 Foxe's *Book of Martyrs*. 1564 Shakespeare and Marlowe born. 1576 The Theatre erected. 1577 Holinshed's *Chronicles*. 1578 John Lyly's *Euphues*. 1579 North's translation of Plutarch's *Lives*. Spenser's *Shepherds Calendar*. 1582 Hakluyt's *Divers Voyages Touching Discovery of America*. 1586 Sir Philip Sidney dies (born 1554). 1590 Marlowe's *Tamburlaine*, Sidney's *Arcadia*, Spenser's *Faerie Queene* (first three books). 1593 Marlowe killed. 1599 Spenser dies. 1600 Hooker dies (born 1554).

STUARTS

Ruler	Political, Social, Religious Events	Literary Events
James I, 1603–25.	The Scots King James VI succeeds to the throne of England as James I: England and Scotland are thus united. 1605 The 'Gunpowder Plot': an attempt to blow up the English Parliament. 1611 Authorised Version of the Bible. 1620 The Pilgrim Fathers land in New England, America. (This is a great period of colonisation in the New World.)	1603 Florio's translation of Montaigne's *Essays*. 1608 John Milton born. 1616 Shakespeare dies. Francis Beaumont dies (born 1584). Cervantes dies. Chapman's *Homer* appears. 1621 Burton's *Anatomy of Melancholy*. 1625 Bacon's *Essays*. John Fletcher dies (born 1579).
Charles I, 1625–49. [*cont. over*]	1628 Cromwell becomes a Member of Parliament. 1629 Charles dissolves his Third Parliament. (For the following eleven years he ruled without a Parliament, and the doctrine of the 'Divine Right of Kings' was widely promulgated.)	1626 Cyril Tourneur dies (born 1575?). Bacon dies (born 1561). 1631 John Dryden born. John Donne dies (born 1573?).

Ruler	Political, Social, Religious Events	Literary Events
Charles I, 1625–49.—*cont.*	1634 Charles demands Ship Money. 1640 The 'Long' Parliament. 1641 Rebellion in Ireland. 1642 Commencement of the Civil War: the King and his 'Cavaliers' against the Parliament and its 'Roundhead' supporters. The theatres are closed. 1647 Charles surrenders to Parliament. 1649 Charles executed and England declared a 'Commonwealth'.	1632 Dekker dies (born 1570?). 1633 George Herbert dies (born 1593). John Donne's *Poems.* 1634 Marston dies (born 1575?). Chapman dies (born 1559?). 1637 Ben Jonson dies (born 1574?). Milton's *Comus.* 1640 Massinger dies (born 1583). 1645 Milton's *Poems.* 1649 Crashaw dies (born 1613?).
The Commonwealth, 1649–53.	1651 King Charles II attempts invasion of England. Defeated, he flies to France. 1653 Cromwell dismisses the 'Rump' Parliament and becomes Lord Protector of England.	1651 Hobbes's *Leviathan.*
The Protectorate of Oliver Cromwell, 1653–8.	1657 Cromwell declines the English crown. 1658 Cromwell dies and his son Richard is named Protector. He resigns however in 1659 after holding office less than a year. From then till the Restoration of 1660 England is governed by Parliament.	

STUARTS RESTORED

Ruler	Political, Social, Religious Events	Literary Events
Charles II, 1660–85.	1662 Act of Uniformity passed: non-conformist clergy deprived of their livings. 1665–7; 1672–4 England and Holland at war. 1665 The Great Plague. 1666 The Great Fire of London. 1679 Habeas Corpus Act passed. (*Note:* an age of scientific enquiry. The Royal Society is established.)	1660 Pepys's Diary begins. 1663 Butler's *Hudibras,* Part I. 1667 Jeremy Taylor dies (born 1613). Cowley dies (born 1618). 1667 Milton's *Paradise Lost.* 1673 Molière (French dramatist) dies. 1674 Milton dies. Herrick dies (born 1591). 1678 Marvell dies (born 1621). Bunyan's *Pilgrim's Progress.* 1680 Rochester dies (born 1647). 1685 Otway dies (born 1652).
James II, 1685–8.	James tries to re-establish Catholicism. He attempts to allay opposition by Declarations of Indulgence. In vain, for Protestants appeal to William of Orange (in Holland) for help. 1688 William lands and James flies to France. On his abdication William and Mary are proclaimed King and Queen.	1687 Newton's *Principia.* 1688 Bunyan dies (born 1628) Alexander Pope born.

HANOVERIANS

Ruler	Political, Social, Religious Events	Literary Events
William and Mary, 1688–1702.	1689 Toleration Act passed. Bill of Rights passed. 1690 William defeats James, who has landed in Ireland in an attempt to raise forces and re-establish himself. 1694 Mary dies.	1690 John Locke's *Two Treatises of Government* and *Essay Concerning Human Understanding.* 1691 Etherege dies (born 1634). 1695 Vaughan dies (born 1622). Congreve's *Love for Love.* 1700 Dryden dies.

Ruler	Political, Social, Religious Events	Literary Events
Anne, 1702–14.	1702 England declares war against France and Spain. 1704 Battle of Blenheim. Gibraltar taken. 1707 Scots Parliament passes Act of Union. First Parliament of Great Britain. 1709 Battle of Malplaquet. Duke of Marlborough victorious. 1713 Peace of Utrecht.	1702 First daily paper established —*The Daily Courant*. 1704 Swift's *Tale of a Tub*. 1709 Steele begins *The Tatler*. 1711 Pope's *Essay on Criticism*. The *Spectator* begun by Addison and Steele.
George I, 1714–27.	1715 Jacobite Rebellion (attempt to re-establish rule of Stuarts). Walpole Prime Minister. 1717 Triple Alliance: England, France, Holland. 1718 England at war with Spain.	1716 Wycherley dies (born 1640). 1719 Defoe's *Robinson Crusoe*. 1726 Vanbrugh dies (born 1664). 1726 Swift's *Gulliver's Travels*.
George II, 1727–60.	1729 Peace between Britain, France and Spain. 1739 England again at war with Spain. 1742 France declares war against England, Holland and Maria Theresa. 1743 Battle of Dettingen: France defeated. 1744 Louis XV declares war on Britain. 1745 Charles Edward (Young Pretender) lands in Scotland, takes Carlisle, retreats to Scotland. 1746 Jacobite rebels defeated at Culloden. 1748 Peace of Aix-la-Chapelle. 1751 Clive of India captures Arcot. 1752 Britain adopts new-style calendar. 1759 Battle of Quebec. Wolfe defeats French. 1760 Completion of British conquest of Canada. (*Note*: This is a period of intense conflict between Britain and France, conducted in the New World and India as well as Europe.)	1729 Congreve dies (born 1670). 1730 Thomson's *The Seasons*. 1731 Defoe dies (born 1660). 1740 Richardson's *Pamela*. 1742 Young's *Night Thoughts*. 1744 Pope dies. 1745 Swift dies (born 1667). 1749 Fielding's *Tom Jones*. 1751 David Hume's *Enquiry Concerning Principles of Morals*. 1755 Dr. Johnson's *Dictionary*. 1760 Sterne's *Tristram Shandy*. Macpherson's *Ossian* hoax.
George III, 1760–1820. [*cont. over*]	1763 End of the Seven Years' War. 1770 Cook discovers New South Wales. 1773 Tax imposed on tea by British strongly resented in Boston, America. 1773 Warren Hastings, Governor-General of India. 1775 Americans rebel against British 'tyranny'. 1776 Declaration of American Independence. 1783 After many military defeats, the British acknowledge American Independence. 1783 Pitt appointed Prime Minister. 1786 Impeachment of Warren Hastings. 1788 Prince Charles Edward ('Young Pretender') dies. 1789 Bastille in Paris stormed. French Revolution begins. 1792 Royalty abolished in France; Republic proclaimed. 1793 Louis XVI executed. 1796 Rise of Napoleon: victories at Lodi, Milan, Bologna. 1798 Battle of the Nile: Nelson defeats French fleet. 1802 Treaty of Peace between France and Britain (short-lived, however); war resumed in 1803. 1804 Napoleon made Emperor. 1805 Battle of Trafalgar: Nelson's victory and death. 1813 Battle of Leipzig: defeat of Napoleon.	1762 Rousseau's *Social Contract*. 1763 First meeting between Dr. Johnson and James Boswell. 1765 Walpole's *Castle of Otranto*. Percy's *Reliques of Ancient English poetry*. 1766 Goldsmith's *Vicar of Wakefield*. 1768 Thomas Gray's *Poems*. 1770 Thomas Chatterton (author of the Rowley fabrications) dies (born 1752). 1771 Gray dies (born 1716). Tobias Smollett dies (born 1721). 1774 Goldsmith dies (born 1730). 1775 Sheridan's *The Rivals*. 1776 Gibbon's *Decline and Fall of the Roman Empire* (first part). Adam Smith's *The Wealth of Nations*. 1784 Dr. Johnson dies (born 1709). 1786 Burns's *Poems*. 1789 Blake's *Songs of Innocence*.

Ruler	Political, Social, Religious Events	Literary Events
George III, 1760–1820.—*cont.*	1814 Napoleon deposed, banished to Elba. 1815 Napoleon escapes. Battle of Waterloo. Napoleon sent to St. Helena. 1819 'Peterloo' massacre (Manchester Reform meeting dispersed by the military).	1791 Boswell's *Life of Johnson*. 1798 The *Lyrical Ballads* of Wordsworth and Coleridge appear. The Romantic era is launched. 1808 William Cowper dies (born 1731). 1812 Byron's *Childe Harold*. 1816 Coleridge's *Kubla Khan* and *Christabel*. 1817 Jane Austen dies (born 1775).
George IV, 1820–30.	1821 Napoleon dies at St. Helena. 1821 Greek Declaration of Independence. (Turks massacre 40,000 at Scio.) 1828 Repeal of Test Act in England (the development of greater religious toleration). 1830 Louis Philippe declared King of the French. 1832 English Reform Bill passed.	1821 Keats dies (born 1795). 1822 Shelley dies (born 1792). 1824 Byron dies (fighting for Greek Independence). 1827 Blake dies (born 1757).
William IV, 1830–7.	1833 Slavery abolished in British colonies.	1832 Scott dies (born 1771). 1834 Coleridge dies (born 1772). Lamb dies (born 1775). 1836 Dickens publishes *The Pickwick Papers*. 1837 Carlyle's *The French Revolution*.
Victoria, 1837–1901.	1838 'Great Western' steamer crosses the Atlantic. 1839 Chartists riot at Birmingham. (The Chartists were agitating for certain political and electoral reforms.) 1840 Penny postage introduced. 1842 Great Chartist demonstration in London. 1848 Widespread revolutionary movements on the Continent. French Republic proclaimed. 1851 Submarine telegraph between Britain and France. 1851 The Great Exhibition in Hyde Park, London. 1854 War between Britain and Russia. Armies land in the Crimea. 1856 End of Crimean War (Russians defeated). 1857 Indian Mutiny breaks out. 1861 American Civil War begins. 1863 Slavery abolished in America by decree of President Lincoln. 1865 Lincoln assassinated. Civil War ends. 1868 Disraeli Prime Minister. Resigns, succeeded by Gladstone. 1870 Franco-Prussian War (ends 1871). 1874 Gladstone ministry resigns. Disraeli succeeds. 1875 Britain purchases Khedive's shares in the Suez Canal. 1878 Cyprus ceded to Britain. 1879 Wars in Zululand (this is the period of British colonisation in Africa).	1845 Newman enters the Catholic Church. 1847 Charlotte Brontë's *Jane Eyre*. Emily Brontë's *Wuthering Heights*. Thackeray's *Vanity Fair*. 1848 Karl Marx's *Communist Manifesto*. 1850 Wordsworth dies (born 1770). Tennyson's *In Memoriam*. 1855 Browning's *Men and Women*. 1859 De Quincey dies (born 1785). George Eliot's *Adam Bede*. Tennyson's *Idylls of the King*. The Darwinian theory. 1861 Palgrave's *Golden Treasury*. 1865 Matthew Arnold's *Essays in Criticism*. 1866 Newman's *Dream of Gerontius*. 1867 Marx's *Das Kapital*. 1868 Browning's *The Ring and the Book*. 1870 Dickens dies (born 1812). 1872 Samuel Butler's *Erewhon*. 1882 Rossetti dies (born 1828).

[*cont. over*]

Ruler	Political, Social, Religious Events	Literary Events
Victoria, 1837–1901.—*cont.*	1882 Cairo occupied by British troops. 1886 Upper Burma annexed. 1887 Queen Victoria's Golden Jubilee celebrations. 1893 Irish Home Rule Bill rejected by House of Lords. 1894 The Dreyfus scandal in Paris. 1895 Ashanti expedition. 1897 Queen Victoria's Diamond Jubilee. 1899 Boer War begins (South Africa). 1900 Relief of Mafeking. Boxer outbreak in China. Transvaal annexed to Britain. (*Note*: A great period of industrial and colonial development. Railways were built, steam-ships used, the spirit of philosophical and scientific enquiry was very strong. Reason was much in conflict with religion.)	1889 Browning dies (born 1812). Hopkins dies (born 1844). 1890 Gilbert publishes some of his comic operas. 1892 Tennyson dies (born 1809). 1894 Stevenson dies (born 1850). 1895 Pinero's *The Second Mrs. Tanqueray*. 1896 William Morris dies (born 1834). Hardy's *Jude the Obscure*. Housman's *A Shropshire Lad*. 1898 Shaw publishes some plays. Wilde's *Ballad of Reading Gaol*. 1899 Wilde's *Importance of Being Earnest* published. 1900 Ruskin dies (born 1819). Conrad's *Lord Jim*.
Edward VII, 1901–10	1902 Treaty between Britain and Japan. Boer War ends. 1903 Coronation Durbar at Delhi. 1904 Russo-Japanese War begins (ends in 1905). 1909 Old age pensions come into operation in Britain. Constitution of South African Union signed at Bloemfontein.	1903 George Gissing dies (born 1857). 1908 Arnold Bennett's *The Old Wives' Tale*. 1909 J. M. Synge (Irish playwright) dies (born 1871). Swinburne dies (born 1837). Meredith dies (born 1828). 1910 H. G. Wells's *Mr. Polly*.
George V, 1910–36. [*cont. over*]	1911 Italy declares war on Turkey. 1912 Chinese Republic established. 1913 Irish Home Rule Bill passed. The death of Scott and his Antarctic expedition reported. 1914 The First World War begins. 1917 America enters the War. 1918 Armistice signed. 1919 Peace Conference in Paris. Alcock and Brown fly the Atlantic. 1920 First meeting of the League of Nations. 1926 General Strike. With newspapers either reduced to a single sheet or not appearing at all, broadcasting comes into its own as an important information service. 1929 Graf Zeppelin successful in intercontinental flights. American slump. Wall Street crash. 1930 R101 destroyed on maiden flight: 48 lives lost. 1931 Great floods in China. Coalition Government in Britain. 1932 Manchuria becomes Japanese puppet state Manchukuo. 1933 Hitler appointed Chancellor. Reichstag fire. 1934 Austrian Nazis murder Dolfuss, Austrian Chancellor. Hitler becomes Dictator. 1935 Saar plebiscite for return to Germany. Italo-Abyssinian War begins. League of Nations sanctions against Italy fail.	1913 D. H. Lawrence's *Sons and Lovers*. 1915 Somerset Maugham's *Of Human Bondage*. 1916 Henry James dies (born 1843). James Joyce's *A Portrait of the Artist as a Young Man*. 1917 T. S. Eliot's *Prufrock and Other Observations*. 1918 Hopkins's *Poems*. 1922 T. S. Eliot's *The Waste Land*. James Joyce's *Ulysses*. 1924 E. M. Forster's *A Passage to India*. Sean O'Casey's *Juno and the Paycock*. Conrad dies (born 1857). 1928 Thomas Hardy dies (born 1840). 1929 Hemingway's *A Farewell to Arms*. 1930 D. H. Lawrence dies (born 1885). Wyndham Lewis's *The Apes of God*. 1931 Arnold Bennett dies (born 1867). 1932 Huxley's *Brave New World*.

Ruler	*Political, Social, Religious Events*	*Literary Events*
George V, 1910–36.—*cont.*		1933 Galsworthy dies (born 1867). 1935 Eliot's *Murder in the Cathedral.*
Edward VIII, Jan.–Dec. 1936 (abdicated). George VI, 1936–52.	1936 Edward VIII succeeds George V. Spanish Civil War. Rhineland remilitarised. Edward abdicates in favour of brother, George VI. 1937 Japan begins attempted conquest of China. 1938 British navy mobilised Sept. 28. Munich agreement Sept. 29. 1939 Italo-German pact. Anglo-Polish treaty. Germany invades Poland Sept. 1. Britain declares war on Germany Sept. 3. 1940 Germany advances westward. Dunkirk evacuation of British troops. Battle of Britain. British victory. 1941 Germany invades Russia. Philippines invaded by Japanese, to whom Hong Kong surrenders. Japanese attack Pearl Harbour. U.S. in war. 1942 Java, Singapore surrender to Japanese. 1,000 bombers raid Cologne, first daylight raids on Ruhr. Germans halted at Stalingrad. Battle of El Alamein. Rommel in full retreat. 1943 Churchill, Roosevelt and Stalin meet in Teheran. U.S. bombers attack Germany. Allied invasion of Sicily. 1944 Allied forces in Rome. Paris liberated. First V-2 falls on England. Arnhem landing. Last German offensive in the West. 1945 U.S. landing on Luzon. Russians take Warsaw. Yalta conference. Dresden bombed. Russians take Berlin. War with Germany ends. Atom bombs on Japan. World War II ends. 1946 Nuremberg sentences on Nazis. Goering commits suicide. 1947 India and Pakistan assume dominion status. Breakdown of four-power conference on Germany. 1948 Mahatma Gandhi assassinated. The Berlin airlift. Malayan Communist Party outlawed. 1949 General Mao Tse-Tung proclaims People's Republic of China. Chinese Nationalist Government sets up headquarters in Formosa. 1950 30-year alliance Treaty between China and Russia. First U.S. super-fortresses arrive in Norfolk, England. American and British troops in South Korea. 1951 Festival of Britain. Germany admitted to Council of Europe. Colombo Plan begins. Japanese peace treaty (Russia, China and India not parties to it).	1936 Auden and Isherwood's *The Ascent of F6.* Kipling dies (born 1865). Housman dies (born 1859). Chesterton dies (born 1874). Huxley's *Eyeless in Gaza.* 1937 Wyndham Lewis's *The Revenge for Love.* 1938 Wells's *Apropos of Dolores.* 1939 Yeats dies (born 1865). Joyce's *Finnegans Wake.* Priestley's *Johnson Over Jordan.* Eliot's *The Family Reunion.* 1940 Hemingway's *For Whom the Bell Tolls.* Mann's *Lotte in Weimar.* Snow's *Strangers and Brothers.* Greene's *The Power and the Glory.* 1941 Joyce dies (born 1882). Virginia Woolf dies (born 1882). Woolf's *Between the Acts.* 1942 Waugh's *Put Out More Flags.* 1943 Greene's *The Ministry of Fear.* 1944 Huxley's *Time Must Have a Stop.* Hartley's *The Shrimp and the Anemone.* 1945 George Orwell's *Animal Farm.* 1946 Camus's *Caligula.* 1947 Lowry's *Under the Volcano.* 1948 Mann's *Dr. Faustus.* Ionesco's *The Bald Prima Donna.* Mailer's *The Naked and the Dead.* 1949 Eliot's *The Cocktail Party.* Orwell's *Nineteen Eighty-Four.* Miller's *Death of a Salesman.* Huxley's *Ape and Essence.* 1950 Bernard Shaw dies, aged 94. Orwell dies, aged 47. Hemingway's *Across the River and into the Trees.* 1951 Whiting's *Saint's Day.* Powell's *A Question of Upbringing.* Salinger's *The Catcher in the Rye.* James Bridie dies (born 1888).

Ruler	Political, Social, Religious Events	Literary Events
Elizabeth II, 1952–	1952 Death of King George VI. Elizabeth II assumes throne. Japan again a sovereign and independent power. Emergency in Kenya. Eisenhower U.S. President.	1952 Dylan Thomas's *Collected Poems*. Cary's *Prisoner of Grace*. Beckett's *Malone Dies*.
	1953 Queen Elizabeth II's coronation. Hunt, Hillary, Tenzing climb Everest. Piltdown skull declared a partial hoax.	1953 Beckett's *Watt*. Angus Wilson's *Hemlock and After*. Eliot's *The Confidential Clerk*. Kingsley Amis's *Lucky Jim*. Dylan Thomas dies (born 1914). Churchill wins Nobel Prize for Literature.
	1954 U.S. hydrogen bomb exploded at Bikini. Food rationing ends in Britain.	
	1955 Death of Einstein. City of London a 'smokeless zone'. Pope advocates limitation of nuclear test explosions.	1954 Golding's *Lord of the Flies*. Isherwood's *The World in the Evening*.
	1956 Khrushchev denounces Stalin. French leave Indo-China after eighty years. Anglo-French offensive in Egypt. Russia invades Hungary.	1955 Beckett's *Waiting for Godot*. O'Neill's *Long Day's Journey into Night*. Nabokov's *Lolita*. Newby's *The Picnic at Sakkara*. J. F. Donleavy's *The Ginger Man*.
	1957 Tokyo protest against Pacific nuclear tests. Sibelius dies. Russia's Sputnik I. Jodrell Bank radio telescope in operation.	
	1958 Sputnik I disintegrates after 1,367 circuits of the earth. Bertrand Russell launches Campaign for Nuclear Disarmament. Khrushchev premier of Russia. Third U.S. earth satellite. De Gaulle President of France. First U.S. moon rocket fails. Pius XII dies. John XXIII succeeds him.	1956 Osborne's *Look Back In Anger*. Snow's *Homecomings*. Durrell's *Justine*. Angus Wilson's *Anglo-Saxon Attitudes*.
		1957 Pinter's *The Dumb Waiter*. Spark's *Memento Mori*. Iris Murdoch's *The Sandcastle*.
	1959 Castro overthrows Batista regime in Cuba. Russia launches Lunik I round sun. Pope John announces Ecumenical Council. Jodrell Bank radios message to U.S. via moon. World's population (2,800 million) increasing annually at rate of 45 million. Russia's Lunik III photographs back of moon.	1958 Ionesco's *Rhinoceros*. Pinter's *The Birthday Party*. Sillitoe's *Saturday Night and Sunday Morning*. Burgess's *Malayan Trilogy* completed. Pasternak's *Doctor Zhivago*. Kerouac's *The Dharma Bums*.
	1960 Sharpeville shooting in South Africa. U.S. to resume underground atomic tests. Agadir destroyed by earthquake. Ghana proclaimed a republic. Premier of Jordan assassinated. Senator John Kennedy elected U.S. President. Archbishop of Canterbury visits Pope in Rome.	1959 Bellow's *Henderson the Rain King*. John Arden's *Sergeant Musgrave's Dance*.
		1960 Pinter's *The Caretaker*. Bolt's *A Man For All Seasons*. Albert Camus dies in road accident.
	1961 Russian satellite with dog aboard launched and landed safely. Insurrection of part of French army in Algeria quickly quelled. Russia's Major Titov circles earth seventeen times. Soviet sector of Berlin sealed off from Western sectors. Negotiations begin for Britain's entry into Common Market.	1961 Ernest Hemingway dies. Iris Murdoch's *A Severed Head*. Waugh's *Sword of Honour* completed. Osborne's *Luther*. Heller's *Catch-22*.
	1962 Britain launches satellite Ariel from Cape Canaveral. French leave Algeria after 132 years. Telstar launched. U.S. Mariner II launched towards Venus. 21st Ecumenical Council opens in Rome.	1962 Whiting's *The Devils*. Burgess's *A Clockwork Orange*. Nabokov's *Pale Fire*.
	1963 Britain refused entry to Common Market. Pope John dies. Paul VI elected. Great British mail-train robbery (£2.5 million). Black freedom march on Washington. Nigeria a republic. President Kennedy assassinated. End of Second Vatican Council.	1963 Robert Frost, Aldous Huxley and Louis MacNeice die. Suicide of Sylvia Plath. Baldwin's *The Fire Next Time*.
[*cont. over*]		

Ruler	Political, Social, Religious Events	Literary Events
Elizabeth II, 1952– —*cont.*	1964 Shakespeare quatercentenary celebrations. Britain's Blue Streak rocket fired from Woomera. U.S. Civil Rights Bill enacted. Harpo Marx dies. Lyndon Johnson U.S. President. Kenya a republic. 1965 Churchill dies. President Johnson says U.S. action in South Vietnam to continue. Australian troops land there. Americans land in Dominican Republic to quell civil war. China explodes second atomic bomb. British ban on television cigarette advertising. 1966 Death of sculptor Giacometti. Britain imposes trade sanctions on Rhodesia. Luna 9 lands on moon. Successful landing of Gemini 10: docking and space walk. 1967 Six-day Arab-Israeli War. American bombing of North Vietnam to continue. Pope issues encyclical *Populorum Progressio*. Biafra secedes from Nigeria. China explodes her first hydrogen bomb. First European colour television begins on BBC second channel. Che Guevara killed in Bolivian jungle. Human heart transplant at Cape Town. 1968 Africans in Rhodesia hanged in defiance of Queen's reprieve. Martin Luther King assassinated. Senator Robert Kennedy shot, dying next day. Papal encyclical *Humanae Vitae* condemns all forms of artificial birth control. London demonstration against Vietnam war. U.S. President orders halt to bombing of North Vietnam. Apollo 8 moon mission. 1969 Eisenhower dies. Nigerian federal forces capture Biafran capital. De Gaulle resigns as President after referendum defeat. Maiden voyage of *Queen Elizabeth II*. Spain closes frontier with Gibraltar. U.S. moon landing. British troops police Ulster. Ho Chi Minh, North Vietnam President dies. Russia and U.S. ratify nuclear non-proliferation treaty. 1970 Bertrand Russell dies. Israeli air attacks on Egypt. U.S. President Nixon promises withdrawal of another 150,000 troops from Vietnam within a year. More troops in Ulster. Splashdown of Apollo 13 after complex rescue operation. Worldwide concern about pollution of sea, rivers, air. General de Gaulle dies. 1971 America's eleventh year in Vietnam War. Apollo 14 launched successfully to moon. Western table tennis teams in China, leading to wider entente. Lieutenant Calley convicted of murder of Vietnamese civilians. Rolls-Royce collapses. Stravinsky dies.	1964 Edith Sitwell dies. Albee's *Who's Afraid of Virginia Woolf?* Philip Larkin's *The Whitsun Weddings*. Sartre declines Nobel Prize. Christine Brooke-Rose's *Out*. William Burroughs's *Nova Express*. 1965 T. S. Eliot dies. Edward Bond's *Saved*. Waugh's revised *Sword of Honour*. Sylvia Plath's *Ariel*. Muriel Spark's *The Mandelbaum Gate*. Mailer's *An American Dream*. William Faulkner dies. 1966 Evelyn Waugh dies. Arthur Waley (translator from Chinese) dies. Malamud's *The Fixer*. 1967 Robert Lowell's *Near the Ocean*. Thom Gunn's *Touch*. Angus Wilson's *No Laughing Matter*. Golding's *The Pyramid*. Naipaul's *The Mimic Men*. 1968 Herbert Read dies. Mailer's *The Armies of the Night*. Theatres Act in London abolishes censorship. John Updike's *Couples*. Durrell's *Tunc*. 1969 Doris Lessing completes *The Children of Violence*. Nabokov's *Ada*. Bellow's *Mr. Sammler's Planet*. Elizabeth Bowen's *Eva Trout*. 1970 C. P. Snow's *Strangers and Brothers* completed. Ted Hughes's *Crow*. Patrick White's *The Vivisector*. Dan Jacobson's *The Rape of Tamar*. Durrell's *Numquam*. E. M. Forster dies. 1971 Powell's *Books do Furnish a Room*. 1972 Ezra Pound dies. Elizabeth Bowen dies.

Suggestions for Further Reading

PART 1. GENERAL SURVEYS AND REFERENCE BOOKS

The Cambridge History of English Literature (C.U.P.)
A Companion to English Literature—Gillie (Longman)
The Pelican Guide to English Literature (Penguin)
Writers and Their Works (Longman for the British Council)
Oxford Companion to English Literature (O.U.P.)

PART 2. HISTORICAL BACKGROUND, SPECIAL STUDIES AND ANTHOLOGIES
      OF PROSE AND VERSE

Chapters 1–5
BENNETT, H. S. *Chaucer and the 15th Century*, O.U.P. 1947 (Oxford History
      of English Literature, II, 1).
BREWER, D. S. *Chaucer in His Time*, Longman 1964.
CHAMBERS, E. K. *English Literature at the Close of the Middle Ages*, O.U.P.
      1945 (Oxford History of English Literature, II, 2).
COULTON, G. C. *Art and the Reformation*, C.U.P. 1953.
COULTON, G. C. *Medieval Panorama: the English Scene from Conquest to
      Reformation*, C.U.P. 1938.
HUIZINGA, J. *The Waning of the Middle Ages*, Penguin 1965.
KNOWLES, D. *The English Mystical Tradition*, Byrnes & Oates 1961.
KNOWLES, M. D. *The Evolution of Medieval Thought*, O.U.P. 1962.
LEGGE, M. D. *Anglo-Norman Literature and its Background*, O.U.P. 1963
LEWIS, C. B. *Classical Myth and Arthurian Romance*, O.U.P. 1932.
LEWIS, C. S. *The Allegory of Love*, O.U.P. 1936
LOOMIS, R. S. (ed.) *Arthurian Literature in the Middle Ages*, O.U.P. 1959.
POWICKE, F. M. *The Reformation in England*, O.U.P. 1941.
RENWICK, W. L. and ORTON, H. *The Beginnings of English Literature to
      Skelton*, Cresset 1952.
SCHLAUCH, M. *English Medieval Literature and its Social Foundations*, Heffer
      1956.

STENTON, D. M. *English Society in the Early Middle Ages,* Penguin 1951.
WADDELL, H. *The Wandering Scholars,* Constable 1927.
WESTON, J. L. *From Ritual to Romance,* C.U.P. 1920.

14th Century Verse and Prose, ed. K. Sisam. O.U.P. 1921; rev. 1955.
15th Century Verse and Prose, mod. ed. A. W. Pollard. Arber's English
    Garner, 1903.

Interlude—The Bible
DAICHES, D. *The King James Version of the English Bible,* C.U.P. 1941.

Chapters 6, 7, 8 and 10
BINDOFF, S. T. *Tudor England,* Penguin 1950.
BRADBROOK, M. C. *The Growth and Structure of Elizabethan Comedy,*
    Penguin 1963.
CRAIG, H. *The Enchanted Glass: The Elizabethan Mind in Literature,* Black-
    well 1936.
ELTON, G. R. *England Under the Tudors,* Methuen 1955.
ELTON, G. R. *The Tudor Constitution,* C.U.P. 1960.
HILL, C. *Society and Puritanism in pre-revolutionary England,* Secker &
    Warburg 1964.
KNIGHTS, L. C. *Drama and Society in the Age of Jonson,* Penguin 1962.
LEWIS, C. S. *The Discarded Image: an Introduction to Medieval and Renaissance
    Literature,* C.U.P. 1964.
NEALE, J. E. *Queen Elizabeth,* Penguin 1960.
ROSSITER, A. P. *English Drama from Early Times to the Elizabethans,*
    Hutchinson 1950.
ROWSE, A. L. *The England of Elizabeth: the Structure of Society,* Macmillan
    1967.
SIMON, J. *Education and Society in Tudor England,* C.U.P. 1966.
TREVOR-ROPER, H. R. *Religion, the Reformation and Social Change,* Macmillan
    1967.

*The Thought and Culture of the English Renaissance: an Anthology of Tudor
    Prose,* ed. E. M. Nugent, C.U.P. 1955.

Chapter 9
BRADLEY, A. C. *Shakespearian Tragedy,* Macmillan 1904.
BURGESS, ANTHONY. *Shakespeare,* Cape 1970.
DANBY, J. F. *Shakespeare's Doctrine of Nature,* Faber & Faber 1949.
ENRIGHT, D. J. *Shakespeare and the Students,* Chatto & Windus 1970.

GRANVILLE-BARKER, H., and HARRISON, G. B. (eds.) *A Companion to Shakespeare Studies*, C.U.P. 1934.

GRANVILLE-BARKER, H. *Prefaces to Shakespeare*, Sidgewick & Jackson 1927.

HUNTER, R. G. *Shakespeare and the Comedy of Forgiveness*, Columbia U.P. 1965.

KNIGHT, G. W. *The Wheel of Fire*, Methuen 1949.

KNIGHT, G. W. *The Imperial Theme*, Methuen 1951.

KNIGHTS, L. C. *Some Shakespearian Themes*, Chatto & Windus 1959.

KNIGHTS, L. C. *An Approach to Hamlet*, Penguin 1960.

KOTT, J. *Shakespeare Our Contemporary*, Methuen 1967.

SPENCER, T. *Shakespeare and the Nature of Man*, C.U.P. 1943; 1949.

SPURGEON, C. F. *Shakespeare's Imagery and What it Tells Us*, C.U.P. 1935.

TILLYARD, E. M. W. *Shakespeare's History Plays*, Penguin 1962.

TILLYARD, E. M. W. *Shakespeare's Last Plays*, Chatto & Windus 1938.

TILLYARD, E. M. W. *Shakespeare's Problem Plays*, Chatto & Windus 1950.

TILLYARD, E. M. W. *The Elizabethan World Picture*, Chatto & Windus 1943.

WILSON, J. DOVER (ed.) *Life in Shakespeare's England*, Penguin 1944.

WILSON, J. DOVER *What Happens in 'Hamlet'*, C.U.P. 1951.

Chapter 11

ELIOT, T. S. *'Metaphysical Poets' in Selected Essays*, Faber & Faber 1932.

EVANS, M. *English Poetry in the 16th Century*, Hutchinson 1955; 1967.

KNIGHTS, L. C. *'The Social Background of Metaphysical Poetry' in Further Explorations*, Chatto & Windus 1965.

WILLIAMSON, G. *The Donne Tradition*, O.U.P. 1930; 1958.

WILSON, F. P. *17th Century Prose*, California U.P. 1960

WINNEY, J. *A Preface to Donne*, Longman 1970.

Elizabethan Prose, ed. D. J. Harris. Longman 1968.

The Metaphysical Poets, ed. Helen Gardner. Penguin 1957.

Elizabethan and Jacobean Prose, 1550–1620, ed. Kenneth Muir. Penguin 1956.

Chapters 12 and 13

ASHLEY, M. *England in the 17th Century*, Penguin 1952; 1967.

ASHLEY, M. *The Greatness of Oliver Cromwell*, Hodder & Stoughton, 1957.

CLARK, G. N. *The 17th Century*, Clarendon Press 1929; 1947.

FIRTH, SIR CHARLES. *Essays Historical and Literary*, O.U.P. 1938.

HILL, C. *The Century of Revolution, 1603–1714*, Nelson 1961.

HILL, C. *The Intellectual Origins of the English Revolution*, O.U.P. 1965.

KEAST, W. R. (ed.). *17th Century English Poetry*, O.U.P. 1962.

LYONS, SIR H. *The Royal Society*, C.U.P. 1944.

PAUL, R. S. *The Lord Protector*, Lutterworth Press, 1955.

POTTER, LOIS. *A Preface to Milton*, Longman 1971.

TREVELYAN, G. M. *The English Revolution 1668–1689*, Butterworth 1938.

WEDGWOOD, C. V. *17th Century English Literature*, O.U.P. 1950; 1951.

WEDGWOOD, C. V. *Poetry and Politics Under the Stuarts*, C.U.P. 1960.

WHINNEY, M., and MILLAR, O. *English Art, 1625–1714*, O.U.P. 1957.

WHITEHEAD, A. N. *Science and the Modern World*, C.U.P. 1926.

WILLEY, B. *The 17th Century Background*, Penguin 1962.

The Oxford Book of 17th Century Verse, eds. Sir Herbert Grierson, and G. Bullough, O.U.P. 1934.

17th Century Prose 1620–1700, ed. Peter Ure. Penguin 1956

Chapter 14

BOAS, F. S. *An Introduction to 18th Century Drama*, Clarendon Press 1953.

KNIGHTS, L. C. '*Restoration Comedy: The Reality and the Myth*', in *Explorations*, Chatto & Windus 1946.

LOFTIS, J. (ed.). *Restoration Drama: Modern Essays in Criticism*, O.U.P. 1966.

NICOLL, A. *A History of Restoration Drama 1660–1700*, C.U.P. 1923; 1952.

NICOLL, A. *A History of Early 18th Century Drama 1700–1750*, C.U.P. 1925; 1952.

NICOLL, A. *A History of Late 18th Century Drama 1750–1800*, C.U.P. 1927; 1952.

Chapters 15 and 16

BUTT, J. *The Augustan Age*, Cresset Press 1950.

CASSIRER, E. *The Philosophy of the Enlightenment*, O.U.P. 1951.

GEORGE, M. D. *Hogarth to Cruikshank: Social Change in Graphic Satire*, Penguin 1967.

GRUNDY, C. R. *English Art in the 18th Century*, 'Studio' 1928.

HEARNSHAW, F. J. C. (ed.). *The Social and Political Ideas of Some English Thinkers of the Augustan Age*, Harrap 1928.

HUMPHREYS, A. R. *The Augustan World*, Methuen 1954.

LEAVIS, F. R. *Revaluation*, Penguin 1964.

LEAVIS, F. R. *The Great Tradition*, Penguin 1962.

MACLEAN, K. *John Locke and the English Literature of the 18th Century*, O.U.P. 1936.

MARSHALL, D. *English People in the 18th Century*, O.U.P. 1956.

PLUMB, J. H. *England in the 18th Century*, Penguin 1950; 1963.

RICHARDSON, PROF. A. E. *An Introduction to Georgian Architecture*, Art & Technics 1949.

STEPHEN, SIR L. *English Literature and Society in the 18th Century*, Duckworth 1904.

SUTHERLAND, J. R. *A Preface to 18th Century Poetry*, O.U.P. 1948.

WATT, I. *The Rise of the Novel: Studies in Defoe, Richardson and Fielding*, Penguin 1963.

WILLEY, B. *The 18th Century Background*, Penguin 1962.

The Pelican Book of English Prose II–III, ed. K. Allott. Penguin 1956.

The Oxford Book of 18th Century Verse, ed. D. Nichol Smith. O.U.P. 1926.

Chapter 17

ABRAMS, M. H. *The Mirror and the Lamp: Romantic Theory and the Critical Tradition*, O.U.P. 1953.

BATE, W. J. *From Classic to Romantic*, O.U.P. 1946.

BEACH, J. W. *The Concept of Nature in 19th Century English Poetry*, Macmillan 1936.

BOWRA, SIR C. M. *The Romantic Imagination*, O.U.P. 1950.

BRYANT, SIR A. *The Age of Elegance*, Collins 1950.

DOWDEN, E. *The French Revolution and English Literature*, O.U.P. 1904.

ELTON, O. A. *A Survey of English Literature, 1780–1830* (2 vols.), E. Arnold 1912.

GRANT, A. *A Preface to Coleridge*, Longman 1973.

HOBSBAWN, E. J. *The Age of Revolution. Europe 1789–1837*, New English Library 1962.

JAEGER, M. *Before Victoria: Changing Standards and Behaviour, 1787–1837*, Chatto & Windus 1956.

KLINGENDER, F. D. *Art and the Industrial Revolution*, Royle Publications 1947; rev. 1968.

PURKIS, J. *A Preface to Wordsworth*. Longman 1970.

READ, SIR H. *The True Voice of Feeling: Studies in English Romantic Poetry*, Faber & Faber 1953.

THOMPSON, E. P. *The Making of the English Working Class*, Penguin 1968.

WHITEHEAD, A. N. '*The Romantic Reaction*' in *Science and the Modern World*, C.U.P. 1926.

WILLEY, B. *19th Century Studies*, Penguin 1964.

The Pelican Book of English Prose IV, ed. J. Allott. Penguin 1956.
The Oxford Book of English Romantic Verse, ed. Sir H. S. Milford. O.U.P. 1935.

Chapter 18

ASHCROFT, T. *English Art and English Society*, P. Davies 1936.
BAKER, J. E. *The Re-Interpretation of Victorian Literature*, O.U.P. 1950.
BELL, QUENTIN. *Victorian Artists*, Penguin 1968.
BRIGGS, A. *The Age of Improvement*, Longman 1961.
BRUCE, MAURICE. *The Shaping of the Modern World*, Hutchinson 1958.
CECIL, LORD D. *Early Victorian Novelists*, Constable 1934.
CHAPMAN, R. *The Victorian Debate: English Literature and Society 1832–1901*, Weidenfeld & Nicolson 1968.
CHESTERTON, G. K. *The Victorian Age in Literature,* Williams & Norgate 1913.
CLARK, G. K. *The Expanding Society: British 1830–1900*, C.U.P. 1967.
GAUNT, WILLIAM. *The Aesthetic Adventure*, Penguin 1957.
GRIERSON, SIR H. J. C. *Lyrical Poetry from Blake to Hardy*, Hogarth Press 1928.
HALÉVY, E. *The Growth of Philosophic Radicalism*, Faber & Faber 1949.
HALÉVY, E. *History of the English People in the 19th Century*, Benn 1936.
HUNT, J. D. *The Pre-Raphaelite Imagination: 1848–1900*, Routledge & Kegan 1968.
IRVINE, WILLIAM. *Apes, Angels and Victorians*, Weidenfeld & Nicolson 1955.
LEAVIS, F. R. *New Bearings in English Poetry*, Chatto & Windus 1932; 1950.
LEAVIS, F. R. *The Great Tradition*, Penguin 1967.
RUSSELL, B. *The Scientific Outlook*, Allen & Unwin 1931.
SOMERVILLE, D. C. *English Thought in the 19th Century*, Methuen 1929.
STEEGMAN, J. *Victorian Taste*, Nelson 1970.
THOMSON, D. *England in the 19th Century*, Penguin 1950.
WILLEY, B. *19th Century Studies: Coleridge to Matthew Arnold*, Chatto & Windus 1949
WILLEY, B. *More 19th Century Studies: a Group of Honest Doubters*, Chatto & Windus 1956.
YOUNG, G. M. *Victorian England*, O.U.P. 1936.

The Pelican Book of English Prose V, ed. K. Allott. Penguin 1956.
The Oxford Book of 19th Century Verse, ed. J. Hayward. O.U.P. 1964.
The Victorians, ed. G. Grigson. Routledge & Kegan 1950.

Chapter 19

ARCHER, W. *The Old Drama and the New*, Heinemann 1923.

BENTLEY, E. R. *The Playwright as Thinker: A Study of Drama in Modern Times*, Hale 1946.

BENTLEY, E. R. *The Modern Theatre*, Hale 1948.

HUDSON, L. *The English Stage 1850–1950*, Harrap 1951.

NICOLL, A. *A History of Early 19th Century Drama 1800–1850*, C.U.P. 1930.

NICOLL, A. *A History of Late 19th Century Drama 1850–1900*, C.U.P. 1946.

ROWELL, G. *The Victorian Theatre*, O.U.P. 1956; 1967.

SHAW, G. B. *Our Theatres in the Nineties*, Constable 1932.

Chapters 20 and 21

ALVAREZ, A. *The Shaping Spirit*, Chatto & Windus 1958.

AMIS, K. *New Maps of Hell—A Survey of Science Fiction*, Victor Gollancz.

AYER, A. J. et al. *The Revolution in Philosophy*, Macmillan 1956.

BURGESS, ANTHONY, *The Novel Now*, Faber 1971.

COMFORT, ALEX. *The Novel & Our Time*, Phoenix House 1948.

CROSSMAN, R. H. S. (ed.). *The God That Failed*, Hamish Hamilton 1950.

ELIOT, T. S. *Poetry and Drama*, Faber & Faber 1951.

ELIOT, T. S. *Notes Towards the Definition of Culture*, Faber & Faber 1948.

ESSLIN, M. *The Theatre of the Absurd*, Penguin 1970.

FLUGEL, J. C. *Man, Morals and Society*, Penguin 1955.

FORSTER, E. M. *Aspects of the Novel*, Edward Arnold 1949.

FORSTER, E. M. *The Development of English Prose between 1918 and 1939*, E. Arnold 1945.

FORSTER, E. M. *Two Cheers for Democracy*, Edward Arnold 1951.

FRASER, G. S. *The Modern Writer and His World*, Longman 1953.

FREUD, SIGMUND. *Civilization and Its Discontents*, Hogarth Press 1930.

GRAVES, ROBERT, and RIDING, LAURA. *A Survey of Modernist Poetry*, Heinemann 1927.

HOGGART, R. *The Uses of Literacy*, Penguin 1958.

HUBBARD, H. A. *A Hundred Years of British Painting 1851–1951*, Longman 1951.

ISAACS, JACOB. *An Assessment of 20th Century Literature*, Secker & Warburg 1951.

LEHMANN, J. *Penguin New Writing*, Penguin.

MACBETH, G. *Poetry 1900–1965*, Longman 1966.

MUIR, EDWIN. *Transition Essays in Contemporary Literature*, Hogarth Press 1926.

MUMFORD, LEWIS. *The Culture of Cities*, Secker & Warburg 1940.

PEVSNER, N. *Pioneers of Modern Design*, Penguin 1960.

PINTO, V. DE SOLA. *Crisis in English Poetry 1880–1940*, Hutchinson 1951.

POPPER, K. *The Open Society*, K. Paul 1945.

RIESMAN, DAVID. *The Lonely Crowd*, O.U.P. 1950.

RUSSELL TAYLOR, J. *Anger and After*, Penguin 1969.

TRILLING, LIONEL. *The Liberal Imagination*, Secker & Warburg 1951.

TRILLING, LIONEL. *Beyond Culture*, Penguin 1967.

WARNOCK, G. J. *English Philosophy since 1900*, O.U.P. 1958.

WHYTE, W. H. *The Organization Man*, Penguin 1960.

WOOTTON, BARBARA. *Social Science and Social Pathology*, Allen & Unwin 1959.

The New Poetry, ed. A. Alvarez. Penguin 1962.

The Faber Book of Modern Verse, ed. Michael Roberts. Faber & Faber 1951.

Index